THE MODERN AMERICAN WINE INDUSTRY:
MARKET FORMATION AND GROWTH IN
NORTH CAROLINA

STUDIES IN BUSINESS HISTORY

Series Editor: *John Singleton*

THE MODERN AMERICAN WINE INDUSTRY: MARKET FORMATION AND GROWTH IN NORTH CAROLINA

BY

Ian M. Taplin

Routledge
Taylor & Francis Group

LONDON AND NEW YORK

First published 2011 by Pickering & Chatto (Publishers) Limited

Published 2016 by Routledge
2 Park Square, Milton Park, Abingdon, Oxfordshire OX14 4RN
711 Third Avenue, New York, NY 10017, USA

First issued in paperback 2015

Routledge is an imprint of the Taylor & Francis Group, an informa business

BRITISH LIBRARY CATALOGUING IN PUBLICATION DATA
Taplin, Ian M.
The modern American wine industry: market formation and growth in North Carolina. – (Studies in business history)
1. Wine industry – United States – History. 2. Business networks – United States – History. 3. Wine industry – North Carolina – History. 4. Business networks – North Carolina – History.
I. Title II. Series
338.4'76632'00973-dc22

ISBN-13: 978-1-138-66151-6 (pbk)
ISBN-13: 978-1-8489-3136-7 (hbk)

Typeset by Pickering & Chatto (Publishers) Limited

CONTENTS

Dedicated to Cindy and to the memory of my parents

LIST OF FIGURES AND TABLES

PREFACE

Several years ago I attended an MBA class presentation at my university in which students, working in groups, had put together a marketing plan for a local cooperative winery. Their diligence in background research on the industry was admirable and undoubtedly they devoted many hours pondering ways in which this particular firm could leverage its uniqueness and stand apart from the competition. They had access to much financial details and revenue streams, were on the cutting edge when it came to possessing analytic tools to evaluate financial reports and were clearly cognizant of the latest marketing theories that are appropriate for small businesses. Yet at the end of the presentations I couldn't help but think that they had missed the essence of the wine industry in North Carolina. They had seen everything through the lens of competition and therefore their recommendations – professional and thorough as they seemed – focused entirely on how the company's strategic growth could be predicated upon their enhanced competitive position *vis-à-vis* their neighbours.

As anyone knows who has examined an industry in its infancy, where the learning curve is steep and information is spotty, imprecise and often inaccurate, there is the recognition that to survive new firms typically enter into cooperative relationships, sharing information that would be an anathema to firms in established industries. During this period of infancy, interactions between firms and reciprocal relationships between actors are forged that contribute to the growth of a network. Thus clusters are born which provide the framework for further innovation and organizational learning. Instead of competition being the driving force behind industry growth, cooperation and reciprocity become normative and emerge as constituent features of the developing marketplace.

While the new institutional thought in economics has helped us be more sceptical of adducing rational behaviour to actors in all market transactions, it is within the realm of sociology where theorizing on the social construction of markets has enabled us to better understand how market formation is intricately linked with social relations. In earlier research that I did on small firm growth in Italy, I also came to appreciate the work that economic geography contributed to this debate by specifying how interdependency between firms could facilitate knowledge transfer and maintain market stability. It is with such a cluster analytic framework that I first started thinking about the dramatic growth of wineries in North Carolina. It seemed that if I was to understand this growth it had to be with intellectual tools that went beyond mere acknowledgement of entrepreneurial endeavour. Instead, if one thought about it as a process of market formation and cluster development, both an agglomeration of increasingly structured but often still informal relationships, then one would be better able to understand why the industry has been so successful in its current form when earlier periods of growth met with failure. Crucial to this analysis is the role networks play as transmission belts for knowledge and information transfer. When I started my interviews with winery owners and winemakers, everyone emphasized that they freely and enthusiastically shared information with others, particularly newcomers. They attributed the successful growth of the industry in part to this exchange of knowledge yet also acknowledged that there was little in the way of formal institutional supports that would structure such interactions. It is precisely such swelling up of information and tacit knowledge that has been disseminated widely through interactions that constitutes the dynamism of this embryonic cluster. It is such richly detailed micro-level interactions that form the basis for my own analysis, enabling me to trace the evolution of an industry and the formation of a new market in rural North Carolina.

An earlier iteration of Chapter 4 was published (with R. Saylor Breckenridge) in *Research in the Sociology of Work*, 15 (2005), entitled 'Entrepreneurship, Industrial Policy and Clusters: The Growth of the North Carolina Wine Industry'. Similarly, some of the ideas contained in Chapter 5 and 6 were first developed (again with R. Saylor Breckenridge) in a working paper entitled 'How Large Firms Create Industry Norms and Legitimacy: The Growth of the NC Wine Industry', *Cahiers de Recherche*, CEREBEM, Bordeaux Ecole de Management, #103–6, and subsequently 'Large Firms, Legitimation and Industry Identity: The Growth of the North Carolina Wine Industry', published in *The Social Science Journal*, 45 (2008).

Presentations on this work were made at the Department of Sociology, University of North Carolina, Charlotte; Department of Sociology, North Carolina State University; Management and Organizations group at Duke University; Bordeaux Ecole de Management; and Wake Forest University Business School. I am thankful for the many useful comments I received from individuals at these institutions during and after these presentations. Thanks go to R. Saylor Breckenridge who was my research collaborator in the early studies and who has often helped me think through many of the key ideas that are contained in this book; Arwen Hunter who provided research support on the earlier historical aspects; Wei Zhao, Paul Escott and Lisa Keister who made useful comments on specific chapter drafts; plus my colleagues in the Department of Sociology at Wake Forest University who listened to my stories about North Carolina wine and made suggestions about issues to consider. I would also like to acknowledge the input from my students in several wine MBA classes at Bordeaux School of Management. Having been urged to think strategically about wine industry growth, they came up with ideas and suggestions that have helped me clarify my own thinking on the subject.

I am particularly grateful to a number of friends whose expertise in the area of wine is much greater than mine. These include my Wake Forest colleagues E. Clay Hipp (who is also a small vineyard owner), the late Bob Swofford (who as a chemist helped me understand more about the technical properties of grapes and wine that I ever wanted to know!) and, in Bordeaux, François Durrieu and Christophe Estay. Two friends in Napa Valley, California, Doug Shafer and Russ Weiss, have endured hours of conversations with me whilst I picked their brains about winemaking and running a winery. Both of them happen to do the latter extremely well and were monumental sources of information. I am also grateful for insights into the industry, plus much unpublished archival material, provided by Margo Metzger Knight of the North Carolina Wine and Grape Council. Research assistance from Mary Scanlon, Research Librarian at Wake Forest University, has been fantastic as she helped me identify, obtain and interpret often confusing and contradictory secondary statistics from various agricultural agencies. We both spent many frustrating hours trying to discern trends from data where collection methodologies would abruptly change.

Inevitably one relies upon the past work of others; none so important in my case than the magisterial two-volume study by Thomas Pinney. These volumes provide minute details of the history of wine in America and I would be immensely satisfied if my own work provided a mere footnote to his study.

Finally there are two other groups that deserve acknowledgement. One is the large number of winery owners, grape growers and winemakers in North Carolina who gave freely of their time and answered my questions over the past seven years. All were extremely patient, eager to provide me with as much information as I needed, and were often as enthusiastic about my project as I was. They made data collection easy and enjoyable. Second is the group of friends who have sustained me intellectually over the years. Whilst one can rarely adduce specific comments to particular individuals, one nonetheless subtly incorporates their ideas that when aggregated make you realize the huge debt you owe to such people. These are the people who force you to think clearly on a daily basis. They include Ned Williams, Christopher Dandeker, Doug Fletcher, Roger and Julia Cornish, John Wise, Simone Caron, Jonathan Winterton, Mike Lawlor, Andrew Nixon, M. J. Andersen, W. Frick Curry, Yuahua Shi, Page West, David Coates and Berkeley Miller. To my wife, Cindy, who patiently listened to me describe what I was doing and read drafts of the manuscript and who was unflagging in her encouragement of the project over the years, my gratitude and love is never ending. Thanks also go to Adam and Sarah for continually asking questions as they become the next generation of critical thinkers.

INTRODUCTION

On a crisp late autumn day in 2000 my wife and I were driving on country roads west of Winston-Salem, North Carolina. Located in the north-west Piedmont, with the foothills of the Appalachian mountains visible in the late afternoon sun, this is an area of rolling hills, small towns and rural settlements. The countryside displays a rich and mixed agricultural heritage, just far enough from the expanding suburban sprawl of nearby cities to avoid excessive property speculation. There are dairy farms, soya and corn fields, the occasional tobacco patch and the usual collection of decaying abandoned properties indicative of old ways of rural life that are perhaps no longer sustainable. The traffic is light, the roads narrow and the countryside evokes feelings of nostalgia for an Arcadian past, notwithstanding the occasional rusted pick-up truck and gas station/country store advertising videos and lottery tickets.

Imagine our surprise after cresting a hill when in front of us lay acres of well-tended vines on these rolling hills and several beautiful, expansive and meticulously landscaped homes. Rounding a sharp bend in the road we came across the large sign to Westbend Vineyards. Founded in 1972 by the Kroustalis family, and named after the western bend of the nearby Yadkin River, it covers 60 acres planted with prime *vinifera* grapes. A photograph of the area could easily mislead someone into thinking they were in Sonoma County, California. In fact I subsequently discovered that the road where Westbend Vineyards is located (Williams Road) has on occasion been used to shoot movies that are ostensibly set in California wine country.

I visited the winery on a later date and learned its history. With money from a restaurant supply company that he owned, founder Jack Kroustalis had decided he wanted to grow grapes, chose this land and, against the advice of many in the agricultural community, planted French hybrid vines. The harvested grapes were sold to other wineries in the south-eastern United States but after a decade of this he decided it was time to produce his own wine. In 1988 the winery was bonded and the first Westbend wines were released in 1990. He hired a professional winemaker, assuming that if the venture was to succeed he needed someone who was knowledgeable about viticulture and winemaking. By bringing in a professional, he was also making a statement of intent; that he was determined to transcend the amateurism associated with many 'hobbyist' winemaking activities that had emerged around the country with the growing interest in wine. Making what are essentially dry wines in a region with a predilection for sweet beverages and in a county with no real history of wine consumption was a challenge to say the least. But he and his family persevered and the winery now produces 5,000 cases annually, has won numerous awards for its wines and is the oldest winery in the recently created Yadkin Valley AVA.

Approximately 100 miles west of Westbend Vineyards is the most visited winery in the United States with approximately one million people annually touring the operation. This is Biltmore winery, a part of the rambling Biltmore House and estate near Asheville, nestled in a valley in the western Appalachians. The first vines were planted here in 1971, with French-American hybrids soon supplemented by *vinifera* grapes. The initial idea behind this venture by then owner William A. V. Cecil (a descendant of the house's founder Cornelius Vanderbilt) was to make the estate self-supporting. After early experiments growing different types of grapes, a winery was established and through a combination of locally grown grapes plus juice and grapes bought from out of state, has now grown to a production of 140,000 cases. Troubled times in the 1980s when frosts and bad harvests threatened to bankrupt the venture have been replaced by optimism in recent decades as sales have increased and the winery become an established tourist destination. The hiring of an experienced French winemaker, Bernard Delille, in 1986 and his subsequent promotion to winemaster, plus Sharon Fenchak who joined the winery in 1999 as winemaker and assistant to Delille and is responsible for in-house research and development, brought a more professional footing to the operation. The winery is on an impressive scale and although tours of the facilities are included in the house tours, it is nonetheless a significant accomplishment to have created a 'wine tourism' site in the western North Carolina mountains. Even though grapes for the wine they sell often come from out of state, the physical presence of what appears to be an extremely professionally run operation on a scale that is impressive even for states with established winemaking cultures has done much to solidify the image of North Carolina as a winemaking state.

Drive 100 miles east of the Piedmont towards the coastal plain and one arrives at the small town of Rose Hill where the state's largest (in volume) winery, Duplin, is located. The surrounding countryside is fairly flat, dotted with the occasional industrial-scale hog farm, fields of cotton plus the other usual mixed agricultural products. It is in many respects an unlikely place to find a winery. It was started in 1972 when the Fussell brothers (Dan and David) bought 132 acres of farmland and, following the advice of the North Carolina Agriculture Department, planted 10 acres of muscadine grapes. This grape is native to the region and grows well in the soil and climate of south-eastern North Carolina. The Fussells' business plan was to sell their grapes to a winery in upstate New York but by the time the first big harvest came in 1974 the price offered per ton had more than halved (from $350 to $150). Facing possible financial ruin they decided to make their own wine and tried to establish a winery in Rose Hill where they would make a traditional southern 'sweet' wine from their own grapes.

What they were doing was not necessarily new – the state's first commercial vineyard, Medoc vineyard, was founded in 1835 in Halifax county and the state's scuppernong vine can be traced even further back in history to Walter Raleigh's colony on Roanoke island in the sixteenth century.[1] But since Prohibition had shut down the industry, any attempt at rejuvenation would run counter to entrenched views about moral depravity associated with alcohol consumption. This was clearly the case in the town of Rose Hill, whose residents were appalled at the prospect of a winery and furthermore state laws still prohibited wine production. Fortunately family connections with state Senator Harold Hardison did result in a change in the state law and the winery was given the necessary permits to open. Its first site was the back part of the store owned by the Fussell brothers' father, D. J. Fussell, who had used his influence with politicians to have the laws changed.

Learning winemaking through trial and error (mostly error according to the official history of the winery), the brothers bottled their first wines in 1975 (225 'drinkable' bottles) and by 1976 were selling every drop of the 3,500 gallons produced. Their success continued and they bought more and more grapes from other growers who had seen a similar decline in their earlier expectations for this as an easily sold crop to out-of-state wineries. Some of these farmers formed a cooperative and, together with new investors, provided the resources for the winery at least to get by from the late 1970s into the mid-1980s when they opened their current production facility (1984). By this time they were producing 200,000 gallons of wine.

Changes in the preferential laws that provided beneficial tax treatment to North Carolina-produced wines occurred in 1983.[2] Designed earlier to promote grape growing and winemaking, the laws were deemed unconstitutional by the Attorney General of North Carolina. This move significantly hurt farmers and Duplin saw their wine sales drop dramatically. Consequently they had to cut back on their grape purchases, which eventually led many farmers to stop growing grapes. By 1986 Duplin produced a mere 10,698 gallons of wine.

A change of fortune came in the mid-1990s following studies that indicated health benefits associated with moderate wine consumption and a relaxing of local attitudes towards alcohol consumption. By this time Duplin was able to leverage its local presence and reputation and build new contracts with farmers who once more saw the financial benefits of growing muscadine grapes – this time for sale locally. With a new generation running the winery, currently it is embarking upon ambitious expansion plans that include the construction of a new facility replete with a chapel for weddings, a hotel and restaurants. As of 2008 their production is 266,000 cases of wine.

These are three different but related stories of an industry in its infancy but one that is nonetheless beginning to establish its presence in the state. Duplin's story is more detailed than that of the other two wineries because it chronicles an attempt to resurrect an industry that had flourished in the eastern part of state in the latter part of the nineteenth century. Despite this history, the winery faced economic uncertainty, market unpredictability, legal challenges and variability in institutional support – all of this for an agricultural product with a proven track record of successful harvesting. The fact that they persisted in their efforts and have emerged as the largest winery in the state speaks volumes about entrepreneurial zeal and the growth of conditions that facilitate market formation. For the wineries that were developing elsewhere in the state, their struggle would be even greater since their product (drier *vinifera* grapes) had never been successfully grown in the region, the market for this type of wine was not clearly established, and the general lack of both support and enthusiasm from state agricultural agencies all appeared to conspire against potential success. Yet it is in the central part of the state where the recent rapid growth of wineries has occurred, where a density of wineries has encouraged ancillary supplier industry growth, and where an emerging identity and legitimacy for the infant industry is most apparent.

When I first started my research on North Carolina wines in 2002 there were 25 bonded wineries in the state; currently (2010) there are 92 and estimates of approximately 350 additional grape growers. This rapid growth positions North Carolina as the fastest growing state in terms of new wineries in the United States. Discounting the fact that the base was very small, it is nonetheless an impressive growth rate that shows little sign of abating and thus far only three wineries have closed. Much of this massive growth has occurred in the last decade with the formation of small, what we might call boutique wineries and is located primarily (but not exclusively) in the central portion of the state (the Piedmont region). Although in the eastern part of the state muscadine grapes flourish and wineries such as Duplin in this region have prospered selling primarily sweet wines, the hype associated with wine production has come from the drier wines produced in the Piedmont region. With a better understanding of how to control the pests and diseases that plagued earlier attempts, it appears that weather and soil conditions in this region are favourable to, or at least permit *vitis vinifera* grape production – the type of grapes that most wine drinkers associate with the liquid in their bottles. It is this area that now has three officially designated wine regions (AVAs). Such status does not necessarily guarantee product quality but does endow legitimacy to firms operating within the boundaries and is used to market the product regionally. It is a *de facto* stamp of approval signifying the establishment of an industry's identity. As such it is a measure of the progress made in a very short period of time for a product that has struggled to establish itself amidst a local culture that often is unsympathetic if not outright hostile to alcoholic beverages.

Agricultural Transformation: The Challenge of Grape Growing and Winemaking

Despite opposition to alcohol consumption amongst many in the area, North Carolina has a storied history replete with exploits of those who made and sold hard liquor. As with many farmers in colonial times, difficulty of transporting corn across mountain roads stimulated the more enterprising amongst them to turn their crop into mash which they then distilled into whiskey.[3] Thus was born 'moonshine', the beverage that became something of a staple after the American Revolution. Others had planted apple orchards and used that crop to make apple brandy. Moonshine entered the popular imagination with Prohibition and later the rise of NASCAR. Drivers that won races in the latter competitions had often earlier in the day run bootleg liquor down mountain roads. Even after the repeal of Prohibition in 1933, the pervasiveness of dry counties in much of the south-eastern United States meant that manufacture and consumption of the beverage remained omnipresent.

In light of the above, one has the curious coexistence of those whose religious beliefs result in their trenchant opposition to any form of alcohol and a subculture and local market that has thrived by producing it illegally. It is this context that makes the rise of the wine industry in North Carolina such a fascinating story, set against competing forces that have shaped agricultural practices for centuries.

The three wineries briefly discussed above (together with the others that I will talk about) are part of what appears to be a small yet nonetheless significant event in the rural landscape of North Carolina. But they go beyond being merely footnotes in a story of agricultural change or of plucky individual initiatives. They are instead part of a broader picture of how local economies can be transformed, how change agents interact with institutional forces to reshape economic development processes, and what the consequences of such outcomes might portend for a rural population not always enthusiastically embracing cultural changes and possibly threats to established beliefs. Set against a background of early attempts to establish a market for wine, all of which for a variety of reasons failed, this begs the question of whether the current growth spurt will follow a similar trajectory that results in its demise. Market formation occurred at various stages in the industry's history in North Carolina but recent events suggest the possibility of a more permanent presence because of a combination of factors that were often lacking in the past. Let me briefly explain these disparate forces and show how they shape the emergence of this new agricultural endeavour.

At one level what one sees in these stories is the passionate insouciance of individuals who are prepared to risk what they have to realize their dream. There are some with farming experience who are looking to diversify to another crop, others who have decided that they are at an age when they can try something different and have the resources to do so. There are still others who have become passionate about wine following trips to vineyards in California, Italy or France, and decided that they would like to try making their own wine. Whatever the individual rationale for a winery's founding, the initiative, dedication and determination of these early pioneers has played a significant role in establishing the incipient identity of winemaking in the state.

But let us take this notion of individual resilience one step further. Whilst remaining an agricultural crop, winemaking and the ownership of a vineyard has a cache that somehow can transcend the reality of farm life. To say that one owns a winery can be thought of as exotic or even 'sexy' even though the harsh reality of agricultural labour is a constant reminder of the rigours entailed in such a venture. Some individuals buy vacation homes, yachts or indulge other expensive passions. But owning a winery somehow endows one with a veneer of sophistication, possibly even a semblance of cultural capital inasmuch as one's avowed pursuit is part of an ancient activity that epitomizes (in many but obviously not all people's eyes) what is good in life. After all, wine drinking can be seen by some to be an intrinsically civilizing activity and associated with countries that are deemed civilized.[4]

The individuals who decide to plant a vineyard embrace a long-term venture fraught with uncertainty. The obvious question to ask is why do they do this? This book endeavours to answer that question and although the answers will vary there are some common threads. Because of the long time frame of starting a winery, it inevitably attracts those whose passions about the product are matched by the financial resources necessary to sustain them for years of red ink on their balance sheet. Time and again when asked if they made a profit the owners of wineries would say 'not yet but eventually it needs to be self-sustaining'. Business plans are often developed around a ten-year framework during which time resources from other endeavours are used to cross-subsidize the winery's operations. As one winery owner, in business since 2000, said this is not for the faint of heart! Just when I think we'll make money this year, a summer hail storm or late spring frost destroys half of my grapes and I end up having to buy grapes which means another year of loss (interview with author, 2008)

There are some nonetheless who start a winery with more limited resources. The barriers to entry can be fairly low if one's sights are set at a very modest level. Some locate their winery in their backyard and use the basement for making and selling the wine. Such operations rely heavily upon familial self-exploitation of the type most often seen in immigrant entrepreneurial ventures.[5] They work hard, pool labour and what limited resources they have, and in many cases 'learn on the job'. This is also the reality of many small businesses and in this respect wineries are not too different.

Part of the challenge is the time frame needed to develop the vineyard. After vines are planted it takes three to four years before they are mature enough to yield the quality and quantity of grapes needed for harvesting. After the wine is made from the grapes it needs to be stored in tanks or barrels before bottling which can lead to further months (or years in the case of red wine) before it is released for sale. For even the most ambitious operation it takes four years before they can start to see a return on their investment; realistically for most it is five to seven years. That means four years without any real income from the winery but significant up-front costs. After acquiring the land one buys the vines, plants them and then has to fertilize, spray and manage the vineyard. When the vines begin to mature, there is the capital cost associated with winemaking itself (picking grapes, crushing and de-stemming, fermenting and storing, and ultimately bottling). Some vineyards initially 'outsource' these operations after picking. This saves on overheads but leaves one dependent upon others for crucial parts of the winemaking operation – and these services still cost money. In an industry in its infancy many of these services themselves are only just beginning to emerge.

Despite these daunting conditions, only three North Carolina wineries thus far have failed. Given the high mortality rate of start-up ventures in most sectors of the economy this is quite an achievement. It is a testament to the perseverance of the individuals involved in the wineries. But perhaps it is also a reflection of changing product demand conditions that have led to new entrants and growing industry resilience. In other words have the opportunity structure or the conditions that encourage and reward entrepreneurial activity in this sector changed in recent decades in ways that favour start-ups? Instead of seeing entrepreneurial activity solely conditioned by a supply of willing individuals, are there contextual factors and events that stimulate firm foundings? Recent methodological criticisms of the supply-side obsession in the entrepreneurship literature have focused upon causal forces and conditions that facilitate entrepreneurial activity.[6] In the case of North Carolina to what extent has the social and cultural setting changed in ways that facilitate winery establishment? Related to this, have resource availability[7] and social networks[8] altered to the extent that organizational founding is a product of the interaction between entrepreneurial attributes and broader socio-economic forces? But what exactly might the demand-side perspective on entrepreneurship be telling us about the context of wine in a culture more attuned to beer/spirits or abstinence? Nationally wine consumption is increasing in the United States so it might not be too unreasonable to say that these new wineries are catering to an increased demand for the product. North Carolina has seen a significant influx of educated outsiders (often derogatively referred to by locals as 'yankees') settling in the state, especially around the areas of the Research Triangle and the banking centre of Charlotte. Other parts of the state have seen the migration of retirees, generally wealthy individuals who have been attracted by the relatively pleasant climate and low cost of housing but who also tend be wealthier and well educated. Both groups constitute target populations for wineries since they consist of people who either are knowledgeable about wine and/or have time available to visit wineries. The latter has become part of wine tourism – visits to the countryside as recreational activity – and such lifestyle activities are shaping sector growth. These are important issues that need explication because they go beyond simple truisms about hard-working individuals succeeding in the face of adversity.

In addition to changing demand conditions, what other events in the broader environment possibly have occurred to stimulate winery growth? Public policy can be instrumental in shaping economic activity and I have already alluded to tax laws that were earlier designed to aid a fledgling industry. To what extent has the winery sector been shaped by institutional forces that have not necessarily made success inevitable but at least limited failure? Providing incentive packages, infrastructural support and expert advice, government can essentially underwrite some of the costs associated with industry growth. In the incipient stages of growth such support can be crucial to help individuals cope with a steep learning curve and gain requisite advice for operational efficiency. Even in a neo-liberal market economy there are mechanisms designed to assist firms and new ventures, especially if they are perceived to be of use to the broader economy (job creation, tourism growth, tax revenues, etc.). In the case of winemaking one looks to the local agricultural extension agency and state universities for specialist advice. But according to some in the industry that advice was not as readily available as some winemakers might have hoped for in the early stages of growth.

In recent years, the growth of specialist oenology and winemaking programmes at local community colleges has provided much-needed 'technical' instruction for would-be vintners. How this emerged and what role it plays *vis-à-vis* other specialist programmes within the Department of Agriculture needs explication. In other words what are the politics of local agricultural policy, especially for a product such as wine which has not been part of the rural landscape until recent decades? Some have argued that the North Carolina Department of Agriculture has been too obsessed with the major cash crops in the state (tobacco and soya) and with industrial scale agri-business (hog and chicken farming) to be bothered with more esoteric crops such as grapes where the economic contribution is small. The legacy of Prohibition, the persistence of dry counties and the moral outrage against alcohol consumption in some quarters has led to accusations of politically motivated indifference by state officials towards vineyards. If such is the case how has this affected the growth of wineries?

Resources are an integral part of any sector growth and in the case of vineyards, appropriate available land is necessary. Since most wineries start out and remain small, the demand for large acreages is not high. But the land must be suitable for grape cultivation and in the recent decade such land has become available as farmers have abandoned tobacco growing in North Carolina. Dramatic changes in tobacco production following extensive litigation against tobacco companies over product liability in the late 1990s also produced opportunities for new farmers to diversify their crops. With demand for tobacco declining, some farmers have been looking for alternative crops. Fiscal incentives, with funds from the legal settlement that states signed with the major tobacco companies, have enabled many farmers to try new crops and some opted for vines. In other cases people have inherited land that was hitherto used for tobacco and decided to try their hand at grape growing. In the case of the former one has individuals accustomed to the routines of agricultural life with the practical experience of farming that could facilitate operational efficiency. For others whose agricultural heritage is family-legacy based their enthusiasm for 'getting their hands dirty' is stimulated by a desire to pass on a viable commercial entity to the next generation. How much of the winery growth story is intertwined with the decline of tobacco production? Have the number of farmers and other owners of agricultural land who have embraced grape growing been significant and have they shaped the sector's growth?

As sectors grow and become regionally concentrated, ancillary support industries typically emerge. What often follows are relationships, ties and general links, both formal and informal, between the various actors that fall under the general umbrella of networks. The more established networks become and acquire a regional specificity, the more likely they resemble clusters. Clusters or industrial districts as they are sometimes known can be traced back to Alfred Marshall's writings on the economies of localization and more recently the seminal work by Michael Piore and Charles Sabel.[9] The idea behind these theories is that when a critical mass of firms develops in a particular sector, other specialist firms that service them are encouraged to grow, and that geographical proximity is conducive to innovation because of spillovers in localized knowledge and the overall lowering of transaction costs.

The concept of clusters and networks is pertinent to winemaking in North Carolina since there are people now servicing vineyards with operating equipment, vineyard management techniques (spraying and fertilizer applications) and even marketing skills that in the past were conspicuous by their absence. Does the provision of such specialist firms provide lower input costs and through the growth of a critical mass of localized specialist knowledge contribute to the growth of a cluster? What are the network characteristics of wineries and can one argue that a vibrant winemaking cluster exists? Just because firms are located in the same area does not necessarily mean that they are embedded in localized networks that facilitate collective learning and knowledge diffusion.[10] If a network of interdependency has emerged what role do different firms (and key individuals within these firms) play in fostering learning and establishing governance procedures necessary for legitimizing further sector growth? What is the 'industrial atmosphere' that Marshall talked about that promotes innovation-related knowledge in unstructured ways and is North Carolina but one example of many emerging wine sectors in other regions of the United States and overseas?

In essence this book is theoretically informed history. In it I explain the stages of market formation in terms of the supply of actors and the demand for products that are in turn shaped by institutional and structural forces that provide a framework for operating knowledge crucial for industry survival. The emphasis upon the notion of a cluster to explain the growth of wineries as a network of relationships between individuals, firms and institutions is a crucial part of this analysis but only in so far as it helps us understand recent successes. Given the high growth rate of wineries and their clustering in certain areas of the state, it is instructive to examine what exactly is entailed when firms locate in close proximity to each other in an apparent cooperative effort to share information and technical knowledge crucial to firm survival. Because such relationships involve mutual obligations and expectations, trust and reciprocity emerge to solidify the networks that become embedded in the cluster.

In Chapter 1 I provide an overview of the cluster concept and then discuss the emergence of networks, how they are structured and collective resources generated. Key to this discussion is an assessment of how an incipient cluster attracts new entrants, what their resources are and what contribution they make to the growing legitimacy of the sector. I look at how clusters confer collective resources on localized firms and how performance criteria can be assessed via degrees of embeddedness within the cluster. This chapter examines how cluster governance falls under the scope of leader firms – firms with extensive resources and access to knowledge that permit them to shape the direction of cluster growth. It will also discuss the liabilities of clusters, their isomorphism and possible 'system' failure when external stimuli are effectively excluded. It concludes with an assessment of market functioning and competitive dynamics in clusters.

Chapter 2 chronicles the various largely unsuccessful attempts to establish winemaking as a viable commercial enterprise during colonial times. The reasons are multiple but key was that the types of grapes favoured by Europeans (*vinifera*) were difficult to grow in the climate of North Carolina and because of the local population's preference for, and easy manufacture of, hard liquor such as whiskey and brandy. Despite such obstacles, the initial development of commercial wineries in the state during the 1800s up to and including Prohibition, when the industry collapsed, nevertheless indicates that demand for the product existed if supply conditions could be maintained. Success during this phase was predicated upon the cultivation of muscadines – a grape indigenous to the area and resistant to most diseases. Chapter 3 discusses post-Prohibition growth of the muscadine market and the way in which institutional forces failed to stimulate a revival of the industry until the 1970s when individual initiatives from people with non-farming backgrounds proved successful. The significance of this period is that it illustrates how the absence of key issues can inhibit the growth of a new sector. It was during this time period that early *vinifera* pioneers started their wineries in the Piedmont area and west to Asheville (Biltmore House). In recounting their stories one can examine how collective learning and the availability and transmission of knowledge necessary for successful viticulture of this type of grape became established.

In Chapter 4 I look at the resurgent growth in the 1990s with the focus switching somewhat from muscadine grapes to French varietals and hybrids. Here it is a story of entrepreneurial activity where a supply of individuals whose aspirational lifestyles combined with financial resources to permit industry entrance; the decline of tobacco and associated financial subsidies for crop diversification plus the availability of agricultural land; and the growth of oenology programmes to provide systematic knowledge and information about winemaking. The interaction of changing resource conditions with an entrepreneurial climate that has fostered interest in winemaking further precipitates additional institutional changes that consolidate cluster formation.

By the early years of the twenty-first century it is apparent that several resource-rich firms have emerged and begun to establish a strategic leadership role. By investing in requisite resources, establishing clear quality control parameters, providing information channels for knowledge dissemination as well as general industry leadership, such firms have sustained the legitimacy of the newly established sector by exercising crucial governance functions. At the same time, many newcomers have successfully entered the market by gaining access to extant knowledge and acquired technical viticulture skills at local educational institutions. To what extent have such actions curtailed information flows within the cluster, potentially driving some firms out of the cluster? I discuss these issues in depth in Chapter 5, assessing how the social structure of embeddedness changes, with cooperation becoming part of a more differentiated hierarchical structure.

In Chapter 6 I examine how the industry structure has changed and consolidated around a certain pattern consistent with industry trends in general. In addition to several large, resource-rich wineries, there are small boutique wineries that grow their own grapes and have a full-time winemaker, small wineries that outsource winemaking and vineyard management to outside specialists, and wineries that buy most of their grapes but make their own wine. All of these are in addition to grape growers who sell their grapes to wineries. Within this emerging structure I analyse how knowledge dissemination (crucial to quality production) becomes increasingly available within the dense network whereas information (innovation potential) flows widely to all members (weak ties) of the cluster. Whilst the latter remains a public good, the former becomes a 'club' good with restricted membership. In this chapter I assess how increased cluster density might have affected network interactions. For example are some firms (either old or new) becoming marginal and playing a diminishing role in this structure? With the growth of specialist occupations (vineyard management, pesticide and fungicide spraying firms, crushing and bottling operations, etc.) attracted by the cluster's size growth, has this enabled firms to be less dependent upon informal network relations and rely instead upon formal contractual linkages?

Finally, in the Conclusion, I reflect upon networks as a source of change and a vehicle of innovation and whether there is an optimal size of cluster, both geographically and in terms of firm density. Does the cluster of North Carolina wineries provide allocative efficiency and adaptive processes that are sustainable? At what stage does competition replace cooperation as a normative structuring principle? In the case of the North Carolina wine industry, will its sustained growth continue unabated or will one begin to see an increase in firm mortality rates? As density increases, possible new AVAs emerge and sector legitimacy improves following product quality enhancements, the wine industry in North Carolina could enter a new phase where it establishes itself as a broader regional presence. But this assumes that demand for the product will increase to satisfy growing supply, and that pricing structures which currently reflect operational costs will remain compatible with consumer buying power.

Data and Methods

In many respects this has been an elusive industry to study, especially in the contemporary period. When I started the research in 2002 there were 25 wineries in the state; currently (2010) there are 92 with new ones opening every month. This has stymied my original aim of doing a saturation study of the industry whereby I hoped to conduct interviews with the owners and winemaker in each of the wineries. It left me scrambling to identify newcomers and cognizant that I might be missing some important part of the organizational puzzle. I had also intended to conduct interview with as many growers as possible, aiming initially for 10 per cent. That also proved fraught with problems, not least of which being able to identify exactly who was growing grapes for sale to wineries rather than merely for table consumption. Historical records were also scarce, even identifying wineries and grape growers in the nineteenth century when the industry became established for the first time. Eventually I have been able to conduct interviews with 48 winery owners or winemakers and 7 grape growers. Included in this number was each of the large wineries, all of those that started in the 1980s and 1990s, while the others were derived from a random sample of wineries in each of the principal regions (clusters) of the state.

Since this is a study of people and processes, it seemed appropriate to hear the stories of those involved. This sort of ethnographic research is incredibly time consuming and inevitably leaves one at the methodological mercy of critics who claim that the sample might be biased, too small, insufficiently representative, etc. To counter these arguments I do believe that one gains such rich, detailed and contextual information from hearing individual narratives that it enables one to build a much more complex picture of routine interactions than one could ever gain from simple surveys. I was able to build upon my initial interviews in a snowballing fashion, soliciting ideas for further questions from respondents as well as asking them to delineate carefully their view of the organizational world they inhabited.

Each firm I visited I asked questions from a structured questionnaire (see Appendix A) but left open numerous opportunities for respondents to tell their own stories in ways that they felt best suited their situation. Given my initial hypothesis about the role of knowledge sharing in cluster formation I needed to find out how they cognitively approached learning in their business, what they perceived their own resources and weaknesses to be, and what strategies they developed to enable their business to grow. But I had to find ways of asking questions that did not lead them in their responses; to discern their own construction of an operational reality and definition of the situation. This was generally easy since most actors immediately started talking about the overall cooperative framework in the industry. From such narratives I was able to impose my own analytic schema to interpret this information.

I spent between two and four hours asking questions about their operation, their reason for entering the business, financial details, the difficulties they encountered and plans for the future. The informants were individuals who were knowledgeable about their own business as well as the industry in general so it provided an opportunity to ask them (in confidence) about the relative merits, problems and performance attributes of other owners/winemakers. I recognize that using key informants does not necessarily produce 'objective' information since their responses are inevitably conditioned by their own social context. However, by matching 'official accounts' from each of the interviews one gains an overall impression of the processes at work in constructing the industry, and cross referencing subjective accounts produces a finely grained picture of how the cluster has been formed and structured. I also attended conferences and workshops designed for grape growers and winemakers in the state and talked with individuals at such venues. I visited educational institutions in North Carolina that provide training and workshops for the industry, met with officials at the Wine and Grape Council as well as those at the Agricultural Extension Agency.

In discussions with winery owners I asked them about suppliers of key resources and followed these leads with further interviews with such individuals (real estate agents specializing in marketing potential vineyard land, suppliers of fertilizer, posts and trellising equipment, packaging, etc.). I relied upon local industry publications such as *On the Vine* to get a sense of what other ancillary products were being advertised (bed and breakfasts and tourism-related items); this enabled me to gauge the broader impact of the industry on the region. I interviewed individuals in the tourism industry to gain their sense of what the wine industry was doing and how legitimate as a destination endeavour it was. I used newspaper stories to gain further insights: during the nineteenth century such records are often all there is factually about the industry; currently they constitute a record of topical concerns for incumbents as the industry has emerged.

I revisited six of the wineries on numerous occasions since I felt that the individuals there were key informants and well integrated in the various networks that I had discerned. In extensive discussions with these people I was able to learn valuable additional details about routine interactions; some of which were formally circumscribed in associational meetings, others of a more informal 'behind the scenes' nature. This was particularly useful as I attempted to make sense of the emerging patterns of governance in the industry. They also pointed me to other key figures that I had overlooked in my earlier round of interviews. Whilst not claiming that information gained from such sources is necessarily objective, it did provide me with a way of assessing processes as well as examining differing subjective evaluations of the industry. In a piecemeal fashion one can construct from such ethnographic work a picture of an evolving process.

For descriptive statistical information I relied upon United States Department of Agriculture Census data, North Carolina Department of Agriculture and Consumer Affairs and then, for more recent information, the North Carolina Department of Commerce. Because of significant changes in the methodology of data collection at the Department of Agriculture, it was difficult to analyse accurately longitudinal trends. It was also difficult to gauge how much of grape production was used for wine and how much for table grapes in earlier periods, hence my reliance upon newspaper and archival records that detail specific regions where production occurred. When I look back upon the research, this aspect of it proved most daunting and frustrating since it was often difficult to interpret the data and I had to be careful not make too many assumptions that might have conveniently suited my argument.

For the colonial period I relied upon archival records of the Moravian settlers which provide a fascinating detailed account of daily life in a region of North Carolina where wine was produced and consumed. That and newspaper accounts of other areas offer nuanced views on the industry in its incipient phase. They also are testament to the trials and tribulations of the early settlers in their struggles to grow grapes.

* * *

What follows is a discussion of micro-level interactions that produce macro-level phenomenon. It is a story of how markets are constructed socially and through routine interactions that create stability. Markets as institutions are in this sense, as Neil Fligstein has argued,[11] self reproducing structures populated by actors who are not always profit maximizers. Whilst most actors embrace organizational learning as a way to minimize uncertainty, they do so in a cooperative fashion that is often different from that conceptualized by neo-classical economic theories. This is then a story of how people cooperate and in doing so shape and structure the subsequent growth of the cluster.

If one drives along country roads in the western Piedmont now (2010) one can see numerous small and several large wineries dotting the landscape. Each year several more open and others are in the planning stage. Some people who earlier opted just to grow grapes now are building their own winery. One winery that opened in 2004 with a 35,000-square-foot Tuscan style facility on 65 acres of vines stands in contrast to a 2.5-acre site opened the following year where the building housing the operation resembles a large tobacco shed.

Signs on the major highways advertise North Carolina wines and the regional trade group, the North Carolina Grape Council, continues to be an advocate for the industry. Elsewhere, private firms advertise 'wine tours' and bed and break-fasts compete for business from oenophiles or those seeking a weekend break. It is evident that something interesting is happening as wineries become more established in North Carolina and the regional press devotes more and more time to talking about them. What this portends for the future is important to assess, but the best way to do that is through understanding how we have reached this level of activity at the present. Hopefully this book will offer some valuable insights into what has happened and why.

1 DISTRICTS, NETWORKS AND KNOWLEDGE BROKERING

In 2008, Princeton economist and *New York Times* writer Paul Krugman was awarded the Nobel Prize for economics. Ostensibly for his work on trade theory, the award nonetheless mentions how his ideas piqued interest in the economics of agglomeration. The notion is that firms can achieve operational efficiencies by co-locating in particular geographic areas. It builds upon the work of Alfred Marshall and Alfred Weber, who argued that regional clusters of firms can maximize the benefits of unique local resources, provide economies of scale across various facets of the operation, and access specialized labour markets and industry-specific infrastructures.[1] For Krugman, the geographical concentration of firms, even in high-wage economies where labour inputs are expensive, can endow advantages that otherwise might not be possible precisely because specialist activities concentrate talent and key resources.[2]

These ideas, alongside those of theorists on industrial districts and the architecture of emerging markets, complement the burgeoning literature on entrepreneurship and enable us better to conceptualize how new firms grow and stabilize, and how their interaction with competitors and suppliers is shaped by institutional parameters. Such a framework is particularly useful in analysing the emergence of the North Carolina wine marketplace. Having struggled for centuries to establish itself as an area of grape growing and winemaking, North Carolina's success of the last decade has been centred on clusters of firms and a cooperative framework of information sharing. The dissemination of knowledge crucial to viticultural success, all too often lacking in previous times, and a social and institutional environment conducive to entrepreneurship, combined to facilitate industry growth. In this chapter I examine the notion of districts and the role that clusters of firms play in such settings; what forces shape the growth of clusters; and how clusters contribute to innovation. I then look at the networks of firms and individuals that are a constituent part of clusters, how actions are embedded within such networks, and the role that leader firms play in eventually shaping cluster governance. Rather than view entrepreneurship as simply a product of individualistic initiatives, I examine the context of such

activity, particularly the construction of an institutional environment that ultimately shapes organizational forms.

In recent years much of the literature on these topics has examined how
interaction between firms is structured and detailed knowledge necessary for
production efficiencies transmitted. However, what are often overlooked are the
mechanisms whereby new firms access requisite knowledge and how that access
varies in accordance with resources and capabilities. Resource and capability variation is inevitable as firms, especially newcomers, have widely different sets of
circumstances that they leverage for operational success. Furthermore, not only
financial capital and operational knowledge condition ultimate success; it is also
a function of social capital. By social capital I refer to the way relationships (networks) can be a valuable resource for individuals because they link them with
key actors who over time can be indispensable sources of crucial knowledge.[3]
Understanding how social capital can both enable and constrain organizational
performance is important for assessing the dynamics of cluster activity and why
some firms appear better positioned to take advantage of knowledge acquisition
than others. If we can grasp the ways that these various activities come together,
then we can gain insights into how a new industry such as winemaking can
emerge in a region such as North Carolina and what factors condition its successful growth.

Clusters and Industrial Districts

Studies that have built upon Marshall's early work on the externalities of specialized industrial locations typically argue that when firms or industries co-locate
in ways that complement each other and share common sets of resources it can
lead to increasing returns to scale. Using the economic success of geographical districts such as Silicon Valley and Route 128 around Boston in the United
States, Baden Wurttemberg in Germany, and the 'Third Italy' such studies have
highlighted the innovative performance of clusters of firms in these areas.[4] Inter-
firm collaboration within such districts is made possible, it is argued, by the
provision of a dedicated infrastructure, a pool of skilled labour and a relevant
education system to sustain such a growth.[5] Not only is knowledge and information transfer easier within such a setting because of face-to-face interaction,
the potential for partnering between firms increases and the resulting growth of
supplier firms in the area can lower operating costs.

Regional clusters of firms have existed for centuries, with far-flung examples
such as the Prato textile industry in Italy and the Japanese silk industry having
their origins in the Middle Ages, and the 300-year-old Geneva-based luxury
watch industry in Switzerland. What they all had in common was an ability to
attract skilled individuals and new ideas from outside the cluster which sub-

sequently acted as a stimulus for public and further private investment.[6] The dynamism and vitality of such regional economies was long ago seen as an engine of economic growth; the greater their success the more dominant they became locally and the more they became a focal point for innovative activity. Because they were often a fertile ground for new ideas they tended to attract precisely those who were not risk averse and stimulated local government investments in supporting activities that sustained such growth. Supplier firms recognized the benefits of acquiring skill sets that could service the cluster and were themselves often recipients of public investment incentives, effectively subsidizing their own location decision.[7] Whenever suppliers or buyers play a crucial role in operational efficiency by virtue of geographical proximity, they can significantly add to innovative performance of core cluster firms.

Despite the apparent economic success of clusters, most studies tended to assume that the benefits of firm concentration were self-evident; that somehow significant advantages accrue from concentration and sharing of a common environment. In recent years a more sanguine understanding of the negative consequences of clusters has emerged. Sorenson, for example, recognized that proximity leading to network density can in fact intensify competition.[8] As more and more firms locate in an area where similar firms already operate, they are also more likely to fail. Moreover, as networks structure and eventually stabilize interactions, such stability can ultimately have the effect of stifling innovation.[9] This is especially likely when external conditions (e.g. consumer taste or institutional support) change.

Notwithstanding such reservations, the economic advantages of clustering are in the area of lowered transaction costs and the benefits of mutual policing.[10] These can and often do outweigh the negative aspects mentioned above, especially when examining other wine regions such as those in Italy and Chile.[11] It is apparent that co-localization implies a climate of understanding and trust, voluntary information and tacit knowledge sharing, plus norms of cooperation and the enforcement of agreements that reduce malfeasance.[12] What is essentially a localized network of organizations thus takes on a life, and interests, of its own.

One of the key ideas in all of these discussions is the notion of trust as a public good. Since market order is necessary for the survival of firms, mechanisms that support interdependent relationships and with that co-operation, consensus and even solidarity are crucial. A minimal degree of predictability is essential for transactions to take place and this is invariably predicated upon established patterns of behaviour and a normative acceptance of rules of order. There is an extensive literature in the social sciences on the problem of social order because uncertainty, intolerance and instability have been commonplace in past societies.[13] Institutionally mediated social relationships designed to forestall conflict are associated with the growth of the nation state, but trust as a social mechanism can reconcile individual motivations and structural constraints at the local level. Stability is achieved when predictability and reliability in relationships and transactions exist, which in turn are a function of normative mechanisms and general cooperation. Norms of reciprocity are crucial building blocks for collaboration and trust is the precondition for cooperation. Individual behaviour, therefore, is shaped by the perceptions of consistency in the behaviour of others, their predictability a function of a stable order.

At one level humans are quite perceptive when it comes to evaluating the trustworthiness of someone with whom they must interact. They do this by weighing the cost and benefits of trusting someone who in many cases is a complete stranger. As long as that trust in not betrayed, individuals instinctively will return favours. The more such individuals work with each other, the more inclined they are to embrace reciprocity as a guiding principle of such interaction, and the more exchange relationships become solidified.[14] In other words behaviour conditioned upon sharing knowledge and information becomes institutionalized as interactions increase. Reputations develop and these become valuable resources for firms. Because newcomers to an industry or sector lack detailed knowledge it is more beneficial (and often less risky) for them to embrace trust than the alternative. As they do this they effectively accept self-policing of transactions since any betrayal of trust can be immediately recognized and acted upon. Eventually such informal mechanisms are reinforced by state institutions and formal associations that monitor transactions and provide rules and regulations for behaviour. But the effectiveness of such a regulatory framework is contingent upon a fairly smooth operational efficiency of daily transactions, and *ipso facto* a continued belief by individuals in the benefits of such transparency.

As more firms cluster in a particular location they can confer further stability to the social order of the local marketplace because trust based inter-relationships become *de facto* guarantors of collaboration. Local community based social relationships, and the rules of behaviour that are embedded in such relationships, help guarantee standards of behaviour which further engender trust and cooperation.[15] The conditions for such collaboration are therefore rooted in the willingness of local actors to share and cooperate because to do otherwise would be inimical to the benefits of clustering. In turn this encourages further synergies between firms that subsequently foster innovation through collective learning. It also strengthens inter-firm networks and encourages the growth of formal institutions that help govern the cluster.

Once established, clusters can provide competitive advantages for firms because they are able to capitalize upon their unique collective assets.[16] The competitive performance of firms in the cluster is a function of horizontal and vertical relationships – the latter consisting of the input–output relations with supplier and buyer firms.[17] The horizontal relationships refer to the density of interaction between similar firms in a geographic location whose proximity permits constant and close monitoring of each other. Supplier and then subsequently buyer firms eventually choose to locate within the cluster because co-location reduces their costs of coordination. Traded and non-traded inputs that are industry specific can increase in number and at lower cost when co-location occurs.[18] According to P. Maskell clustering therefore encourages further specialization, improves knowledge creation and generally overcomes problems of asymmetrical information.[19]

The spillover effects of knowledge can further the competitive advantage of the cluster, thus attracting new firms to the area who seek access to this collective resource. New entrants believe that they can benefit from access to local knowledge and take advantage of local suppliers. The more established and successful the cluster becomes, the more this perception motivates new entrants. Second, the growing legitimacy of the cluster and the absence of notable mortality rates for firms within it encourage entrepreneurial activity for those interested in starting a firm in this sector. The apparent success of small ventures stimulates action by individuals whose resources permit entry. If entry costs are low, as can be the case for a small winery, knowledge barriers can be overcome by gaining access to localized operating norms.

Recent research in the sociology of entrepreneurship has highlighted the role played by interpersonal networks, organizational structure and the broader institutional environment in shaping individual initiatives.[20] As a result of this work, we are better placed conceptually to understand the contextual and behavioural perspective of entrepreneurial behaviour and able to view organizational growth through the interaction of individual volition and broader socio-economic and cultural processes. The contextual factors associated with cluster growth provide conditions that encourage and facilitate entrepreneurial activity; what Glade describes as 'opportunity structure'.[21] Entrepreneurship is therefore context-dependent,[22] with the result that individual agency is partly a function of available resources as well as conditioned by the perception of additional resources that become available following start-up. Entrepreneurial activity increases when a critical mass of firms within a cluster is established and a shared business culture emerges.[23] In turn this acts as a further catalyst for innovation that sustains cluster growth. While it is difficult to determine exactly what a critical mass actually constitutes, we do know from organizational ecology that founding rates for firms are strongly related to the size and distribution of organizational populations.[24] But even then, the absence of institutional supports, as Max Weber noted over a century ago, can severely hamper the efficiency of entrepreneurial activity.[25] Context and demand, social networks and trust, provide the multidimensional complement to social capital in explaining entrepreneurial success.

The joint actions of firms in the cluster trigger new initiatives and encourage further specialization of activities.[26] Such micro-level activity can involve assessments of human capital/motivation variables and their alignment with financial resources. Spin-off firms emerge as incumbents bring their specialized knowledge to pursue niche activities. This increases the division of labour but also permits collective organizational learning and sector upgrading. Because clusters facilitate information gathering, specialized knowledge is channelled through sets of reciprocal obligations and responsibilities among firms in the cluster. Such relationships structure ensuing market activities and become part of elaborate networks within the cluster.

Importance of Networks

Since clusters are predicated upon dense sets of relationships and norms of reciprocal obligation it is important to understand how such interactions are embedded in networks. Networks typically bind together individuals or firms through actions that are mutually beneficial. They can be formal or informal, strong or weak, and short-term versus long-term.[27] Central to their notion is the idea of trust and reciprocity, in which individual behaviour is conditional upon perceived benefits of cooperation and sharing. In other words, networks structure and coordinate relationships between firms (and individuals within those firms) in ways that promote further information and resource sharing. As Ulrich Staber states, networks bind 'firms together into a coherent and innovative system of relational contracting, collaborative product development and multiplex inter-organizational alliances'.[28] Action is therefore embedded in the dense sets of ties that exist between firms, individuals and even organizational bodies in the cluster.

Networks are especially important in new markets since they provide parameters for both individual and inter-organizational interactions. As a cluster develops, the growing density of firms facilitates informal and formal relationships. Brian Uzzi has argued that formal or arm's-length relationships are the type normally found between businesses.[29] They tend to be more contractual, short-term and geared towards routine procedural issues. There is an understanding that general information is shared through such relationships, but it can often remain at a superficial level. Informal, or what he refers to as 'embedded ties', are typically the glue that holds firms and individuals together in a cluster. These are personal relationship based, flexible and longer term, and typically emerge out of implicit understandings of local market activities. They emerge as newcomers realize that access to crucial operating knowledge is privileged but nonetheless accessible through *de facto* membership of the cluster. Likewise, incumbent firms realize that there are benefits to be obtained from sharing knowledge that can improve the overall reputation of the sector. Newcomers can bring new ideas, initiatives and resources that can replenish cluster performance, stimulate innovation or simply improve visibility by adding to existing numbers. Newcomers that are resource rich can of course provide qualitatively different benefits by enhancing the legitimacy of the cluster by bringing instant 'name recognition'. In addition it is likely that such newcomers will possess the requisite operational knowledge to have a significant impact upon product quality, both as individual producers and collectively if they can exercise a leadership role.

The denser the firms in the cluster, the greater the division of labour, the more efficient individual firms can become. While position in the network may vary between firms, those in similar positions will tend to behave similarly in their interactions with other firms because they share common constraints even if they do not interact directly. Firms that occupy such structurally equivalent positions in a network may possess informational benefits over those less advantaged. Since they are not subject to inertial forces, they are more likely to embrace innovation as well as broker information exchanges within the network.[30] Embedded ties within this structural context involve sharing tacit knowledge that can improve problem solving, even if sometimes that knowledge can be proprietary in nature. Because of trust-based relationships and norms that reinforce such reciprocity, inter-organization communication flows involve rich and detailed knowledge. They also facilitate collective problem solving which can be crucial for an emerging industry where individual resources might be limited.

Key to the success of clusters (and networks) is the ease of entry by newcomers since often they are a source of valuable knowledge. Too exclusive a membership can stifle new ideas and new opportunities and prevent new competencies from being incorporated into the network.[31] Over-embeddedness refers to the situation where economic action becomes stifled when network firms become too self-absorbed and ossified.[32] Conversely, dynamic clusters rely upon the flow of new information and maintenance of links outside of the cluster.[33] Network boundaries must be relatively permeable and the structure flexible in order for detailed knowledge to flow freely between firms and individuals in the network. Let us remember that the strength of the network is its ability to generate innovative ideas and embrace a certain amount of change without compromising its stability. In volatile markets, more fluid relationships are necessary than they are in embryonic markets. The architecture of an emerging market is of necessity evolving and flexibility is crucial since market growth is dependent upon the entry of newcomers.

Physical proximity is a key variable for operational efficiency of a network, especially when tacit knowledge sharing is involved.[34] Being physically close to other firms permits routine, sometimes daily interactions that help foster ties and make knowledge transfer much easier. Not surprisingly, network effects on organizational learning are most beneficial when spatial proximity is most pronounced.[35] It is the exchange of knowledge on a personal level that provides the basis for the growth of institutional frameworks and possible formal inter-firm relationships. However, one must discern not just the quantity of contact but also its qualitative dimensions. From professional interactions and casual conversations to direct seeking of detailed knowledge, the linkages can vary greatly. Loosely coupled networks are typically those where interactions are infrequent and only recent, ties are weak and individuals lack intimacy with one another.[36] On the other hand tightly coupled networks, despite the potential for disruption following new entrants, can exhibit knowledge sharing crucial for cluster evolution. Clusters are therefore emergent and fluid, embracing newcomers who can provide density benefits to supplier and even buyer firms. Firms within the network have a common interest in its survival and therefore typically develop a common vision. This reinforces the structural dimensions of the cluster inasmuch as it commits individuals to act in certain ways that maintain operational consistency and integrity.

Measuring Network Efficiency

Having outlined the various components of networks and clusters and shown how their strength lies in the creation of reciprocal relationships, one needs to analyse how knowledge transfer actually happens and the ways in which interactions are structured within networks. This has often been neglected in studies where the existence of a network presumes a level of cooperation and subsequently innovation without actually delineating the process whereby this occurs. Ulrich Staber has argued that even empirical studies of district networks are more likely to be descriptive than analytic and that we need a more rigorous assessment of the causal mechanisms that eventually lead to innovation.[37] We cannot merely assume that because firms locate in a particular area where other firms in the same industry exist that there will be interactions that are mutually beneficial. As noted earlier, it is conceivable that increased density can stifle innovation rather than encourage it.

Discerning the types of relationships that are established in the initial phase, how interactions are initiated and newcomers assess incumbents in terms of trust and whether they have the requisite knowledge that can be acquired are all important parts of the organizational puzzle. In other words, what are the existing sorts of filtering mechanisms that structure eventual knowledge transfer and how do newcomers determine the appropriate routes to gain access to this knowledge? Is there a selection process at work in which only efficient (however that might be determined) firms possess the resources to best understand network dynamics and therefore adapt to them?

The latter presumes an evolutionary perspective to organizational dynamics, a selection process whereby certain new entrants (as well as incumbents) survive by virtue of their ability to contribute to the overall cluster.[38] Furthermore one might assume that new entrants are more likely to be 'accepted' into the network, with requisite knowledge transfer occurring, if they have appropriate resources that incumbents see as potentially beneficial to the network. Therefore 'membership' becomes a two-way process – newcomers seek entry to the industry and are successful because they have appropriate resources; incumbents are more likely to accept new entrants if they are perceived to have the necessary resources for survival.

There are a number of important issues for the functioning of a network that are raised by the above. One relates to the notion of stability, specifically how networks manage the changes in structure that result from new entrants. Second, how do networks overcome basic governance problems that emerge as the number of members increase and interactions become more complex? Third, and related to the former point, how does the density of the network affect the quality of interactions? Are the network ties weaker as the numbers increase or stronger because the overall legitimacy (and status) of the network cluster is heavily dependent upon innovation? A loose coupling assumes that members interact infrequently while a strong coupling implies a great degree of reciprocity. Finally, does an increase in size result in higher rates of organizational mortality?

In terms of network stability, one can reasonably assume that there is homophily associated with individuals in the network inasmuch as those seeking entry to the industry and network share similar assumptions about goals and business activity. Structuring of network activities is often based upon similarity among the individuals, as like tends to attract like and therefore homogeneity usually arises.[39] Because members of a network share similar occupational interests and goals and recognize that individual success is part of the collective reputation, they will work towards maintaining network integrity. Stability becomes problematic when the environment is in a state of flux and uncertainty or when diversity of members is such that routines and interactions become incompatible. Although diversity can enable learning advantages and promote innovation through different but complementary resources,[40] it can also impair trust-based reciprocity. If individuals have different resources it is probable they have different assumptions about their business goals. Such differences can inhibit interaction because individuals are less likely to see mutually beneficial gains. As a consequence the basis for trust is eroded, interactions are more superficial and information rather than detailed knowledge is exchanged. This in turn minimizes the potential for innovation and can eventually lead to hierarchy within the network with a core group of insider firms and a periphery of marginalized actors. This can be problematic for the network or it can merely constitute a recasting of the network structure in ways that enhance efficiency for core firms as is normally seen in organizational evolution.

The growth of a hierarchy of networked firms can endow the cluster with appropriate resource-rich firms whose activities can be benchmarked by others. If a cluster is to grow, it must be capable of encouraging innovation and collective organizational learning. To do this requires firms with appropriate knowledge and skill sets to establish best business practices and standards of operational excellence.[41] Some firms must assume a leadership role in this process and, by virtue of that capacity, are powerful arbiters of activities within the cluster. Not only can leader firms set standards but they can use their powerful position to impose such standards on other firms in the cluster. This can be done through knowledge sharing that demonstrates what needs to be done and how to do it, but also more forcefully by actively discouraging non-performing firms from remaining in the cluster. Such isolation can lead eventually to these firms failing.

Leader firms can play a significant role in cluster governance, inasmuch as they have the resources and capabilities to set high standards as well as take appropriate risks. They typically have the biggest investments, are more committed to a long-term view of the enterprise and have a more professionalized staff. Conversely, large firms can ossify, impede innovation and become complacent. Rather than act as engines of growth they can cling resolutely to old ways, resisting rather than embracing change and hindering operational improvements. History is replete with such examples, most notable of which in recent years is the United States automobile industry. Yet if they do possess dynamic capabilities and foster improved governance, their role can be singularly crucial to establishing legitimacy for the new sector.

Governance is the glue of cluster and networks since it binds firms together under an umbrella of operational legitimacy and it can stimulate organizational learning.[42] Above all, governance is important if firms are to reduce dynamic transaction costs since it coordinates individual transactions and structure interactions. In the absence of formal institutional structures that regulate behaviour, it acts as a stabilizing force. It promotes order, creates a framework for the realization of mutual gains and enables routine self-regulation without cumbersome oversight from external bodies. Such governance often occurs with the growth of 'organizational fields'[43] as new sets of professional ideals, operating standards and technical efficiencies become established.[44]

When most effective, governance also relies upon a leadership role played by key firms to establish operational parameters that sustain competitive advantage. Such standard-setting is only beneficial to the overall cluster if it permits other firms to tap into the specialist knowledge base. Cluster governance works best when leader firms set standards but also facilitate innovation in firms who previously lacked the resources to establish such procedures independently. Thus, organizational social capital rather than individual social capital is the crucial component since the former is a public good. The importance of the link between social capital and network types for overall governance is argued quite convincingly by Inkpen and Tang.[45] While social capital is important for initial embedding of firms in networks, and at this level remains a private good, when network relationships are aggregated into organizational entities it becomes the glue that sustains the ties. Knowledge transfer and innovation are opened to a wider arena of players, enhancing the adaptive capacity of the network as a whole and furthering the efficiency of the cluster.

As leader firms become established and their efficiency determined they are more likely to be sought out by newcomer firms who select them as potential sources of indispensable knowledge. The former's knowledge base is a resource that might be difficult to replicate by new entrants, but the latter is likely to seek out such firms precisely because they are perceived as leaders.[46] The more such firms are sought out, the more credible they become as leaders and the more central they are to the cluster knowledge network.[47]

If leader firms are an important source of stability in cluster governance as networks become consolidated, is there a time when their role becomes less paramount? As the marketplace becomes more established and the density of firms increases, more formal rules of self regulation tend to be adopted. Once clusters have become established they are likely to have generated a series of industry associations that begin to operate in a regulatory fashion for the cluster, thus rendering leader firms less important for standard-setting. Together with other institutional frameworks, such as local government bodies concerned with issues like soil and water conservation, agricultural development and alcohol regulations to mention those specific to winemaking, member associations govern sector activities in ways that require adherence to certain standards. What Amin and Thrift refer to as intra-cluster 'institutional thickness' can further networking and the diffusion of knowledge.[48]

Membership-based industry associations exercise collective responsibility to promote the industry in ways that ensure operational standards. It is in the best interests of such associations to maintain certain behavioural parameters for member firms since this enhances the overall reputation. To do otherwise is inimical to their basic mandate. The emergence of such associations generally marks the 'formalization' of the cluster since now it has the collective resources that merit formal interactions and systematized knowledge exchange. It can also provide opportunities for benchmarking that can improve product quality, as well as create a more coherent organizational identity. While lacking enforcement powers, the pressures that such associations can bring to bear on individual firms can be important tools in limiting free-rider action. Formal sanctions against

individual firms are limited but the close inter-relationships that exist within
the network can be an important source of informal constraints. Knowingly to
violate basic operational precepts can and often will result in opprobrium being
heaped upon the offender, followed possibly by denial of subsequent knowledge transfers. Such is the emerging pattern of normative behaviour that such
associations are a product of and a mechanism for its maintenance, with their
governance role increasing exponentially.

Arguably, the more developed a cluster becomes, the greater its status and
therefore the bigger the potential loss associated with aberrant behaviour. Consequently, formal associations acquire greater power as the cluster becomes
established, and are more likely to use that power to impose agendas upon members.[49] As they do this they tend to assume the governance role hitherto held
by leader firms, although the latter's position and role in the hierarchy is not
entirely diminished.

In some cases, industry associations can represent firms and even localized
clusters at different stages of development. Recent entrants to the marketplace
can benefit more from industry associations than earlier entrants when such
organizations were in their infancy. Similarly a developing cluster will look
more readily to affiliate with such organizations as a way to improve their overall identity and expedite organizational learning at the firm level. In such cases
they are less likely to look to more established leader firms than they are to avail
themselves systematically of knowledge transfer made possible by association
affiliation. As this happens, the nature of information flows is transformed and
formalized, embedded ties are formally and informally structured, and knowledge systematized around a common set of practices. This in turn can promote
efficiency and subsequently improved sector legitimacy.[50] But it can also lead
to organizational mortality as individual firms lacking requisite skill sets depart
the sector. Crucial to understanding this organizational evolution is an assessment of how firm liabilities become exposed, how individual firms leverage their
operational strengths to overcome market adversity and whether the collective
effort of the cluster can significantly shift aggregate performance to limit the
liability of newness.

Wine Clusters

In the above conceptual outline I hope to have demonstrated the utility of using
the notion of clusters in which networks act as conduits of valuable knowledge
to frame my analysis of the rapid growth of the wine marketplace in North Carolina. North Carolina is not unique in witnessing a growth of firms in this sector;
states such as Virginia, Texas and Pennsylvania amongst many others have seen
growth patterns in recent decades. My interest in the North Carolina case stems

from the recent rapid growth of the industry after decades if not centuries of intermittent success followed by spectacular collapse. To what can one attribute the recent growth when previous efforts failed or revolved round a small number of firms?

Academic studies of wine regions in the United States have typically focused upon the growth of specialist firms in an organizational space that is separate to that occupied by generalist firms;[51] or how firms pursuing high status aspirations within a sector can establish performance parameters that further endow reputation and legitimacy.[52] In such instances, attention has focused upon California and the growth of the wine cluster there with recent studies showing how market differentiation has further occurred around classification systems that signify different attributes.[53] Outside of the United States, studies of Chile and Italy have examined the link between innovation systems and cluster knowledge networks.[54] Such studies typically evaluate performance alongside comparative positioning, noting how new firms position themselves within a cluster and use that to leverage a national and even international identity.

Clearly the North Carolina wine industry remains at best a regional phenomenon but it nonetheless behoves us to understand the dynamics of this current growth and determine whether such growth constitutes a platform from which a broader market identity can be attained. The apparent high degree of cooperation that has fostered sector growth, has led to improved firm operational performance and enhanced quality, features that characterize the importance of clusters for learning and innovation.[55] The informational advantages that accrue to firms participating in a network demonstrate how collective resources can be seen as the aggregate of individual transactions, but also how they influence both individual firms as well as the evolution of the network.[56]

As we examine these issues empirically, a number of key themes are of paramount importance. First of all we need to understand exactly how the cluster has emerged and when and at what stage it became an effective organizational concept. After several centuries of mostly failed experiments, wineries started to flourish in the first decades of the nineteenth century only to collapse during Prohibition. Their limited resurgence in the 1970s was focused upon a handful of firms in different parts of the state pursuing different market segments for their product. There were few firms during these initial periods and they were regionally quite isolated from one another. Their success was notable given the longevity of several of them, as we shall see in the next chapter. But they did not exhibit the density that has come to characterize the current situation.

This brings us to the next issue; what is the optimal number of firms necessary for a cluster to become established? At precisely what stage do the activities of individual firms acquire the requisite density and frequency of interactions for cluster benefits to emerge? In a related vein, is there an identifiable time period

when the marketplace generates sufficient 'hype' or desirability to influence significantly the decision of newcomers to enter the market? Since the rapid growth
of wineries in North Carolina occurred in the 1990s, it could be asserted that
this signifies the 'take-off' stage when incumbents were demonstrating success
(however that might be measured), institutional supports were developed and
winemaking in the regions of the state became a legitimate activity rather than
a quirky curiosity. During this time network activities should have developed
sufficiently to make knowledge sharing a dynamic collective resource. However,
this begs the question of whether at different times in an industry's evolution
there are different mechanism for information and knowledge sharing. Does
organizational learning occur outside of clusters (probably yes)? At what stage
do interactions acquire the reciprocal benefits and trust-based sharing that characterizes embedded relationships? Once this question is answered we can then
start thinking about how these interactions are structured and how key players
start to broker activities within the cluster.

We also need to specify clearly how knowledge is shared and be able to demonstrate tangible operational benefits that accrue to individuals and the clusters
as a whole. Prior to the twentieth century it is very difficult if not impossible to
determine the extent of knowledge sharing between individuals and organizations. But one can deduce from historical records and newspaper accounts that
individuals did collectively confront various viticultural issues to gain a better
grasp of basic growing conditions, even if at times their optimism took prec-
edent over the harsh reality of crop failure. In recent decades, with the formal
dissemination of basic techniques and an awareness of what works and what
does not, it is apparent that most types of grapes can be grown in the state. The
crucial test of industry success, however, remains whether requisite quality levels
can be continuously maintained.

Quality measures are a fairly clear indicator of industry progress and presumably one could also look at sales figures as a measure of firm success. Awards
won at regional competitions, restaurant placement of wines and general blind
tastings are all proxy measures of quality and denote the overall legitimacy of the
industry. But it is necessary to be clear about the conduits whereby these accom-
plishments are made possible. Leader firms will be identified and their role in
shaping the marketplace growth documented. Individuals in such firms, with
the organizational capital that sustains their operations, are a crucial part of the
overall success equation but we need to be specific about what exactly they have
done to underwrite industry growth. How has their presence and behaviour
shaped regional activities? Digging deeper into individual histories and seeing
how they coordinated daily activities will provide a nuanced perspective on this
process, as too will an assessment of how institutional actors come to play an
increasingly important role in providing governance and operational guidelines.

As local community colleges in the state start offering viticulture and oenology programmes, and the Department of Agriculture provides more specialist advice on winemaking and grape growing, it creates the institutional density that supports firms and network activities.

In order to explore these complex interactions and marketplace formation, we need to step back and examine the early history of winemaking in North Carolina and see how these initial developments shaped industry evolution. In the next chapter I look at events surrounding early winemaking activity in the state, the formative years of winery growth and how this early success was doomed by Prohibition – the recovery from which took much longer than in other areas of the country. A marketplace for wine emerged but it often had to compete with locally manufactured hard liquor as the beverage of choice. Because of the latter's ubiquity, winemaking suffered the moral opprobrium levelled at what were perceived to be the ills of alcohol consumption and this further compounded the tribulations many grape growers were facing in their fights against disease and pests. When wine was successfully made, it was to meet local and regional demand of quite distinct constituencies.

2 FROM THE BEGINNINGS TO PROHIBITION

My Lord, [Duke of Bedford]

    I have been engaged in a very laborious work for these fifteen years by past, in civ-ilizing a wild barbarous people and endeavouring at least to bring them on a par with our neighbouring colonies. The reason of my small success is owing to the inequality of their Representatives in Assembly. When that is redressed I hope matters will go smoothly. In the meantime I have employed myself in attempting to raise and pro-duce such commodities as Great Britain imports from countries of a parallel latitude, and I can with pleasure inform your grace that I have brought wine and raw silk to a good degree of perfection and if I had my arrears paid I don't doubt but to turn the minds of the people of this province pretty universally this way.

I am, with great respect, &c.,

GAB JOHNSTON (1749)[1]

The author of this letter, Gabriel Johnston, was Governor of North Carolina. Fifteen years earlier he had written to the Board of Trade in London claiming that he had had some success in planting vines around the Cape Fear River and with appropriate financial support could conceivably develop a wine industry in the colony. At that time he had couched his appeal in mercantilist language, ask-ing for a subsidy so that wine could be produced in the North Carolina colony and then shipped to England. Not only would this obviate the need to pay 'ready money to foreigners' for wine, it would discourage the colonists from entering manufacturing in competition with England.[2] Now he was writing to ask for more money, claiming success in his early venture into winemaking and invok-ing the latitude argument (North Carolina was in the same latitude as the major wine-producing regions of the lower Mediterranean) that would be a standard rationale for others who planted European vines in the mid-Atlantic region.

    What his success had been we are not certain although it does seem likely that his inflated notion of successful winemaking was more a ploy to solicit funds from England using popular ideologies of the day than it was to sustain his various and sundry agricultural endeavours. In their response, the commis-sioners sensibly, and predictably (as bureaucrats are wont to do), asked him to furnish evidence of his wines.[3]

Whether he did or not we do not know. But his persistence in attempting to secure funds for his various enterprises in the face of marked reluctance by his paymasters back in England is matched only by the naive enthusiasm with which people in the colonies had earlier embarked upon winemaking. Not only the planting of mulberries for raising raw silk and olive trees for oil, vines had also been claimed by Johnston to be particularly suited to both the climate and soil of the Carolinas. In this he was merely echoing the claims of settlers a hundred years earlier who had enthusiastically argued that the colony could be founded 'in the hope of producing a rich commodity of wine'.[4] The fact that people were still arguing this without much wine to show for their troubles a century later suggests an excessive optimism in the face of incessant failure.

Johnston's policy, if that is what it can be called in hindsight, was apparently to look for ways to keep the population employed and producing commodities that could demonstrate the value of the whole colonial enterprise. If it meant he had to bend the truth a little, then presumably he felt this was necessary when dealing with fickle inhabitants whom he clearly held in broad disdain. Ultimately we do not know if he produced any wine (doubtful for reasons we shall soon discover) or even whether he seriously believed he could on a regular basis given the impediments that even he must have realized he was facing. His persistence in his appeals to London was not uncommon during these times, with lines of communications severely stretched, transport unreliable and distances immense given the modes of travel. As with his successors who echoed the same sentiment, he argued that with just a little more financial assistance, winemaking could be successful. How much money and time would be thrown at such endeavours for the next 300 years or so is a tribute to man's perseverance in the face of reason.

Vines but the Wrong Grapes

When the first settlers arrived on the shores of what is now North Carolina and Virginia in the late 1500s and early 1600s, it seems from the few written accounts that they did in fact see large quantities of native grapes that were undoubtedly *vitis rotundifolia*, better known as muscadine or scuppernong. However, we need to be cautious about such early accounts of abundance as they were frequently written for an audience back in England and designed to paint an 'Arcadian' picture of the new lands to attract potential settlers. Nonetheless, we now know this grape variety is native to the region and the vines do grow to an impressive scale.[5] When Verrazano explored the Cape Fear River in what is now the area around Wilmington, he reported a land 'so full of grapes ... in all the world, the like abundance is not to be found'.[6]

The settlers in the Virginia colony were the first to demonstrate an almost unbridled enthusiasm for grape growing in their attempts to make wine. Operating with the impeccable logic of seventeenth-century settlers, it was deduced that since 'a rich profusion of grapes adorned the woods of the colony',[7] wine could easily be made. All that was lacking were individuals who could properly 'dress' the vines and understand some of the more subtle nuances of winemaking. Vines were replanted and tamed and wine was made, much of it by individuals whose knowledge of such processes was at best rudimentary. The resulting product was often described as 'sour' and clearly different to the tastes of European grapes (*vinis vinifera*) that these people were accustomed to. Consequently, the settlers persisted with their *vinifera* experiments. A 1623 law passed by the Virginia colonial assembly required every householder to plant ten vines, yet various competitions between 1651 and 1693 that offered prizes for wine production resulted in no winners.[8] Yields seemed to vary widely but no significant amount of wine appears to have been made, notwithstanding exaggerated claims, and was consumed locally.[9]

It was now assumed that the problem lay not in the vines but in the absence of people skilled to manage them and make the wine. Appeals to attract skilled *vignerons* from France to help with these endeavours produced some results in terms of individuals but little in wine.[10] These winemakers were encouraged to bring European grapes since winemaking trials with the native grape were proving less than successful. But either they were less skilled than they pretended (possibly) or the *vinifera* vines they imported were ill-suited to sandy soils and climate of the mid-Atlantic region (most definitely); wines of appropriate quantity or quality were not forthcoming.

The problem was not the cold winters that the locals thought caused the loss of leaves and the eventual death of the vines; instead it was insect-borne diseases and pests. Vines take from three to five years before they yield a viable crop and during that time the vines conceivably did grow thereby encouraging a false optimism of the bounty to come. There was also probably great variability in the rate and intensity of the diseases when they struck, due to climatic variations. But strike they always eventually did. Downy mildew might desiccate some leaves whilst others went untouched; black rot would result in some fruit surviving whilst others shrivelled;[11] the end result was always that the vines died. The native grapes were immune to these diseases but unfortunately they did not produce the sort of wine that the locals were accustomed to.

Why did these early colonists persist in the face of such failures? Partly, the explanation lies in the lack of generalized learning whereby obvious flaws could be transmitted to others. Because of the general isolation of such endeavours, and the absence of a framework to disseminate what worked and what did not, most of the early grape growing and winemaking was individualistic and motivated by an unbridled enthusiasm for replicating agricultural practices that worked in Europe. The fact that the vines appeared to be growing in the first few years after planting, and when diseases did start to appear the crop was not uniformly destroyed, further delayed recognition of the problem.

Second, early colonists were caught up in the ideological fervour of economic opportunism that saw the colonies as a source of profit. There are constant references to the desirability (and more dubiously the viability) of silk, vines and olive oil amongst their writings.[12] Whilst oil is perhaps a natural desire given its importance in cooking and as a lubricant, silk and wine are more luxurious products. Yet they figured prominently throughout that first colonial century with little actual evidence of any of these products being produced on a commercial scale. Perhaps they were the product of wishful thinking and a desire to find suitable treasures comparable to the gold of South America of which the Spaniards at least had concrete evidence. Such luxuries would certainly play well back in London, satisfying government accountants as well as piquing the imagination of would-be settlers and investors. There were also serious claims made about the similar latitude of the colonies to the Mediterranean region, and *ipso facto* a presumption that Mediterranean-style crops could be successfully grown in the Americas. The fact that England is on a similar latitude but with a completely different climate from Newfoundland did not appear to sway this reasoning.

In retrospect it is difficult to determine whether the early settlers were overly optimistic or incredibly naive when it came to identifying the agricultural activities that would sustain the new colonies. It was also probably conditioned by the structure of agriculture in the Colonies together with transportation impediments. Much of North Carolina's agriculture was small-scale and subsistence oriented, primarily because the state lacked access to markets that would have encouraged growth of cash crops. As C. Cathey argued, agriculture became increasingly unprogressive because the incentives for excellence were not present.[13] The generally low levels of education amongst the predominantly rural population further compounded the problems. It is worth noting the comments by a local official, Elkanah Watson, who wrote in 1786, 'Perhaps no state had at that period performed so little to promote the cause of education, science, and arts as North Carolina ... The lower classes of that region were then in a condition of great mental degradation'.[14] Damning words indeed but also quite prescient when it came to understanding why attempts at innovation such as grape growing so frequently failed. However, the abundance of land and the relative ease with which some crops could be grown did little to encourage innovation, although agricultural societies that were formed in the early 1800s did eventually lead to agricultural reforms by mid-century.

The seventeenth and eighteenth centuries are replete with attempts to make wine but it was only in the late 1770s that regular cultivation occurred, and this with a domesticated native grape called the Alexander.[15] By the beginning of the nineteenth century it was finally clear that if there was to be a future for winemaking in America, it had to be with native grapes or possibly hybrids. No less an oenophile authority than Thomas Jefferson summarily stated in 1809 that, 'it will be well to push the culture of this grape (Alexander) without losing time and efforts in the search of foreign vines which it will take centuries to adapt to our soil and climate'.[16] It was in North Carolina, however, that some of the earliest success with native grapes finally occurred.

North Carolina's Own: Scuppernong

The muscadine (*vitis rotundifolia*) grapes, that grow on the large vines that legend credited Sir Walter Raleigh with discovering on Roanoake Island and referred to subsequently as the Mother Vine, have become popularly known as scuppernong.[17] The grapes do not grow in bunches but in clusters, with each grape the size of a cherry. The vines themselves are often huge, the size of tree trunks and each one can yield a ton of fruit. However, when fermented the result is a strong-tasting and bitter wine; hence the need for sweetening and other doctoring to transform it into a palatable if not slightly musky tasting beverage. It was this less than desirable flavour that had led to the experiments with *vinifera* grapes, all of which had ended in failure. When such ambitious plans were finally abandoned and attention focused upon utilizing native grapes, it paved the way for renewed interest and the eventual success in North Carolina of scuppernong.

One of the first to chronicle the apparent bounty of native grapes in North Carolina was the Surveyor General John Lawson. His writings in the first decade of the eighteenth century suggest a veritable abundance of various types of grapes which undoubtedly fuelled the winemaking fantasies of many a subsequent farmer in the region.[18] He recognized the need to improve the harvested product through grafting but was unsure of exactly what the right combinations should be.[19] His enthusiasm for advocating the harvesting of these grapes for wine perhaps explains the broader public optimism reflected in the claims of Governor Johnston cited earlier. Subsequent governors were more sanguine in their assessment of the potential, arguing that 'the rich wines need proper vine dressers to improve them'.[20] In other words, appropriate techniques for cultivation and individuals with skill-sets to facilitate this were needed. The fact that many still subscribed to the idea that wine could be a valuable commodity in the future meant that experiments continued.

How successful these experiments were and how extensive winemaking was during the latter part of the eighteenth century and early nineteenth is difficult to determine. From the fairly meticulous records of the Moravians who had settled in North Carolina during this period, however, one gains a partial understanding of its importance in one community. We cannot necessarily generalize from this small sample but one can understand how information about viticulture was transferred into the region and an embryonic market emerged.

Moravians and a Market for Wine

Situated in the central part of the state better known now as the Piedmont region, the Moravian settlements were flourishing communities by the late eighteenth century, the population having migrated south from Pennsylvania and originally from Europe. Moravians used wine in their religious services and had taverns for more secular leisure activities. Most of this wine was secured from overseas sources but demand outstripped supply so local sources were sought. This however, proved an uneasy task as is indicated in their various records, highlights of which below provide a summary of their concerns.

According to the 23 April 1776 Minutes of the Salem Boards, an Act of Parliament in England had cut off all commerce with the West Indies thus making supplies of wine for their communion difficult to obtain.[21] Five days later, they record that they were 'nearly out of Communion wine, and discussed how to get more. Mr Lock, who deals in wine, has some to sell, but at 12sh. per gallon. If we cannot get any cheaper we will have to buy from him.'[22] And on 13 May they discussed the possibility of using wine made from wild grapes in the Lovefeasts since tea, coffee and sugar had become very expensive. On 22 July 1780 they reported that, 'As the Communion wine is nearly out, the wine in the Tavern shall be bought from Br. Meyer for hard money.'[23] In the 1781 Minutes of the Salem Boards, they note, 'Br. Shaffer has some good wine made from wild grapes, which he is willing to sell for use in Holy Communion. Br. Herbert shall be asked to buy as much as he can for this purpose.'[24] Another Moravian community in this area at Bethabara noted similar wine shortages in 1781.[25]

By the 1790s alcohol sales were sufficiently robust to prompt the need for a licence to sell wine and beer in these communities and this is one of the first indications of government involvement in this industry. It had been standard practice to give wine to bearers and mourners at funerals but in February 1803 that practice was terminated, either because the beverage had become too expensive and scarce or the imbibing of alcohol was now deemed insufficiently reverential at such sombre occasions.[26] Given low life expectancy and large families funerals were a fairly frequent event at this time, so it is not inconceivable that much wine was consumed.

Finally, looking at inventories of supplies to the communities, one can see the importance of wine amidst other commodities deemed essential for daily life. For example, an account of Br. Johannes and company's move to Salem from Bethlehem on 21 September 1785 has wine (2.5 gallons of Teneriff wine, 9 gallons of claret and 2 boxes with 24 bottles) constituting almost 20 per cent of their expenditures and more than their cost of ham and dried beef (other items were coffee, barley, rice and sugar, plus implements for cooking and eating).[27]

The above provide a number of interesting insights. First it is clear that wine was increasingly being made to meet the demands of this community, but often of insufficient quantity. From this one deduces that either the Moravians drank much wine, albeit in frequent attendance at Holy Communion, or that the supply was so unreliable as to create periodic shortages. Harvests were probably unpredictable so even the native grapes that were used did not always produce the desired volume. Who exactly made the wine we are not certain but it was more than one or two members of the community since different names are listed as potential suppliers. Since many Moravians were from central Europe where winemaking was an established practice and its consumption part of daily life,[28] one can presume that those who made the wine in North Carolina had some practice at the process. We know that native grapes were used and this was probably scuppernong. It was presumably 'doctored' to provide a taste that might be somewhat similar to the wines of Europe, or at least to make it palatable. A typical procedure was to add apple or peach brandy (both of which were made locally) that fortified the wine but also stabilized it. As to quantity, records do indicate that as early as 1769, three Moravian settlements made nineteen hogsheads from wild grapes.[29] Most of the wine was made for personal consumption, but given norms of self-sufficiency that characterize pre-industrial agricultural communities many people in the community probably made wine or bought it from their neighbours. Given the references cited earlier of locals being approached to sell wine for Communion it seems that a significant number tended vines and harvested the product to make wine in sufficient quantities to generate an occasional surplus that could be sold locally.

The existence of taverns tells us that wine was also made for commercial sale. However, relative to other alcoholic beverages, wine was not the main beverage of choice at such establishments. An inventory of liquor at the tavern in Salem in 1807 shows 924 gallons of whiskey, 455 gallons of Apple and Peach Brandy, 137 gallons of Rum, 5 gallons of Gin, 30 gallons of Coniack, 8 barrels of Cyder, 60 gallons of Malaga wine and 20 gallons of Sicily wine.[30] Clearly whiskey was the local beverage of choice, was the least expensive and probably the easiest to make locally.[31] What exactly Malaga and Sicily wine were, whether they were imported or simply a label given to a style of locally made wine, is difficult to determine. But the relatively modest quantities of wine for sale might suggest that local individual production was sufficient (most of the time) to meet individual needs whereas other liquor was something that was purchased at the tavern.

Second, it does appear that a market of sorts had emerged for the making and selling of wine in this community, thus affording a semblance of legitimacy for the embryonic industry. Although much of the wine that was made was for domestic consumption, there was sufficient impetus for individuals to tend vines in ways that would maximize their harvest potential and hence create a surplus for sale. Whereas previous colonial-era accounts are witness to a desire to make wine, here we see the growth of a veritable demand for the product that is matched with a nascent ability to supply it.

Given the demand for wine, in both sacred and secular settings, and the existence of contractual arrangements for its local sale, the resulting formalization of exchange relations in a proscribed community setting gave winemaking an identity. Those who made wine, whether from native grapes or their experiments with hybrids, now had a marketplace (however limited) in which to purvey their product. Past exaggerated claims of winemaking success earlier in the century could now be supplanted by concrete examples of a commodity that was bought and sold and which was subject to the vagaries of supply and demand fluctuations that mark normal market operations. For this the Moravians deserve credit as the community that injected life into what had been a largely unsuccessful endeavour.

Early Winemaking Elsewhere in North Carolina

Regional interest in making wine continued despite the failures of *vinifera* cultivation and eventually this led to more experiments with native grapes such as muscadines. In early nineteenth-century records there are numerous references to winemaking in the state and plentiful comments on the abundance of grapes. When the weekly Raleigh newspaper, the *Star*, reported that 1,368 gallons of wine had been manufactured in a county which returned only 384 militia, there was considerable interest in what exactly was happening there.[32] And an earlier edition of the same newspaper on 21 December 1809 reported 'an extraordinary and excellent kind of grape' in north-eastern North Carolina and then proceeded to detail the winemaking process. Subsequent articles in that newspaper make reference to the increased cultivation of grapes, emphasizing the beneficial aspects of such endeavours for both commerce and 'as a means of improving the morals of our country'.[33] Once again, winemaking was being seen through the lens of commercial activity but now given a moral imperative to further justify its embrace.

Undoubtedly much of this enthusiasm had less to do with a fervent interest by locals becoming budding oenophiles than actively discouraging the huge quantities of hard liquor that were consumed at that time. It should be noted that North Carolina was not necessarily exceptional in this indulgence. Throughout the colonies whiskey was ubiquitous, with George Washington apparently the largest distiller; 11,500 gallons of corn whiskey were made annually at his Mt

Vernon home. John Hancock in Boston was another large producer and on 4 July 1776 all of the signers of the Declaration of Independence drank home-brewed whiskey.

A study of Edgecombe County, North Carolina, reveals that in the late 1700s the Carolinians 'imbibed alcoholic beverages on a grand scale' and that 'drinking at William Maund's funeral so exceeded expectations that a man had to be sent to Tarboro twice to purchase more rum'.[34] The 1810 Census of Manufactures for North Carolina reported 5,424 stills producing 1,386,691 gallons of whiskey and brandy; an amount far outstripping whatever wine was produced.[35] It has also been suggested that some of that whiskey and brandy was in fact added to wine to make it more palatable or suitable to the needs of a population long accustomed to hard liquor.[36] Subsequent reports argue that the wine continued to be a blend of three-quarters grape juice and one quarter apple brandy or 'a compound of grape juice, cider, honey and apple brandy'.[37]

Notwithstanding the primacy of alternative cheap beverages, interest in better understanding the scuppernong grape and how it could be used to make wine is evident from none other than Thomas Jefferson, who had secured a barrel of the 'Carolina wine' in 1820, most probably from gentlemen planters around Edenton and the area adjacent to Albermarle Sound.[38] He made several additional purchases and although convinced that the producers were keeping the best wine for themselves he nevertheless ordered a thirty-gallon barrel in 1823.[39] This evidently prompted local producers to plant more vines as well as encouraging diversification by those whose earlier attempts at *vinifera* grapes had failed, as well as focusing attention on how best to tend the vines and create hybrids through grafting.[40] Experiments with other native grapes (*vitis labrusca* and hybrids called Norton and Alexander – both the product of grafting native grapes and *vinifera*) were tried especially after the War of 1812 made the import of European wines more expensive.

What had started with the Moravians had now spread to other regions of the state, especially the coastal areas. Farmers, rich and poor, were apparently experimenting with fermented juice, making wines from wild grapes then sub-sequently cultivating their own vines. By the early decades of the nineteenth century, according to Pinney, scuppernong had become the *de facto vin de pays* for the poor in eastern North Carolina.[41] The *American Farmer* of 1 October 1819 commented

> Many farmers near Fayetteville in North Carolina have for years past drank excellent wine of their own making from the native grape ... Wine is made along the Cape Fear River from Fayetteville to the sea, a distance of near seventy miles, and the farmers use it as freely as cider is used in New England. It is common for a farmer to make eight or ten barrels of wine annually for his own use, and many sell considerable quantities.

Once again winemaking was being touted as a cottage industry that could enrich the state but also efforts were being made to disseminate important information for would-be winemakers. Such support was given further encouragement when the State Board of Agriculture distributed vines in the state between 1823 and 1830.[42] In 1827 the state legislature attempted to expand grape cultivation to the western part of the state by granting 500 acres in Wilkes County to a Frenchman for the express purpose of growing grapes.[43] We have no record of his success, if any, in this endeavour. Finally, the widespread use of wine-related names for towns throughout the state (Tokay, Medoc, Cognac and Niagara) suggests the pervasiveness of winemaking or at least a broad familiarity with it.[44]

Growth of Commercial Winemaking

The mid-nineteenth century marks the beginnings of successful commercial winemaking on the east coast of the United States, with areas in Ohio and Missouri leading the way, followed by New York. German immigrants were in the forefront of these activities and although many of their ventures subsequently failed, they nonetheless heralded a more scientific approach that was furthered by viticultural publications such as George Husmann's 1863 *Essay on the Culture of the Grape in the Great West* and his *1866 The Cultivation of the Native Grape, and Manufacture of American Wines*. A product of post-Civil War enthusiasm for a newly united country, the latter became the bible for many grape growers in part because it offered detailed instructions for the various stages in vineyard management and winemaking.[45] In New York state experiments were under way to replace earlier failed attempts at growing *vinifera* with native grapes such as catawba and Isabella (the latter probably originating in South Carolina). A Frenchman named Jean Jacques founded the first successful winery at Washingtonville on the banks of the Hudson in 1839. Through various ownerships, and by making sacramental wine during Prohibition, the company still exists, thus making it the oldest winemaking enterprise in continuous operation in the United States. Another who was successful was Charles Champlin, whose Pleasant Valley Wine Company made a sparkling wine that was eventually called Great Western[46] – a brand that has remained popular to the present time.

In North Carolina, scuppernong continued to flourish and witnessed its first significant commercial success in Halifax County, several decades earlier than the industry's growth in Ohio and New York. A schoolteacher and preacher from New York named Sidney Weller had purchased a 400-acre farm in Brinkleyville, Halifax County, in the 1820s. Since the property was practically derelict, he started virtually from scratch and created a flourishing nursery, a crop-yielding farm and eventually in 1835 a winery that he subsequently named Medoc Vineyard. According to the 1840 census, his vineyard was six acres, the largest in the state, surpassed nationally only by Nicholas Longworth's winery in Cincinnati. North Carolina at that time was the leader in the Union for winemaking.[47] He sold his wine at between $1 and $6 a gallon to markets as far away as New York, New Orleans and St Louis.[48] The bulk of his wine was scuppernong, but with some Norton and a *labrusca* called Halifax, and he attributed much of his success to allowing his vines unchecked growth on trellises rather than pruning as others had done.[49]

In addition to wines he also sold grapes and vine cuttings, exhibiting them at local fairs, and formulas for making an assortment of wines including champagne and the ever popular but now more expensive to obtain Madeira from native grapes. He was also an enthusiastic advocate for winemaking, for example giving a presentation on 'Wine-making as practiced in North Carolina' at the first meeting of the American Agricultural Association that appeared in the first volume of the *Monthly Journal of Agriculture* in 1845.[50] He was tireless in promoting the whole concept of winemaking as an Arcadian endeavour as well as being a morally uplifting and culturally respectable activity.

> If only as a pleasurable employment for hours of relaxation from business, attention to cultivation of vines would afford present compensation to a tasteful, virtuous mind. A number of vines, in regular order, is beautiful and agreeable to the sight especially in season of leafing and bearing. Then becoming ripe, the Scuppernong and some other choice of grapes, perfume the air around some distance with a delightful healthful fragrance. As an article of innocent luxury, no family of settled residence should dispenses with rearing a few vines, at least.
>
> Sidney Weller (1832)[51]

These were stirring words indeed for both budding pastoralists and gentleman farmers. For Weller scuppernong was the perfect grape for the region and he encouraged many people whom he met to grow some of the grapes. At the time of his death in 1854, his vineyard, however, was only yielding forty to seventy barrels a year, suggesting that despite the hype and his local fame, his output was quite minimal. It has been said that he was better at promoting wine than growing it,[52] which might explain the gradual demise of his enterprise. His son John continued the business until the Civil War, after which it was eventually resuscitated by the Garretts, to whom we shall turn shortly.

At the same time as Weller was proselytizing on behalf of scuppernong, a physician turned viticulturalist named Joseph Tongo had chosen North Carolina over Virginia and Kentucky for his vineyard and was determined to make Wilmington the Bordeaux of America, again with scuppernong as his eventually successful crop. Like Weller he was tireless in advocating the economic advantages of wines and raisins and went so far as to establish a school were pupils could 'be taught besides all the practical and scientific details of grape and fruit-raising &c, the art of making wine, and of taking care of it at all peri-

ods of ripening'.[53] He planted grafted *vinifera* vines but, when they eventually
succumbed to the diseases that had afflicted earlier experiments in the previous
century, he returned to scuppernong. His school never got off the ground so one
can presume that whilst there was interest by locals in making wine, there was
not much inclination for the systematic and formal study that he was advocating. Perhaps the fees were too high (tuition of $100 for those bringing a slave or
$150 for those without a slave and needing board and washing); or perhaps the
grape was deemed so easy to make wine from (as he continuously claimed) that
no one saw the necessity of being schooled in viticulture. Whatever the explanation for the school's failure, he nevertheless merits importance because of the
attention he brought to the need for a more professional and scientific approach
to winemaking. Others would subsequently concur with his advocacy, but over
a century later.

Institutional Support

While many localized experiments were enabling individual learning about viticulture during the first decades of the nineteenth century, there were a number
of important innovations nationally that shaped the growth of the industry.
These included the emergence of agricultural and horticultural societies that
advocated specialist skills, often through the use of experimental sites, needed to
improve production techniques; grape and wine grower organizations to facilitate the exchange of information; as well as the growth of publications geared
towards improving farming methods. The agricultural branch of the Patent
Office created an experimental garden in Washington in 1858 in which grapes
were a speciality and within a year had 25,000 seedlings of fifty different grape
varieties.[54] At this site systematic experiments with native grapes, *vinifera* and
hybridization were conducted. When the Department of Agriculture was formally created out of this office in 1862, it continued to promote a rational and
scientific approach to viticulture and winemaking. This was supplemented by
the growth of publications such as *American Farmer* (first published in Balti-
more in 1819) and the *Horticulturalist* (1846), which systematized much of the
information about crop production and, together with newly published books,
offered 'scientific' advice to farmers.

Nineteenth-century state and county fairs were also an important way for
winemakers to get their product to a wider audience as well as to have its quality judged. This informal way of benchmarking proved useful since it enabled
winemakers to see what sorts of wines won awards. Some wines were even
entered into overseas fairs such as London's 1851 Great Exhibition where they
were judged alongside more established European producers. Whatever success
occurred for American producers it was inevitable that such activities encour-

aged some type of information sharing in the winemaking areas. If nothing else it enabled winemakers to understand viticulture techniques from other's experiences rather than relying upon the costly trial and error that had marked many of the past failures.

Finally, it is evident that despite so much uncertainty surrounding winemaking, those in power (early presidents were enthusiastic advocates of the industry) were still prepared to support it as an endeavour worthy of incentives. In addition to land grants to individuals willing to experiment with grape growing, the state also waived taxes on wine in the early years of the Republic.[55] The investments made in the Patent Office's agricultural branch referred to above are yet another indication of how the government remained committed to furthering knowledge on the technical aspects of winemaking. This form of support was vital since it encouraged a professionalism that had been absent in the past and also underwrote the necessary study of hybridization. Attempts to grow *vinifera* were finally being seen as futile, but more and more people realized that grafting native vines to the imports might in fact be a way around the problems.

By the late 1850s the Patent Office in Washington, precursor to the Department of Agriculture, had undertaken a study of oenology and grapes in various regions, with the North Carolina scuppernong identified as the sweetest. Samples were then sent for chemical analysis to Dr Charles T. Jackson in Boston who at that time was funded by wine dealers in New England. His assessment was positive, liking scuppernong the best of the many grapes/wines that he tested and claiming that it is 'the best thus far produced in the United States'.[56] He noted that perhaps more skill in the manufacture of the wine was necessary, and less whiskey additive, but that with improved cultivation methods muscadines could flourish.[57]

Collapse and Rebirth

At the time of the Civil War, there were at least 25 wineries in North Carolina and many more vineyards, in addition to the many farmers who fermented grapes for their own consumption. A market had been established, viticulture techniques improved and Scuppernong was proving to be the signature grape that could be easily turned into wine. Because grape yields were so high (significantly more tonnage per acre than hybrids), costs were fairly low and it was easy to harvest. Even if it continued to be doctored with hard liquor, it was nonetheless a successful outcome to the centuries-old quest to establish winemaking in the mid-Atlantic region. North Carolina dominated the national market at this time but that dominance proved short lived with the outbreak of the Civil War.

The Civil War damaged the industry in two ways. First there was the loss of manpower as white farmers left the land to fight, then, following emancipation, slaves were lost. By the war's end, most of the landowners were bankrupt and capital scarce. Second, regulatory retribution resulted in winemaking licences being revoked. When the South seceded, winemakers ceased payment on their federal bonded licences since the latter's authority was deemed illegitimate. Following defeat, they were therefore not licensed by the federal government and the Union forces opted to punish them by refusing to let them renew these licences.[58] This effectively shut down the industry in the state with the exception of those people making wine for home consumption. Furthermore, disruptions to the transportation system in the South made it difficult to ship products even if they were able to make wine for commercial sale.

Despite lingering questions over the quality of scuppernong,[59] it was a grape that did not need much labour, hence was suited to resource-starved North Carolina in the immediate aftermath of the Civil War. When transportation networks and cities were rebuilt and commerce was resuscitated, commercial wineries began to revive. Together with fruit growing in general (particularly peaches), wine and grapes were in demand because they could supply a burgeoning national market made more accessible by new railroad links and eventually refrigeration.

Wine production was still concentrated along the eastern coastal area of North Carolina although it was beginning to spread westward through the state. For example, Whiteville was originally named Vineland where the firm of Ellis and Company had a flourishing business in muscadines that was bought out in 1872 by one of its partners and continued until the end of the century to be a major supplier of this grape.[60] Commercial vineyards were also located in the Tryon area and the Waldesian immigrants had established a winery in Valdese. There are numerous references to excellent vineyards around Fayetteville where mature vines produced 'bountiful harvests'[61] and where the Tokay Vineyard, rumoured to be the largest east of the Rockies, had thirty-odd grape varieties on a hundred acres.[62] The latter dated from the 1840s and was restored with the help of an established vintner, Allen McBuie, in 1865 before being purchased by Colonel William Greene in 1879. By then it had become a professional operation, replete with warehousing, cellars, four fermenting tanks and storage casks of a capacity of 600–900 gallons. Annual production was 20,000–30,000 gallons of most of the major native varietals.[63] Finally the Bear Winery in Wilmington was producing 200,000 gallons of mostly muscadine by the early 1900s.[64]

As demand for grapes grew, so did production of them increase in areas hitherto deemed more appropriate for other crops. The Sandhills area saw farmers switch to grapes and fruit from lumbering, although here Niagara, Delaware and Concord grapes complemented the scuppernong which still attracted high prices in nearby towns. Southern Pines saw the creation of two large vineyards, encouraged in part by the dissemination of detailed information on viticulture by state agencies. By the turn of the century, cultivation of scuppernong and other native grapes had been thoroughly analysed and grafting knowledge systematized because so much attention had been directed by such agencies, which saw grapes as a viable way of sustaining growth in rural communities. Halifax County, however, the site of Weller's Medoc Vineyard was still the most important area for scuppernong in the state and this vineyard remained its most historic.

Undoubtedly the major success story of the late nineteenth century was the winery and wine business developed by the Garretts from Weller's old Medoc Vineyard. Charles Garrett had returned to North Carolina after the Civil War having prospered in the clothing business in New York, and in 1867 established with his brother the C. W. Garrett and Company winery. In 1871, the five acres of predominantly scuppernongs but also Concords and a small quantity of other native grapes yielded 3,000–5,000 gallons; twenty years later that figure was 175,000 gallons.[65] His son Paul entered the business in 1877 and he became the principal salesman for the wine. However, a family quarrel over who would take over the company following the death of its founder led Paul to leave and set up his own company, Garrett and Company. It was with this company that he firmly put scuppernong on the national map in the early twentieth century.

With scuppernong as his central product, and a marketing finesse that led to the tremendous success of his signature wine from that grape which he called Virginia Dare (after the first child born to settlers in the colony), he oversaw an expansion of sales that embraced much of the east coast. The growth of cities and an increased interest in drinking wine or wine-based cocktails, especially amongst women, drove much of these sales. The demand for his wine was so great that it soon surpassed North Carolina's capacity to supply scuppernong grapes and he was constantly forced to plead with local farmers to supply more. He built up a network of farmers who would supply him with scuppernong grapes, promising to pay them a set amount per bushel. This signifies the emergence of a local network of suppliers whose production was coordinated to a certain extent by this incipient marketplace. Many of the farmers employed very different viticulture techniques, hence quality (and often quantity) varied considerably. Because of his rush to obtain grapes Garrett was less able to work with them to gain the requisite experience that could produce consistency. In this sense, the relationships were purely contractual rather than exhibiting the sort of knowledge transfer that would transform the industry a century later.

Because of such shortages and the fact that Virginia Dare had become the most popular wine drink in the United States by the first decade of the twentieth century, Garrett had to modify its formula, adding to it increasing proportions of bulk juice from California wine. He also diversified his offerings and found success with a claret made from the Norton grape, a port and sherry in addition to fruit wines such as blackberry and strawberry. He was tireless in his efforts to promote not only his wine but the etiquette of serving and drinking it; in other words building a culture of consumption amongst a population more geared towards hard liquor.

Prohibition and Industry Decline

Despite the growing popularity of his wine, an equally popular prohibition sentiment had emerged in North Carolina and the South during the nineteenth century. Temperance movements had been active in the state since the early 1800s; not surprising perhaps given the huge quantities of alcohol that were consumed. The fact that liquor was taxed so low, was easy to make and remained cheap probably did not help encourage abstemious behaviour. However, much of the early agitation was geared towards saloons and the sale of liquor. The Anti-Saloon League had been a pivotal player in limiting alcohol sales in rural counties prior to and after the Civil War and by the end of the century had more than 20,000 speakers preaching prohibition in churches and other public places throughout the country. Alcohol consumption was seen by some as yet another moral abomination, alongside slavery, that needed to be abolished. For others it was viewed as an impediment to worker efficiency and industrial productivity.[66] Opponents looked increasingly to local option laws whereby a majority of voters in a town, county or state could vote to ban alcohol sales. By 1900, 37 states had these laws. In North Carolina attention was shifting towards the production as well as the sale of alcohol and more and more counties were voting to go dry. After several failed attempts to impose state-wide prohibition, a referendum on 26 May 1908 resulted in a vote of 113,612 for prohibition and 69,416 against it. This applied to both the sale and manufacture of 'intoxicating liquors' and became law on 1 January 1909.

It is rather ironic that just when the wine industry was finally becoming commercially viable, a cultural climate opposed to alcohol in general would effectively destroy these achievements. North Carolina was not alone in seeing a groundswell of opposition to alcohol; but the rural nature of the state and the role played by conservative religious groups did provide it with early sustenance and subsequent majority appeal. Other states had passed legislation that banned public drinking but had found it difficult to enforce.[67] Also, proponents of wine drinking argued that it was a drink of temperance rather than intoxication; best seen perhaps in Paul Garrett's various exhortations to understand the finer points of serving and drinking wine. But the dry forces in North Carolina proved resilient and pressed their case more forcefully at the end of the nineteenth century, with the final measure of their success seen in the referendum.

Garrett had been aware of the rising local prohibitionist sentiments and in response had moved his operation north, first into Norfolk, Virginia, in 1903 and then in 1912 to the Finger Lakes region of New York. Each time marked a further expansion of his business so that by the time Prohibition was enacted nationally (the Eighteenth Amendment and Volstead National Prohibition Act in 1920) he had extensive holdings in wineries and vineyards, plus a storage capacity at his new facility for 10,000,000 gallons of wine.[68] He tried to find ways around Prohibition by doctoring his wine so that it could be sold for medicinal purposes (Virginia Dare Tonic) and establishing a cooperative organization to market grape concentrate called Vine-Glo (that allowed people to make wine legally in their own homes) but neither matched the early success of his muscadine wines.

Through such measures he succeeded in staying in business throughout Prohibition but this was not the case for the many North Carolina farmers who had been his principal suppliers. Despite his exhortations in the early 1900s to plant more vines, most farmers were reluctant because of the growing prohibitionist sentiment. They saw no reason to waste time and resources on planting vines whose yield in three to four years could not be made into wine. In this sense, their reluctance was a product of Garrett's early success because by then he was paying generously for wine grapes thus discouraging alternative crop development. With that lucrative outlet likely to be terminated, they abandoned expansion plans and switched to other fruit crops.[69]

Prohibition effectively ended winemaking in North Carolina, at least on a commercial scale, and most of the wineries fell into disrepair. Because the state went dry in 1908, it experienced a longer period of non-production than many other states. When repeal of Prohibition came in 1933, provisions of the amendment permitted states to continue to ban or limit alcohol sales if they so wished. North Carolina did, voting two to one against the repeal. Several years later, however, the state sanctioned local decision-making over alcohol sales and manufacture granting the right on a county by county basis under the regulation of the Alcoholic Beverage Control Boards.[70] The 10 May 1935 Act ratifying this decision permitted the manufacture of wines and also instructed the State Department of Agriculture to facilitate grape growing and viticulture. The eastern part of the state promptly voted to go wet, perhaps because of its earlier commercial success and history of winemaking. Despite a rebirth in this activity, it would be several decades after the Second World War before significant industry growth would occur and once again it was with scuppernong. Even then, government regulations would dampen the initial growth.

Conclusion

From its early colonial origins to the turn of the twentieth century the rise and fall of the North Carolina wine industry is marked by a number of repeated themes. At one level it represents the triumph of hope over reason. One can only applaud the persistence of the early settlers to produce wines from European vines that flourished then withered and died. For a variety of reasons enumerated above, they continued with these endeavours until the end of the eighteenth century before realizing that the abundant supplies of native grapes would probably be a more viable alternative. It is at this stage that North Carolina was able to establish its imprint on winemaking in America with its signature grape, the muscadine popularly known as scuppernong. Having understood the concept of *terroir* (muscadines grow well in the region, *vinifera* do not) local producers mastered viticultural techniques that enabled them to sell a wine, the demand for which continued to fluctuate. The industry grew only to be stymied by the disruptions of the Civil War. The latter half of that century saw a rebirth and the emergence of a national market for the region's wines. Prohibition put an end to this successful period, however, but not before the commercial success of winemaking had been established thus posthumously legitimizing those early failed endeavours.

The fortitude of early winemakers is quite remarkable since many of them lacked knowledge about viticultural techniques. From the outset official enthusiasm for winemaking was notable, yet institutional supports to make it possible were not equally forthcoming. When they finally came in the nineteenth century, most would-be winemakers had long ago abandoned attempts to grow grapes from imported vines and concentrated their efforts on managing the native vines. Because of the latter's abundance, all they had to do was ferment the grapes and find some other suitable alcohol as an additive – activities that were not immensely difficult tasks but ones that did lead to considerable variation in the finished product.

The growth of markets for wine did induce farmers to increase efforts at improving quality and quantity but informal mechanisms for the transfer of knowledge between winemakers were limited. There were still too few farmers making wine and, despite being concentrated in certain regions, contact between producers was probably not that extensive. Given the fluctuations of crops and the vicissitudes of the marketplace, the one thing that could be said to have been institutionalized was uncertainty. Contractual relations between suppliers and buyers undoubtedly existed but these were more arm's length and formal, of the type found amongst self-interested actors in atomistic settings. Relationships were not embedded in ways that could have facilitated trust and the development of governance structures that might have addressed problems of quality and reliability of production. The embryonic nature of the market, and the fact that it experienced two decisive periods of collapse (the Civil War and then Prohibition), made the development of long-term cooperative ties between key actors difficult to sustain. Consequently, interactions were calculative and short term and not surprisingly an implicit structuring of the market that would have enabled coordination to have emerged was impeded. Added to these problems was the lack of density of actors; just when demand for wine increased and resources for new entrants seemed likely, Prohibition sentiments came to the forefront and stifled that growth.

Paul Garrett did play a significant leadership role in the industry but his time was limited and his role of industry advocate did not translate into providing fine-grained tacit knowledge transfer that could have injected operational vitality into the industry. He was a marketing genius who knew how to make money selling wine but he lacked the discipline and attention to detail that was necessary to coordinate his suppliers and provide them with requisite production skills to maintain quality and quantity levels. Earlier, relationships between the Moravians who made wine were probably more embedded than their counterparts a century later. But their efforts were largely local in scope with little inclination (or even resources) to build a market for their product outside of their immediate community. The preference for alcoholic beverages amongst the colonists was considerable but this was largely satisfied by the supply of apparently prodigious quantities of cheap whiskey and brandy. Just when an incipient market for wine was emerging to supplement the preference for hard liquor, the forces of temperance had gained sufficient clout to mount what they thought was the final solution to the dissolute behaviour of so many North Carolinians. Even though Prohibition rules permitted manufacture of a certain quantity of wine for home consumption, there is little evidence of North Carolinians enthusiastically embracing this option. Instead, it seems their preference for whiskey and brandy, the manufacture of which was illegal, apparently continued unabated. This appeared to be a satisfactory solution to meeting local needs for alcohol, thus rendering wine production unnecessary.

3 POST-PROHIBITION TO THE 1990S

North Carolina is the original habitat of the scuppernong grape. The counties of the Upper Coastal Plain are well adapted to its culture and in these counties there are many home vineyards. In several of these counties there are commercial vineyards most of which have been allowed to deteriorate during the last several years. It is believed that it is possible to revive the grape industry and to expand it within this and other southern states. This will give a considerable section a new non-competitive industry which can be used to supplement the income rehabilitation of families.

North Carolina Emergency Relief Administration (1935)[1]

The above comes from a report from an agency that was part of the Federal Emergency Relief Administration (FERA) created to deal with the poverty that accompanied the Depression. In the south, with its high preponderance of tenant farmers and sharecroppers, the plight of rural agriculture was extreme especially when surplus acreage in tobacco and cotton were eliminated. Finding an alternative crop for small plots of land, and for farmers with little in the way of resources, was one of the most pressing concerns of that era. Once again, wine was deemed worthy of coming to the rescue and alleviating the endemic poverty of the region. And it was the scuppernong grape that would be central to this endeavour. However, to be successful, farmers had to be made aware of the market opportunities for grapes when it was not clear that such a demand existed. It remained a crop with potential, but a potential suffused with concerns over prohibitionist sentiments and inadequate information of how such a crop could be marketed locally.

In this chapter I examine post-Prohibition efforts to revive the industry. The attention initially focused upon scuppernong since by now farmers in the eastern part of the state had realized how easy it was to grow, especially since it was resistant to many of the diseases and insects that had ravaged earlier attempts at alternative grapes. However, supply was not the problem. Despite some initiatives from the government and an apparent market for the juice in parts of the United States, the south and particularly North Carolina still clung resolutely to anti-alcohol sentiments.

Despite the persistence of winemaking activities in other states during Prohibition,[2] albeit often through modifications of 'home brew', North Carolina remained resolutely dry when it came to grape fermentation. The absence of a culture of wine drinking in the region meant that what grapes were grown would probably be shipped out of state. If members of the local population fancied a headier brew there was always whiskey and brandy that continued to be made illegally and relatively cheaply. Because attitudes towards alcohol consumption had become polarized (you either abstained completely or drank too much), it did little to encourage a nascent market of moderate wine drinkers because all alcohol consumption had become stigmatized. Those that imbibed did so outside of the law, generally with hard liquor.[3] Consequently there was little if any 'cultural' space for such a beverage and this further discouraged farmers from planting vines. It was only when health problems associated with tobacco were acknowledged in the 1960s that finding alternative or additional crops for tobacco farmers became a priority and such moral opprobrium could be partially countered.

As if the anti-alcohol culture was not enough, would-be vintners on the east coast still struggled to grow grapes that would make a palatable wine. In the years immediately following the repeal of Prohibition, the wine industry on the west coast re-emerged but on the east coast, the grapes that grew in profusion typically were small, low in juice, had insufficient sugar and too much acid. The resulting wine made from such grapes had strange and often unpleasant flavours. The exception to this was the ubiquitous muscadine but it grew best in regions of the south that suffered the harshest and longest from Prohibition. Efforts to grow this grape and make wine commercially in the next few decades were more the product of agricultural and poverty reduction initiatives than they were to satisfy an emerging market of oenophiles. While they stimulated grape production and encouraged a few farmers to begin winemaking on commercial terms, their successes varied. It was only after experiments at hybridization produced a viable grape suitable for European tastes that could be grown in the east, followed by a better understanding of what caused *vinifera* to fail, that an incipient wine market became established in North Carolina during the 1970s. Even then the numbers of wineries were small and the one 'corporate' operation (Biltmore Estates) was very much the exception to the typical vineyard owner who was experimenting in a trial-and-error fashion with small acreage and limited production. However, once it was recognized that most grapes varietals could be successfully grown in the state, the emphasis shifted to making sure viticultural information became available, encouraging entrepreneurial initiatives for industry entrants, then persuading the local population to purchase the final product. Each of these hurdles would be gradually overcome, with varying degrees of success, by the late 1990s.

Solving Rural Poverty

Concerns over the plight of southern agriculture had been endemic since the nineteenth century, particularly the preponderance of undercapitalized tenant farmers, small plots and the low educational levels of the rural population. The Civil War and its aftermath had exacerbated these earlier problems and the Great Depression further fuelled the marginal nature of so many farmers in the region. Finding crops that could be suitable both in terms of a market for the products as well as items that could be feasibly grown by such a population were central to many of the relief efforts that were spawned in the 1930s. Perhaps not surprisingly, attention in North Carolina focused upon expanding existing grape growing since vines were known to grow quite easily; all that needed doing was to develop an infrastructure to market the product.

Through funds disseminated by the FERA to subsidiaries such as the North Carolina Relief Administration, the aim was first to feed the local population then provide them with a viable income source. Small tracts of land were to be provided, and existing growers of grapes were encouraged to produce rooted cuttings for distribution to relief clients as well as for sale to other southern states lacking in the requisite scuppernong vines. Emphasizing scuppernong or broadly muscadines would be an inexpensive way of utilizing existing resources in a cost-effective manner. It was estimated that muscadine vines could yield three tons per acre and, with proposed prices of $35 per ton, that would be sufficient to supplement a farm family's income if not necessarily entirely support it.[4] According to Clarence Gohdes there were vines growing along the eastern counties of North Carolina that produced sufficient quantities of grapes and cuttings for the growers to amortize their costs.[5] The vines and grapes were apparently there; what was needed was some type of coordinated action to get them systematically to market.

Reports from FERA indicate the sale of North Carolina vines to Louisiana and Georgia plus contracts with winemakers there to buy grapes at $35 a ton in three years' time (when the vines would presumably be mature enough to yield a harvest).[6] It appears that the inimitable Paul Garrett was the person responsible for such purchasing promises as he was the only one with the resources and infrastructure to make bulk production of juice. He had continued to complain about the inadequate supply of scuppernong grapes in North Carolina so it was inevitable that after Prohibition's repeal he would join the rural relief bandwagon in advocating further planting. He was convinced of the great potential for grape growing in the eastern part of the state and claimed that, if additional acreage could be provided, he would establish a plant in Manteo to process the grapes. Hitherto, he had shipped whatever grapes were grown in North Carolina to his plants in Virginia to be made into wine there. If he could secure an increased supply of local grapes it would relieve him of securing supplies from California as well as help to solve the local unemployment problem.[7]

How much wine was actually made in the state during the late 1930s is difficult to determine. Figures on grape harvests are imprecise because all too often they include table grapes. In the early part of 1935 vines were planted throughout the south, including North Carolina in response to Garrett's prompting. But within a year interest in such a grand project apparently faded as farmers either failed to appreciate the potential benefits of viticulture or merely decided there might be other more viable crops. Despite Garrett's eloquent appeals, the legacy of Prohibition in the state was too omnipresent and this effectively impeded market formation and discouraged all but a few farmers to continue with their experiments.

Limited Growth

According to the 1940 census only two licensed commercial wineries were listed in the state. As for grape growing, it is difficult to determine from official data sources how much could be and was used for winemaking versus jams and jellies.[8] The decline in the number of farms growing grapes, from 75,313 in 1945 to 9,871 in 1954 and then 3,394 in 1964 does indicate that grape growing amongst farmers was being replaced by other crops, of which tobacco did figure prominently. For the next couple of decades, what grapes were grown for winemaking were typically shipped out of state to be processed to make sweet wine.[9] While the recipients of these grapes were mainly the adjacent states of Virginia or South Carolina, some were sent to Canandaigua Wines in upstate New York, the firm that had acquired the Virginia Dare brand name. Under the tutelage of M. E. Sands and his son Marvin, the winery produced a range of wines from *labsrusca* grapes as well as muscadines labelled Hostess or Mother Vineyard Scuppernong.[10] It seems the link with the North Carolina mother vine remained a powerful marketing tool for wineries that made muscadine-based wines. For example, the largest winery in Virginia in the 1950s, Richard Wine Cellars (established 1951), bought many grapes from North Carolina growers and in 1955 acquired the name Mother Vineyard. Although they used muscadines to flavour their wines they, like Garrett before, had supply problems.

In 1950, ten farmers in Onslow County, North Carolina, planted 25 acres of scuppernong to supply an out-of-state winery. However, five years later when the vines were producing quality grapes, that winery would not buy them at any price. Consequently one of the farmers, Raymond Hartsfield, built his own winery (Onslow Wine Cellars) as a market for these grapes. This encouraged further vineyard expansion by the other area farmers plus by the late 1950s increased demand from wet states for grapes stimulated further production. Another brief success story was that of the Tenner Brothers Winery in Charlotte, established in 1935 to make wine from muscadine grapes as well as other fruits such as blackberries and peaches. After reaching a capacity of 600,000 gallons in 1949, however, it relocated to South Carolina in 1953 when that state offered more lucrative tax concessions for locally produced wines.[11]

In an attempt to secure a more reliable supply of grapes, in 1961 Richard Wine Cellars offered North Carolina grape growers significant financial incentives in the form of five-year contracts to purchase grapes at $200 per ton and a free supply of plants. This piqued the interest of some farmers and grape harvests did increase. In 1962, 150 acres of commercial vineyards existed, 100 of which were concentrated in Onslow County where the New River Grape Growers Association was formed. Such was the out-of-state demand that the sole commercial winery in North Carolina (Onslow Wine Cellars) closed in 1968 because the proprietor found it more profitable to sell his grapes to Virginia than making wine himself.[12]

Despite attempts by the federal government to promote winemaking as an agricultural pursuit that was separate from the distilling and brewing industries, and even to classify wine as an article of food,[13] such efforts continued to run counter to the prohibitionist sentiments. In 1933 Assistant Secretary of Agriculture, Rexford Tugwell, had drawn up plans to develop a research programme for viticulture and oenology and went so far as to construct a model winery at Beltsville, Maryland, near Washington, DC. The impetus for this programme was to avoid repetition of previous mistakes, particularly inferior products that flooded the market, and thus to establish a firm scientific footing for winemaking research.[14] But the plans failed to materialize at levels Tugwell felt were necessary to reshape the industry and he faced powerful interests in Washington who were firmly opposed to winemaking.[15] The shadow of Prohibition and the moral reprehension that was associated with alcohol meant that winemaking would struggle to gain acceptance and legitimacy amongst a broad segment of the population that was culturally unfamiliar with such a beverage. Even though advocating grape growing as a solution to rampant poverty and unemployment in the south made perfect sense to many in the Federal government, it nonetheless ran counter to the dry sentiments that prevailed in North Carolina. To have the government underwrite the costs of liquor production was too much for the conservative senators and congressmen of the so called 'Bible Belt' and they were quickly able to quash this FERA initiative.

Ironically, the lack of enthusiasm for grape growing and winemaking did not mean that the local population embraced teetotalism. Far from it if one relies upon anecdotal evidence and comments such as that from the late Will Rogers who quipped that southern citizens 'stagger to the polls to vote dry'.[16] Whiskey was still the preferred alcoholic beverage and continued to be made (mostly illegally), was relatively cheap and easily available. In this respect the demand for wine was probably insignificant, at least by individual consumers because they could satisfy their alcohol desires with existing cheaper beverages. Table wine was not a normal part of meals in the region; the preference being soft drinks or corn liquor late in the day.[17] The absence of local demand for wine suggests that production pressure probably came from people like Paul Garrett who were seeking a supply for a broader market. But his efforts were insufficient to pique the interests of a local population as potential consumers of the product, neither was he able to stimulate sufficient production. When he died in 1940, however, perhaps the greatest advocate (and benefactor) of scuppernong was lost.[18]

Resurgent yet Intermittent Institutional Support

Institutional forces continued to play an advocacy role for grape growing as a way of mitigating agricultural depression and marginal farming. By the 1960s southern states were still wrestling with rural poverty and finding suitable crops that were economically viable for smallholdings was uppermost in their endeavours. Once again attention focused upon viticulture. However, the perennial concern over encouraging winemaking in areas where prohibitionist sentiments prevailed seemed somewhat diminished given the growing enthusiasm for federal policy that was looking for new sources of revenue that could be found in taxing alcohol.

Immediately following the repeal of Prohibition in 1934 the Liquor Taxing Act was passed that led to 5 cents a gallon tax on table wine and 10 cents for fortified wine. From this modest but controversial excise tax emerged a complicated array of federal regulations governing the production and shipment of wine between states that persists to this day. As Thomas Pinney notes, 'this notion of wine as a productive source of tax revenue was not lost on the states' whose eagerness for ways of buttressing their own budgets led to the eventual imposition of their own levies.[19] The federal policy towards wine and subsequent regulatory powers instituted under the Federal Alcohol Control Administration (FAC) was a reaction to lingering fears of the criminal elements during Prohibition days as well as a way to mollify the continued influence of prohibitionists. But once in place, as with any revenue-generating programme, even one involving a product deemed by many to be morally reprehensible, it proved long-standing. States also had their rights enshrined as to the sale of alcohol and were able to impose their own regulations and local taxes. Thirty years after Prohibition's repeal, North Carolina politicians began to see wine less as a source of moral degeneracy and more as means to promote economic development, agricultural diversification and particularly revenue (through taxes). This translated into modest policies and programmes that emanated from the state agricultural agency in the 1960s. But problems nonetheless persisted.

Whilst grape growing had been increasing during the early 1960s (stimulated by out-of-state sales) and associations of growers had been formed, detailed horticultural and viticultural knowledge was still lacking, especially when it came to other varietals such as concord and bunch grapes. If quantities were to be increased then better cultivation methods were needed. Since harvesting grapes occurs at similar times to tobacco and cotton, adequate labour supplies would also be necessary. Finally, the absence of production and marketing systems to handle any increase in volume, together with inadequate investments in facilities for processing the juice, continued to plague industry growth.

Solutions to the above were all the focus of attention by the agricultural extension service that published a report on the viability of muscadine grape growing in 1966.[20] Essentially, it argued that any expansion of muscadine growing should be linked with the growth of a wine industry in the state. To continue to ship grapes and juice in higher volumes out of state was unlikely given the infrastructural problems mentioned above. It did not make economic sense to expand production locally to satisfy distant demand when the marginal cost increases were so high. But if wine was to be made for local consumption, it would have to be competitive on price and quality lines with California. Imports of wine into the state from California and overseas were increasing during this time so an incipient market of oenophiles appeared to be developing. Therefore, the report recommended a series of rationalization measures to improve the efficiency of local growers that focused upon optimum farm size and resource use.[21] This, it was hoped, might stimulate an indigenous wine industry that might, however inconceivable such a proposition might sound, have a local appeal. Now that the door was open to making wine, albeit slightly, ensuring the quality of the finished product became important. But the problem was the lack of technical resources in the state for viticulture except for muscadines. As a consequence, anyone interested in growing hybrids and especially *vinifera* was forced to go out of state for information – an obstacle that impeded early efforts to successfully grow the latter varietals.

If it is to be Wine it will be Muscadine

In the year prior to the report's publication the state had committed funds towards research and improved technical support. Senator Carl Vitners from Onslow County introduced SB 167 in 1965 and the North Carolina state legislature began funding research on various aspects of muscadine growing and marketing. They allotted $145,000 to the State Agricultural Experiment Station and $21,000 to the agricultural extension service with the specific purpose of encouraging alternative crops to the mainstays of tobacco and cotton. The former was under threat following growing recognition of the health problems associated with smoking. Cotton was being produced more efficiently and in larger quantities elsewhere in the south and overseas. Both were typically produced on smallholdings in North Carolina and it was felt that muscadines could provide a useful supplement or even alternative to such crops. At this time an experimental winery was established at North Carolina State University under the auspices of the Food Science Department with the aim of researching winemaking techniques, examining additional grape varietals suitable for North Carolina's climate and soils as well as developing recipes for muscadine wine.

Since there appeared to be a demand for the grapes, albeit often from outside of the state, the political forces in Raleigh hoped they could capitalize on the continued popularity and distinctiveness of the grape (its musky flavours) and encourage local farmers to acquire the necessary knowledge to grow it, store it and even ferment it successfully. Some mention of potential uses with jellies, juices and jams was also made, perhaps to placate the dry forces that still held sway in the state capital.

The variable demand for muscadines became more pronounced, especially as out-of-state wineries gained access to cheap grapes from California and the market for varietal jug wines increased. Since most of the grape demand came from outside of the state, local producers were often at the mercy of a market over which they had little control and frequently did not understand fully. Given the continued lack of local interest in wine, efforts to stimulate in-state wineries were generally stymied. In 1964 and 1965 there was only one bonded winery in North Carolina and by 1970 there were no commercial wineries in the state.

State government, ever concerned with real and potential problems in the agricultural sector, nonetheless persisted in their attempts to resurrect a wine industry in the state. In 1972 the legislature reduced the annual winery licence fee from $1,000 to $100 and cut the tax imposed upon table wine made from local grapes from 60 cents to 5 cents per gallon (it went up to 87 cents for out-of-state wines). The logic here was that if earlier taxes could be a source of revenue, cutting them might encourage consumption and in the long run see a greater increase in income. Perhaps responding to this initiative, the New River Grape Growers Association reorganized and expanded its membership, becoming the North Carolina Grape Growers Association in 1973. The purpose of the association was to promote research and education across all facets of the production process, to use advertising to encourage wine consumption and to be a general informational source for its members so they could be aware of new trends relative to the grape business. These aims have remained in place since then.[22]

In 1974, a new winery, Deerfield Vineyards Wine Cellars, was opened by George and Benbury Wood near Edenton. The family had been growing muscadine grapes on their 80-acre farm and decided to try making wine rather than selling grapes to out-of-state wineries. They began with a 13,000 gallon capacity but soon expanded that to 50,000 gallons by 1980. Unfortunately when the principal owner died that year, the winery closed down – suggesting yet again that so much of the impetus for winemaking initiatives remained individualistic, despite the promptings of the state legislature. Although the Grape Growers Association had encouraged a collective approach to viticulture, there were few willing to take the leap into actual winemaking, preferring instead to ship their grapes or juice out of state.

In 1977 another attempt to demonstrate the economic benefits of winemaking was advocated by the Agricultural Experiment Station; in this case a report issued out of North Carolina State University on the economic opportunities for a profitable winery.[23] By detailing operational data for three different sized wineries (20,000, 100,000 and 200,000 gallons) the report analysed resource utilization, technical requirements, consumer market potential and revenue streams. Again, the emphasis was upon muscadines but at least in this instance significant attention was placed on the potential for stimulating in-state sales. Also, there was emphasis placed upon profitability outcomes although much of the data was based upon winery operators and equipment manufacturers that were clearly not in North Carolina. Many North Carolina counties were still dry in the mid-1970s so no matter how one pitched the viability of winemaking (broad regional economic benefits, appeals to entrepreneurial initiative, or even trying to convince existing farmers to experiment with a new crop), it still attracted moral opprobrium from many in the state. Perhaps the pervasive dry sentiments that acted as cultural impediments to winemaking neutralized whatever entrepreneurial initiatives might flourish amongst local farmers. So despite occasional exhortations from the state legislature, those that did embark upon winemaking were clearly swimming against the tide. When they succeeded it was yet again evidence of the triumph of hope over reason.

Muscadine Revival: Duplin Wine Cellars

In 1976 Duplin Wine Cellars was opened in Rose Hill by Dan and David Fussell.[24] Four years earlier the Fussells had bought 132 acres of farmland and, following recommendations by the North Carolina Agriculture Department, planted 10 acres of muscadines. They intended to supply the upstate New York market for these grapes where the price per ton was $350 in 1972. However, by 1974, just when their vines were beginning to yield sufficient quantities of grapes, the price per ton had fallen to $150. Selling at that price they could not even cover their costs so as a last resort they decided to make their own wine from the grapes. This required the establishment of a winery – no easy task in

their area where pervasive dry sentiments were further compounded by the owners' total lack of knowledge about winemaking. Confronting these obstacles, first
their father, D. J. Fussell Sr, used his contacts with local politicians, particularly
Senator Harold Hardison of Deep Run, to circumvent the town of Rose Hill's
opposition to such an endeavour and gained a permit to start a winery in the
town. Using the back part of Fussell Sr's store for this embryonic operation, they
then set out to learn as much as they could about winemaking, relying heavily
upon the experiences of individuals associated with the now defunct Deerfield
Winery.

By their own account, it was learning by trial and error with the emphasis
upon 'mostly error' but in 1975 they produced 225 bottles of 'drinkable' wine
(their quote). The following year their 10 acres yielded 3,500 gallons and they
sold out of their entire production. Subsequent years produced 20,000 gallons
(1977), 30,000 gallons (1978) and 60,000 gallons (1979), although by the latter
years they were receiving grapes from other growers in the area who had decided
to join their venture as suppliers and whose own vines were now maturing to
yield fruit.

Benefiting in part from the preferential tax rates, Duplin saw its sales gradually increase and they reached a national market for their distinctive product,
capitalizing upon the earlier familiarity with the muscadine or scuppernong
grapes. Dan sold his share of the winery to his brother David in 1978 and production increased through the early 1980s, reaching 200,000 gallons in 1983.
Spurred by the exponential growth in sales they opened a new winery (the current facility) in 1984 and reached out to encourage more farmers to grow and
supply them with grapes. Echoes of Paul Garrett abound as once again a growing
demand for the wines was met with supply shortages. However, this problem
soon disappeared when in 1983 the Attorney General of North Carolina ruled
that the preferential laws designed to promote grape growing and winemaking
were in fact unconstitutional. Without the preferred tax treatment, Duplin saw
their sales plummet to 47,000 gallons in 1984 and 10,698 gallons in 1985. As
one old-time grower said to me as he summed up this early period 'the state
giveth and the state taketh'.

Trying to find a way to counter the sales decline, but with production levels
still high, David Fussell formed another co-op of local farmers and established
the Southland Estate Winery that opened in 1987. Located close to I-95 in
Johnston County, the aim for this winery was to attract tourists and travellers
on the interstate highway and encourage them to buy wine. Sales from the local
area were insufficient to meet the supply so it was imperative to capture a broader
market of travellers. However, the various members of the co-op had different
visions of what could be attained and sales were never at a sustainable level.
The venture collapsed in bankruptcy in 1991, dealing a further financial blow

to David Fussell who had invested heavily in Southland. For the next few years David returned to teaching to help pay the bills whilst Ann Fussell assumed daily oversight of the winery's operations. Sales improved slightly during the early 1990s but Duplin did not have a profitable year until 1995 and that occurred largely because of events external to the industry. Currently Duplin is the largest by volume winery in the state and has recently undergone considerable expansion of its production facilities. As of 2008, it supplements its own vineyards with grapes from 43 growers, to whom it paid $2.8 million that year. Also in 2008, the winery released a wine with grapes that came from cuttings from the 400-year-old Mother Vine on Roanoake Island, North Carolina blended with other hybrid scuppernong grapes. Named Mother Vine, the initial release was of 224 cases selling at $11 a bottle.

Wine and Health

In previous centuries, putative attempts to promote wine drinking as a morally acceptable and desirable alternative to hard liquor were frequent, but generally unsuccessful. As was noted in the previous chapter, this was largely to no avail primarily because access to whiskey and brandy was easy and affordable, plus manufacture and consumption of those beverages were more familiar to most of the settlers who were from Scotland and Ireland. In fairness to the early settlers we must also acknowledge the probable lack of potable water in many areas, thus providing a more solid rationale for liquor as a means of quenching one's thirst. But by the last quarter of the twentieth century such excuses were less and less legitimate.

Despite the enthusiasm for alcohol consumption by some in the state there were omnipresent religious forces that took a dim view of the reprobate behaviour associated with such activity. They proved a countervailing and increasingly successful force arguing along moral, spiritual and even secular grounds (the dangers and inefficiencies associated with drunkenness). By casting aspersions on even moderate alcohol consumption, they gradually delegitimized the informal production and consumption of alcohol. They consolidated their viewpoint by casting any of its die-hard proponents and activists in terms that even a hardened atheist might think twice about rebutting. The subsequent pervasiveness of dry sentiments in North Carolina, with many counties voting to stay dry even after the repeal of Prohibition, confirms the persistence of a *de facto* 'official' anti-liquor culture.[25] This could not even be dented much by agricultural extension agents who were eager to find crops to supplement or even replace tobacco and cotton. Where economic rationales and moral imperatives failed, however, the medical profession threw the nascent wine industry a much needed lifeline in the 1990s.

In the nineteenth century scuppernong brandy was frequently recommended for its medicinal purposes but in 1995 scientists reported that moderate wine drinking was associated with health benefits and longevity, particularly the prevention of heart attacks and strokes. Not only that, but muscadine grapes contained the highest level of resveratol – the substance in red wine that is most beneficial to health – as well as ellagic acid which is a strong antioxidant that inhibits cancer. In fact studies showed that muscadine grapes contained more Resveratol than any other fruit or vegetable.[26] These studies were widely reported in the press and Duplin was able to capitalize on these findings immediately and promote its wines accordingly. Other muscadine producers have similarly invoked such health benefits as they have sought to boost sales.

The apparent health benefits associated with wine consumption were also tied with Mediterranean diets that were being widely praised at this time. Since such diets were intricately associated particularly with red wine drinking, it proved a further boost in legitimacy for those encouraging the growth of a wine industry in North Carolina and helped deflate some of the prohibitionist ardour. But even before these health issues became widely known, experiments at growing non-muscadine grapes in other regions of the state were finally yielding positive results.

The Breakthrough with Hybrids and *Vinifera*

By the beginning of the twentieth century, numerous experiments to grow hybrid vines in the United States had been successful. Hybrids are a cross between two different varieties of grapes that results in a new grape but one with some properties of the original two. The rationale is to find ways of combating inherent weaknesses of certain varietals by breeding grapes that are more resistant to such weaknesses. In the United States, the idea had been to graft European vines to American rootstocks with the aim of creating grapes that had American resistance to diseases and the fruit quality of European varieties. The phylloxera crisis of the 1860s and 1870s in Europe had furthered hybridization since American stocks could be used in Europe to replenish their own depleted grape supply. Since the first hybrids were of poor quality the French soon looked elsewhere for a solution to their problems, but experiments continued in the United States.[27]

Much of the research on hybrids was conducted at Cornell University where it served an eastern market always looking for ways to sustain an interest in winemaking but without the uncertainty associated with *vinifera* grapes. By the 1950s many eastern vineyards were planted with hybrids (two of the best known being Seyval Blanc and Chambourcin) and these grapes were often used to blend with *vinifera* grapes.

After Prohibition, interest in hybrids was accompanied by experiments with *vinifera*, especially given the success of such grapes in California and a desire to make table wines that might appeal to a broad audience. Increasingly it seemed that if a wine culture was to develop in America it would be with *vinifera* grapes since this was what most people thought wine should taste like. As Adams aptly stated when summarizing the American wine industry in the mid-1930s: 'It was making the wrong kinds of wine from the wrong kinds of grapes for the wrong kinds of consumers in a whiskey-drinking nation with guilt feeling about imbibing in general and a confused attitude toward wine in particular'.[28] This captures the essence of the problem that all the muscadine production in the world could not satisfactorily solve.

By the 1950s more and more experiments growing *vinifera* grapes in cold climates (principally the Finger Lakes region of New York state) were being undertaken. If grafting to native rootstocks could be used to control phylloxera, then one of the early, not always understood, scourges of *vinifera* growing could be tackled. While Pierce's disease was still a problem in the south, it was less redolent as one moved away from the coastal plains. Finally, fungicide spraying could now control the various forms of mildew and rot that had decimated earlier growing attempts.

Much of the early research on *vinifera* growing occurred at the Agricultural Experiment Station at Geneva, New York, where experimentation on grape growing and winemaking dated back to the 1880s.[29] It was the work of Dr Konstantin Frank, however, that brought wider public attention to the possibilities of successfully growing *vinifera* in the eastern part of the United States. A Russian immigrant with winemaking experience who came to the United States via Germany, he was determined to redress over 300 years of failure and after various experiments with other New York state wineries (principally at Gold Seal in 1959), opened his Vinifera Wine Cellars in 1962 in Hammondsport. Although much of his initial effort focused on finding appropriate rootstocks to cope with cold weather, he also used techniques that had been earlier developed at Geneva station. He was an avid promoter of *vinifera* and his subsequent successes with Riesling and Chardonnay certainly proved his point that the grapes could be grown and successfully harvested.

It is also important to note that during the 1950s better knowledge about viticulture had been developed in California, principally at the oenology programme at the University of California at Davis. The more formal scientific approach to the subject there resulted in the dissemination of important research and the transformation of winemaking from an art form into a science. The American Society of Enologists had been founded at Davis in 1950 and annual technical conferences on viticulture were accompanied by an academic journal, the *American Journal of Enology and Viticulture*. This not only legitimized research into winemaking, it also provided a forum for broader public access to crucial information. Whereas in the past so much of learning had been through trial and error, now that knowledge was becoming systematized and formalized.

The result of all of the above was that a renewed enthusiasm for growing *vinifera* emerged, starting in New York state but then spreading southwards to the mid-Atlantic region. These new winemaking pioneers came from varied walks of life,[30] but most had accumulated financial resources from prior successful ventures that allowed them the luxury of experimentation. With careful site selection, careful choice of grape variety and careful management, palatable wines could and were made in this region. Yet in almost every case, each winery was acting like an independent experimental station responsible for generating its own varied set of operating knowledge.[31]

By the 1970s *vinifera* enthusiasm had reached North Carolina and several pioneer grape growers and would-be winemakers were determined to succeed with French varietals and hybrids, establishing wineries in the Piedmont and western area of the state. They faced significant obstacles for, as Thomas Pinney succinctly states when describing the problems for growers of non-muscadine grapes,

> North Carolina illustrates the pattern clearly, beginning with the fact that the climate is difficult for the grape (*vinifera*). In the hot summers there is not much cooling at night, a condition unfavorable to grapes; so, too, are the rain that falls during the summers and the very high temperatures that are likely to occur just at harvesttime. Warm spells in wintertime encourage the vine to grow, and then to suffer from spring frosts. And almost the entire range of diseases and pests ... is at home in North Carolina: phylloxera, nematodes, Pierce's disease, black rot, powdery mildew, bitter rot, ripe rot, grapevine root borer, and grape scale.[32]

Despite the ominous tone of such remarks, as one moves east to west across the state the elevation increases so that from the Piedmont westwards some evening cooling is associated with higher altitudes and the area is less humid than the eastern seaboard and less prone to Pierce's disease. Now that many of the aforementioned diseases could be controlled through spraying, the careful selection of rootstocks and general improvements in cultivation practice, it was a question of acquiring the appropriate vines and learning how to manage them. The state agricultural agencies, however, were still more concerned with promoting muscadine cultivation in the eastern part of the state so when alternative grapes were planted for new wineries in other regions, it was often against the advice of the regional 'experts' in Raleigh. In fact many of the *vinifera* pioneers complained at the conspicuous lack of support and relevant information from the state's agricultural offices at this time. Instead information was more likely to come from out-of-state agencies, particularly the established oenology work being done at Cornell University or even that on a smaller scale at nearby Virginia Polytechnic.[33] Interviews with owners of these early wineries all indicated initial frustration at getting adequate information from state sources – a combination of lack of specialist viticultural knowledge and a lack of enthusiasm for *vinifera* growers.

Three *Vinifera* Pioneers

The first wineries to grow and cultivate *vinifera* grapes successfully on a commercial scale in North Carolina were Westbend (1972), Germanton (1981) and Biltmore (1985). Very different in scale and scope they are nonetheless an important part of the industry's next phase of growth in the state and merit description.

As noted in the Introduction, in 1972 Jack Kroustalis used money he had gained from a successful restaurant supply company and bought 14 acres that he planted with *vinifera* varieties – the grapes that produce fine Californian and French wines – and founded Westbend Vineyards. The vineyard is located in Lewisville, close to Winston-Salem, on gently rolling hills in the north-west Piedmont. Ironically he was advised against planting the above vines by the agricultural experts but he chose to ignore them and gained advice from out-of-state viticultural experts. His European background had kept him focused upon producing European-style wines and he was adamant about this when dealing with his critics as well as in searching out appropriate sources for his vines. Eventually his acreage yielded sufficient quality and quantity of grapes for him to sell them to out-of-state wineries – his plan for the initial venture until he acquired the requisite skills and resources for his own winery. With his annual yields increasing, in 1986 he harvested 70 tons of grapes and at that point made the decision to become a bonded winery (1988), making and selling his own wine.

It had not been an easy growth. Since he knew restaurant owners from his earlier business, Kroustalis recalled going from restaurant to restaurant trying to get them to put his wine on the menu. Most of them laughed at the idea of a quality North Carolina wine so he took samples from Westbend and California and urged them and wine shops to do a blind tasting. His wife, Lillian, helped on the marketing side. She noted that it was difficult at first determining what sort of wine people would like so they tried to make as many different varietals as they could. These numbers have since been pared down as they recognized that at their size they cannot make a wine to suit everyone's taste. Lillian also recognized that by selling wine in the tasting room at the winery one was essentially in the hospitality industry. If people came to taste wine they might buy other things as well so she stocked the tasting room with wine-related products. This basic marketing proved somewhat successful as wine and merchandise sales gradually increased – but it was always, by their own account, really hard work.

To help them with winemaking since their own skills were modest and self taught, they hired an experienced winemaker and general manager, Steve Shepard. Shepard had learned winemaking in Pennsylvania (formerly at Shuster Cellars), which along with Virginia had a slightly better developed wine industry than North Carolina. He was one of the first winemakers to bring detailed knowledge of viticultural practices, especially an understanding of rootstock, clones and appropriate soil conditions, and apply them at Westbend. In explaining his rationale for moving to Westbend, he noted the more appropriate climate for growing *vinifera* in North Carolina than the more established Virginia where wineries were already flourishing growing such grapes.[34] That and the ideal elevation in the region provided proper climatic conditions for wine grape growing. But also he recognized that if a wine industry was to develop in North Carolina it was best to concentrate, at least initially, on growing standard *viniferas* like Chardonnay and Cabernet Sauvignon that could be more easily marketed to wine drinkers. Hybrids could follow and in fact have been planted, but in an area that was still culturally not attuned to wine drinking, the more popular grapes would be familiar to neophytes.

The first wine released by Westbend Vineyards was in 1990. Over the years more adjacent land in the area has been acquired, now totalling 60 acres with the winery currently producing 6,000 cases annually. Its current winemaker is Mike Terry, whose early experience was derived from his work at Long Island wineries.

About 25 miles east of Westbend is the small Germanton winery. In the mid-1970s Bill McGee owned a tobacco and dairy farm in Germanton and together with five others he decided to try growing grapes, seeking help from the agricultural extension service. With limited assistance from state agencies, the partnership subsequently formed the Piedmont Grape Growers Association, an umbrella organization designed to foster learning about winemaking in the region. Using an old dairy barn owned by McGee as a cellar, the group founded the Germanton Winery in 1981 and sold their first wine that year – all of it in fact on the first day! They used French and American hybrids and in 1982 they produced 1,000–1,500 gallons of wine.

Bill McGee died in a traffic accident in 1986 and the operation of the winery passed on to David and Judy Simpson who were living on the McGee farm. They bought into the winery in 1987 and kept it operational with the help of the other Grape Council partners. But their own limited knowledge about viticulture and the gradual loss of interest in the venture by most of the partners posed significant problems. As David Simpson said, 'We were just playing and trying to figure it out; we kept trying different things until something worked.'[35] However, as partners left, the Simpsons bought their interest and learned as much as they could about winemaking and grape cultivation from the sole remaining partner. Simpson subsequently became the winemaker but of a relocated and replanted vineyard of a more modest one acre. They reduced the number of grape varieties from 18 on the original vineyard site and concentrated on Niagara, Seyval, Chambourcin and Merlot – a combination of native, hybrid and *vinifera* to meet the varied palate of the area's population. Their strategy has always been to minimize inventory and sell all of their wines as soon as possible – hence the modest scale of the enterprise. Their single acre produced up to 700 gallons of wine but the Simpsons have acquired more land, planted additional vines and currently produce 2,000 gallons annually.

Since the Simpsons' original business was a framing shop they decided to combine the winery with an art gallery, using sales from the latter to help subsidize their oenological enterprise. The growing regional and national fame of the gallery has enabled them to be financially self reliant but also kept the winery at a modest production size because they split their time as gallery and winery owners. With currently two paid employees their winery expenses remain relatively modest. But they have been forced to buy grapes to meet the demand for their wine since the volume needed surpasses that of their own acreage and they are reluctant to expand their land holdings.

Approximately 100 miles to the west of the above two wineries, nestled in a valley in the Appalachian mountains, is Biltmore winery near the town of Asheville. George Washington Vanderbilt (grandson of Cornelius Vanderbilt) created the extensive 250-room house and 125,000-acre Biltmore Estate between 1890 and 1895. A vineyard was planted in 1971 following the prompting of owner and Vanderbilt heir William Cecil as part of attempts to make the sprawling estate self-sufficient. The estate was already a tourist attraction and it was felt that a winery would increase the number of visitors. Because of its higher altitude and concerns over *vinifera* growing that had not been assuaged by the state's agricultural office, the initial plantings were of French hybrids. A 15-acre plot was devoted to the vines and the first wine was sold in 1979. However, as experiments with *vinifera* grapes were yielding success elsewhere and it was understood what needed to be done to protect the vines and grapes from the multitude of diseases affecting them, it was decided to try new plantings of *vinifera*. Given the chateau style of Biltmore and the general Gallic ambience the buildings and grounds were designed to evoke,[36] it also seemed appropriate to make more unambiguously French-style wines. The hybrids (Villard Blanc, Seyval Blanc, Millot and Foch) produced good quality wines from grapes that yielded an impressive 6 tons per acre. But Cecil wanted a fine European-quality wine and took this passion one step further by hiring a French winemaker, Philippe Jourdain, in 1977. Initially Jourdain's role was as consultant since he owned a vineyard in southern France and was professor of viticulture and oenology at the Lycée Agricole in Carcassone. However, in 1979 he became the winery's first full-time winemaker and retired in 1995, to be replaced by another Frenchman, Bernard DeLille, who still holds this position.

By 1981 the winery produced 850 cases of wine from approximately 15 planted acres. The winery was located in an old dairy barn on the estate and 'officially' opened in 1985, although not without a significant setback that could have crippled the venture financially. In 1983 they had spent $12 million planting more acreage but then on the nights of 19–20 January 1985 a severe winter storm saw temperatures in the mountains drop to −27°F. This severely weakened the new plantings if not killing them outright. Overall grape harvests were halved throughout the state by this event and Biltmore lost 65 per cent of their vineyard and for a brief time faced possible bankruptcy. They eventually rebounded and currently produce 150,000 cases annually, 50 per cent of which is sold direct from the winery.

Given the interest in the winery as a tourist destination, and the capacity of the operation, it was realized that local grapes would be insufficient to meet the demand. Juice from California and New York was used to supplement the supply of local grapes, and often from grapes such as Zinfandel which North Carolina cannot grow. Even though the aim is to source many grapes (particularly for white wines) from neighbouring growers, the sheer volume of their sales precludes that from accounting for much more than 20 per cent of their production for the foreseeable future.

Because the winery was designed to be visitor friendly it actually provides a useful tool in the general education of the region's population about wine and winemaking. Sales have been brisk because visitors to the estate would stop by the winery for a tour then undoubtedly buy a bottle (or more) as souvenirs. Biltmore has been assiduous in developing a portfolio of wines that was felt to meet a wine taste profile that the winery developed. This professional approach to marketing is clearly different from the entrepreneurial one developed by the other two wineries discussed in this section. But then Biltmore had extensive resources and a ready-made tourist destination that would bring people into the winery. Thus began Biltmore's evolution to its current status as the most visited winery in North America.

Conclusion: The Struggle for Market Formation

Notwithstanding some efforts by the state agricultural agency to stimulate the growth of a wine industry as a means of alleviating poverty, a marketplace of wineries and wine production barely survived in the decades immediately following Prohibition. Despite some individual efforts to resuscitate grape growing, a collective endeavour never materialized. For the most part, farmers – the target audience of the rural development initiatives – were reluctant to try the crop on a commercial scale. The past problems of finding a reliable market for the crop probably dissuaded many. Attempts to revive a wine industry were also thwarted by the persistence of prohibitionist sentiments, both at the federal level and locally through the 1950s. A dry culture that was pervasive through much of North Carolina, aided and abetted by powerful politicians, trumped the efforts of agricultural experts and those who were arguing for the restitution of an earlier thriving industry that had stimulated economic development in rural areas. The few individuals that persevered experimenting with grape growing were often forced to find markets outside of the state, since the absence of a local market for table wine had not materialized.

Entrepreneurship studies often point to the importance of demand conditions as a predictor of entrepreneurial activity. In the case of North Carolina from the repeal of Prohibition to the early 1970s, it was quite apparent that there was little if any demand for wine amongst the local population since there was no culture of wine consumption. The failure to stimulate a local market for grapes meant that production would be shipped out of state. But exporting a basic commodity left the value-added to accrue elsewhere, thus further limiting resources necessary for the industry's growth potential. Furthermore, an efficient distribution system and infrastructure to ship large quantities of grape juice was not well developed. Even if local production could have been ramped up to meet the, albeit varying, demand of out-of-state wineries, the marginal costs of doing so where not optimal.

When change came it was the state that once more assumed the mantle of industry advocate, encouraging winemaking through a series of financial incentives and technical programmes starting in the 1960s, and often non-farmers who spearheaded the sector's growth. Even then, however, judicial rulings unfavourable to wine producers and a growing enthusiasm for poultry and hog farming furthered by the agricultural lobby indicate the still tentative nature of such a commitment by state agencies. Despite these limited efforts, there were a few individuals who accepted the challenge, although the majority of farmers preferred to stay with lucrative crops such as tobacco or corn that at least had fairly predictable annual yields and a guaranteed market. Those that entered the industry did so as outsiders, non-farmers with resources that covered the start-up costs of a winery and an enthusiasm for a new endeavour. Because their numbers were initially small, knowledge remained localized. Learning was often on-site and derived from technical information supplied by state agencies or from out of state. Amongst grape growers, associations had developed to exchange viticultural details and be an advocacy body, but their collective resources were limited and constrained by the absence of a developed market for their product. Relationships between individuals even in co-ops were fraught with ambiguity and often dissent (cf. Fussell's failed Southland Estate Winery discussed earlier).

Out-of-state relationships were arm's-length and contractual, but also asymmetrical in power terms as the failure to honour contracts by buyers indicated.

It is perhaps ironic that when industry growth began in the late 1970s it was in the central and western part of the state, with grape varietals that were not endorsed by the state agricultural agency. Muscadines could satisfy a local market, where if wine was to be consumed the preference was for sweet wines, but the real potential for growth (and industry legitimacy) would come with *vinifera* and hybrid producers. New entrants to the industry were more committed to making European-style wines that had greater cache than the sweet muscadines. Even at capital- and resource-rich Biltmore, trial-and-error-based learning, particularly over what sorts of varietals would grow best in the region, predominated. Systematic technical knowledge that was available from established research institutions elsewhere on the east coast was helpful but understanding the *terroir* remained a challenge even for the few experienced wine makers who were now employed at the wineries. They persisted in their efforts, often in the face of opposition from local institutional forces, and their slow success nonetheless enabled them to build a local market for their wines.

The initial efforts to demonstrate the viability of successfully growing and harvesting *vinifera* grapes in North Carolina, after 400 years of failure, was eventually sufficient to prompt others to duplicate the practice. It also stimulated further collective efforts to disseminate tacit knowledge and, through a legislative act, the North Carolina Grape Council was formed in 1986. The Council was charged with stimulating the growth of the state's wine industry and funded research into viticulture as well as underwriting promotional and marketing efforts on behalf of the incipient industry. The Council lobbied for further state support and the passage of SB 164 in 1987 appropriated the majority of state excise tax collected from North Carolina bottled wines for the Grape Council. This money was used for further research and promotion and North Carolina State University began devoting resources for viticulture and oenological programmes.

Journals such as the *Vinifera Wine Growers Journal* had practical articles in the mid- to late 1980s on best practices for *vinifera* wineries in North Carolina. One article by Larry Somers clearly delineated the commercial potential for wineries as opposed to the declining profits of tobacco farming; another pointed to the disdain for *vinifera* growing by agricultural specialists in the state despite the fact that Virginia, with similar climate and soils, was prospering with such vines.[37] Such articles not only urged the creation of wineries in the state, they also argued that such ventures were perfect for small plots managed by enterprising individuals as well as farmers who could devote some of their land to viticulture.

The 1990s proved to be the period when interest in starting a winery was piqued, primarily from individuals with resources for such an endeavour. Many of these individuals were inspired by travels to wine regions abroad but lacked detailed knowledge about winemaking. However, their dedication to learning, experimentation and commitment proved vital for the industry's next phase of growth when a critical mass began to develop in certain regions of the state. After decades, if not centuries of failure, it appeared that sufficient numbers of grape growers were able to make a wine that could be sold to a local population apparently interested in embracing this new beverage. As the former's numbers grew, others were attracted to this developing sector and with them came additional resources and eventually better viticultural knowledge and a critical mass that would facilitate more information exchange vital to industry growth.

4 EMERGENCE OF A WINE CLUSTER

Farmers growing conventional crops like tobacco, soy beans, etc. are faced today with the sure prospect that prices for their products are to fall even lower and massive government support is in a steady decline as the Nation struggles with a mounting deficit. It is therefore wise to look for alternative crops to fill the gap. We know of no better way to consider than the 'new' agricultural industry of growing the great European varietal grapes that alone make the finest and most expensive wines.

There are farmers who can devote part of their land not being otherwise used to viniculture, and we are seeing a large number of business entrepreneurs who are looking to invest in this healthy, outdoor enterprise that is so different from the every-day work of the office.

R. de Treville Lawrence (1987)[1]

When Lawrence wrote the above he was speaking as a lobbyist for the Virginia-based Vinifera Wine Growers Association, which sponsored seminars, festivals and sundry meetings designed to teach people how to grow *vinifera* grapes successfully in the mid-south and move away from hybrids. Like many of his predecessors he was making an appeal for winemaking based upon economic logic, recognizing quite presciently perhaps that some of the agricultural staples of North Carolina were facing decline.

The mainstay of many small farms that dotted the North Carolina landscape, tobacco had proved a resilient crop because demand was fairly predictable, raw material costs minimal and the dollar value of tobacco yields quite high. Some farmers used tobacco as a reliable cash cow to supplement other crops; others had inherited small plots that were either leased or farmed on a part-time basis. By the mid-1990s tobacco was still the principal crop by value in North Carolina, with annual earnings of $1 billion and providing 30,000 jobs in the state.[2] However, that was beginning to change following extensive litigation against tobacco companies over product liability. For the first time in many decades the demand for tobacco was uncertain, with a decline both in the quotas for tobacco leaf and the price paid for it at auction. The result was that alternative crops were being sought by farmers and once again grapes emerged as a potentially viable option.

But Lawrence's quote was also designed to capture the attention of non-farmers. Its appeal to an Arcadian vision of rural life resonated among many for whom an alternative lifestyle was desired. Stripped of the physical demands of agricultural toil and the uncertainty of the seasons, winemaking was elevated to an almost idyllic occupation in the minds of people like Lawrence. I am not certain that any of the newcomers to the industry fully subscribed to the rhetorical depictions of gentlemen farmers at one with nature – most were far more pragmatic than that – but they did harbour romantic sentiments about wine and its 'cultured' role in society. It was such an appeal and passion that would ignite the growth of wineries during the coming decade.

As I will show in this chapter, for many new entrants it was an opportunity to change careers and pursue an interest that had often been piqued by visits to wine-growing regions in Europe or Napa Valley, California. Most were not resource-rich individuals but had sufficient capital to acquire land plus vines and sustain themselves financially until the necessary quantities of grapes grew to make some wine. From different walks of life, with different assets and often different goals, they brought their passion to make and sell wine and acquired land. Most had little background in viticulture knowledge. They struggled to learn appropriate techniques, often lamenting the lack of institutional support for their endeavours. But they established a culture of cooperation, exchanging knowledge and encouraging others to enter the industry, thus creating an informal structure that would eventually lead to the growth of a cluster. By effectively lowering start-up costs and entry barriers for others, their role as information incubators was crucial in fostering industry growth and forging its incipient identity.

In addition to those whose winery and winemaking visions remained modest, there were two other groups who shaped the industry growth. One group comprised individuals who were able to bring both extensive capital and a track record of success at other major commercial endeavours. Using these considerable resources to subsidize the winery development and with a long-term profit horizon they would be able to play a significant part in immediately drawing attention to the embryonic industry and even helping in the development of an institutional infrastructure. Other capital-intensive operations would soon follow. Because they were able to hire experienced professionals to run their operations their presence would later prove crucial in establishing industry legitimacy as the wine cluster developed, and their leadership role will be discussed in more detail in the next chapter.

The other group consisted of farmers and owners of agricultural land, some with more modest ambitions who decided to grow grapes to supply wineries and others who decided both to grow grapes and make wine. Facing the stark reality of changes in demand for their staples, some North Carolina farmers were experimenting with grape growing. Between 1976 and 1996 the price per ton of harvested grapes in North Carolina had tripled, from $266 to $757. Such a sustained increase made grape growing attractive to some farmers as well as to those who bought small plots (10–24 acres) for vineyard development. A few farmers had been growing grapes (predominantly muscadines) for supply to existing wineries such as Duplin so for some of them the logical next step was to make their own wine. For others it represented an opportunity to find what they hoped would be a lucrative substitute for tobacco. And for still others it was a way to experiment with a vineyard without the capital costs of winery development. However, the economic viability nonetheless proved daunting for many, particularly the realization of the time frame needed for profitability, and this dampened their potential entry into viticulture.

Earlier studies have argued that the transition from tobacco to grapes by many farmers was a crucial part of the growth of the wine industry.[3] But a closer analysis of the data suggests that fewer farmers than anticipated made the switch. Unlike most would-be winery owners, this group actually had agricultural experience which enabled them to understand the nuances of crop cultivation better. But even more important than these farmers was the localized agricultural transformation that was occurring as tobacco farms were sold. Tobacco quotas were being significantly reduced during this time and substitute crops such as wheat and soya were not producing the anticipated revenue. Combine this trend with many older farmers who lacked offspring interested in taking over the farm, and the result was an increased likelihood of them selling their land. This was especially true of predominantly tobacco farms which were often smaller in size and therefore most attractive to aspiring winemakers and those interested in growing grapes as a hobby. The demise of tobacco farming has been linked in the public eye with the rise of winemaking. This is true but only in so far as many of the people who are growing grapes and making wine on former tobacco land are not the same people who farmed it for tobacco.

It is important to discuss how established farmers proved less enthusiastic about grape growing than one might have hypothesized, especially given the financial incentives they were offered following the decline of tobacco production. Why the one group with agricultural knowledge and experience proved most resistant to embracing this new crop is an interesting question that merits discussion. That their reluctance to grow grapes did not adversely affect the industry's development, ironically perhaps even facilitating the cooperative exchange of information in the incipient clusters, will be examined.

In this chapter, therefore, I tell the intersecting story of these industry entrants with their differing operational goals. To understand this growth fully, however, one also needs to examine the institutional changes and stable resource conditions that have supported this embryonic industry and facilitated its subsequent rapid growth. Although historically the state had been somewhat ambivalent towards winemaking, encouraging when it did muscadine plantings, by the late 1990s it had pieced together incentive packages and support mechanisms that actually assisted *vinifera* growers. The stable resource conditions refer to the availability of agricultural land and capital for its development: the former because tobacco plots were in declining demand; the latter because individuals were entering the industry having had a successful career elsewhere and *ipso facto* the financial resources to sustain them in the initial years. I argue that this critical conjuncture of linked resources and institutions have come together in ways that provide relational attributes and interdependent linkages that further stimulate entrepreneurial activity.

Industry Resurgence

During the 1970s and early 1980s the state had two or three wineries and there was virtually no growth. However the numbers had tripled by 1990 and during the next decade the rate of increase grew significantly –19 wineries by 2000 and 34 three years later. By the mid-2000s a new winery was opening every month. Details of the annual growth of bonded wineries can be seen in Figure 4.1.

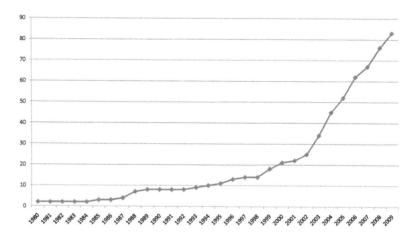

Figure 4.1: Bonded Wineries in North Carolina, 1980–2009. Source: Department of Agriculture and Consumer Affairs.

During that same period of time commercial vineyards also increased as individuals bought land for grape cultivation but not necessarily with the immediate aim of starting a winery. In 1991 there were 68 commercial vineyards; by 1998 there were 128 and by 2001 there were 200. As noted earlier, total numbers of actual vineyards are notoriously imprecise because many of these people bought small plots of land as hobbyist grape growers and failed to register their land as crop-bearing property.[4] Smitten by the wine bug like their winery counterparts, they nonetheless had more limited resources and tended the grapes on a part-time basis. They generally made wine from their grapes at home for personal consumption and did not really see themselves as commercial farmers. However, when local wineries needed extra grapes, some were willing to sell to them providing they could meet the requisite quality stipulations. This informal market transaction provided the incentive for some such vineyard owners to pay more attention to viticultural practices and vineyard management; in some cases it even led to them acquiring more formal training in such areas. Thus began an informal network whereby grape growers forged links with winery owners, and in subsequent years information shared amongst wineries as to who had the best grapes and what sorts of quantities would be available.

Interviews with several such vineyard owners in 2001 confirmed this pattern. One had bought 20 acres of farmland about 20 miles north of Winston-Salem in 1997, not far from where several of the new small wineries were operating, and planted a range of *viniferas* on 3 acres. Another bought 5 acres nearby the following year and planted *vinifera* on 2 of them. Both individuals were professionals who were knowledgeable about wine (but not necessarily winemaking) and were determined to grow grapes and make some wine for their own consumption. Their approach was pragmatic and opportunistic inasmuch as when the vines matured they were able to sell between one half and two thirds of their crop to nearby wineries whose own vines had yet to provide sufficient quantities of fruit. They still (2009) operate along these lines and have no intention, largely because of financial and time limitations, of becoming a bonded winery. Their success has encouraged others to imitate and both noted five additional vineyards have been formed in their vicinity, started by people from similar backgrounds and with similar intent.

The driving force behind the industry's resurgence was, however, to be found in the actual wineries that were founded during the 1990s. It was this spurt of growth that brought attention to a hitherto marginal industry and created an embryonic informal network of winemakers, winery owners and vineyard owners. Within the decade of the 1990s the number of wineries and commercial vineyards had doubled, and the number of wineries would subsequently double again every two years up to the present. Who were the individuals who pioneered such a growth and why did it take off during this period? From the individual stories that follow, one can discern a pattern of trial-and-error learning, a gradual accumulation of viticultural knowledge and the establishment of informal procedures for exchange of tacit operational details.

The New Pioneers: Boutique Wineries

In 1989 Lee Griffin and Marsha Cassedy purchased a 200-acre farm near Tryon in western North Carolina with the intention of planting grapes and making wine. Inspired by their travels to winemaking regions throughout the world, the couple decided to start their own vineyard, initially with French-American hybrid plantings because they were uncertain of what would grow best in their region. Annual experiments with different clones and rootstocks eventually led to concentration on *vinifera* and by 1996 they had 4 acres of vines.

Up to this time they had described themselves as hobbyist winemakers, making small batches of wine and trying different blends. However, continuing to use money from Lee's family textile machinery business that he oversaw, in 1998 they became a bonded winery under the name of Rockhouse Vineyards and that year produced 100 cases of Chardonnay, 75 cases of Chambourcin and 55 cases of Merlot. The following year saw an expansion of the vineyard to its current 10 acres. They recount the times where they worked long hours, balancing different jobs and trying to learn. Lee recalls his trial-and-error experimentation, both in growing grapes and then crafting them into wine ('we made some good salad dressing in those early years' he stated).[5] Like most winemakers they have entered their wines in national competitions and won various medals. But their aim is to remain a small winery, producing what they refer to as hand-crafted wines.

Driving north-east about 50 miles from Rockhouse, one arrives in King's Creek at the 4.5-acre Cerminaro Winery, founded by Joseph and Deborah Cerminaro in 1995 on land adjacent to their house.[6] As part of a 50-acre farm, Joe started planting vines convinced that grapes would grow there given the soil, sun and land configurations. He had grown up in Pennsylvania in an Italian-American family where wine was served daily with meals. He claims that even as a young boy his dream was one day to have a vineyard. When he planted 200 vines, this was his first step towards making the dream come true. He had recently retired and used his savings to buy the vines. But he knew virtually nothing about viticulture and in some cases even basic agricultural practices. His first plantings were of hybrids because he could not afford to lose any grapes and he was not sure how *vinifera* would do. Planting, pruning and harvesting were done by family and friends, with each year more vines added until they reached their current capacity of 500–600 cases of wine annually.

As with many other newcomers to the industry, their comments about the winery are punctuated by numerous references to the tremendous amount of hard work involved and the steep learning curve they faced. As his wife Deborah said 'Like any agricultural thing, it is a lot of work, but you feel so good about the final product. Maybe it wouldn't be quite so rewarding otherwise'. She goes on to say about her husband Joe, 'You just only meet so many people who are so driven. That's how we know it's a passion, because he keeps going and going.'[7]

The winery was bonded in 2001 and by 2002 had a successful (according to Joe's criterion) operation. He was self taught ('I pored over all the books on the subject that I could find') and gained much practical knowledge from visits to Cornell's agricultural programmes. He expressed frustration at the lack of local help from the state agricultural services, but also recognized that the industry's infancy meant limited available local resources. He learned by 'pestering people', asking lots of questions of anyone whom he felt would have useful information. 'I was trying to figure out what would grow, how to grow it, how to harvest it and how to make decent wine' he said, 'and so I had to rely upon what others had done but this was usually in other states'. Because of information scarcity he made mistakes, but he persisted and gradually collected requisite knowledge that would enable him to produce the small quantities of wine made at his house. He still relies upon volunteers to help him at harvest and has no employees. Local people are still enamoured with the concept of a winery in the small town and are happy to pitch in at crucial times. Almost all of his wine is sold direct from the winery and at wine festivals that he attends at various times in the year. They have no plans for expansion and still have the actual winery in their basement.

Another 50 miles further east and one arrives at a restored farmhouse on an 11-acre plot. It is here that two art teachers, Michael and Amy Helton, established Hanover Park winery in 1996 after a month-long honeymoon trip to France had ignited a passion for old-world wines. They planted vines in 1997 and 1998 and turned the 1897 farmhouse into a tasting room and winery. Their first harvest, in 1999, yielded 375 cases. Largely self-taught, but with tutelage from Virginia winemaker Ed Schwab of Autumn Hill Vineyards, Michael eventually gave up his teaching job to devote himself full time to the winery.

In an interview Michael was quoted as saying about the first harvest, 'My single goal – and I remember this very clearly as my concern – was not to embarrass myself'.[8] He also noted how they often felt overwhelmed in the early years ('four tons of chardonnay up close is huge') and how steep the learning curve was despite meeting with winemakers in North Carolina and Virginia. Another trip to France in 2002 enabled the couple to meet with French winemakers, learn additional techniques and expand production. During that trip they found winemakers were more responsive and shared more details than in the past. They attributed this to the fact that they introduced themselves as winery owners and thus established their own legitimacy. Amy retired from her teaching job in 2004 and now runs the tasting room and the distribution side of the business. Their current production of approximately 2,000 cases from 8 planted acres is a mix of *vinifera*, hybrids and some sweet fruit wines. They believe that at this production level they can be profitable and keep full control over the whole process.

However, they continue to experiment, in both viticulture and actual winemaking. Michael has tried different systems of canopy management to improve the quality of his grapes and altered the yield per acre. He has also tried blending to maximize the use of his best-quality grapes to make a 'reserve' type of wine that can retail at a higher price point. In these activities he indicated that he has learnt by doing and watching what others have done. As he says, 'it is a continuous process and you have to be willing to experiment, to see what others' experiments have produced'.[9]

I tell these three stories for illustrative purposes. Of the wineries that were started around this time, and in subsequent years, most have similar individual narratives. At one level they are the epitome of a classical entrepreneurial enterprise. Individuals with an abiding interest in wine find themselves at a stage in life where they have the financial resources and the time to devote to the pursuit of this interest. Some single-mindedly pursued their ambition of owning a winery and acquired land, planted vines, secured the bonding permits, then built a winery and tasting room. Others were more cautious entrants, deciding to move up to becoming a winery after years of growing grapes for sale to established wineries. The latter's resources were often more modest but for both learning was more likely to be by trial and error. Some devoted full-time energies to their projects; others a 'day job' enabled them to cross-subsidize the vineyard and they remained part-time or even 'hobbyist' winemakers.

Most of those who grew grapes specifically for their own winery self-financed their operations or had the support of a small number of partners. The latter were generally friends who were prepared, with similar entrepreneurial zeal, to invest in the venture – more often for the pleasure or status of part-ownership of a winery than for any significant financial rewards. Largely self-taught, most of these newcomers faced a steep learning curve in the initial years of their operation. With limited access to local knowledge, even when technical information was available it was very different from the practical skills that are necessary on a daily basis. Most did have the benefits of family labour or the help of friends at peak times of the year, so costs were contained somewhat. The uniqueness of a winery in a particular area, which in some respects hindered growth because of information shortages, also proved beneficial. As one small winery owner told me in an April 2003 interview,

> When we opened the county was dry and locals were either hostile to the venture or at least downright sceptical. But a number of the neighbours were also curious. When they saw us working out in the fields, planting vines – doing essentially agricultural work – they would come by and chat. In fact one elderly man showed up one day and then just started coming back every day, offering to help out. He became our first unofficial, unpaid employee. I think his presence helped us gain credibility among the locals and he was certainly useful around the place.

Another commented on how relatives showed up at various times of the year and 'pitched in'. He went on to say,

> We just bought a bunch of food and set it out and at the end of the day we would collapse exhausted by the barn, eating and drinking the [home-made] wine from the previous year. We could never have afforded to pay anyone at that stage. But at the same time there wasn't really anyone around with the skills that we needed. People were used to working in the fields but didn't know anything about viticulture. So there wouldn't have been any point in hiring people. (interview with author, May 2003)

Even though the wineries had done the requisite soil tests and been careful in selecting rootstock and vines, it was still unclear what grapes would grow best in this area. Similarly when it came to harvesting and making the wine, these newcomers were trying to figure out what was the best way, how to prune, when to pick, and how to manage the whole fermentation process. Initially, gaining knowledge even from official resources was difficult. One small owner said that he had to go out of state to learn winemaking because specialist help was not available locally when he started in the mid-1990s. Another commented,

> We were scrambling trying to figure out what to do. I talked with folks up in Virginia and then at Cornell. It was even hard trying to get good information on cuttings. But gradually I got in contact with others who were doing the same thing around here and we started talking more about our problems. This enabled us to find some collective solutions and the more we asked questions and sought resources (just basic equipment and fertilizers mostly) the more we found folks would start supplying the things that we needed. It was a real sense of learning by doing but constantly sharing with the others like us when we found something that worked or didn't. (interview with author, 2003)

Initially banks were not keen on loaning money for wineries because there was no proven end product or local experience of doing due diligence on the venture. Real estate agencies were unaccustomed to dealing with agricultural property that would be potential vineyard sites. Other basic supply sources for routine vineyard maintenance were not readily available locally and even technical support was typically available only out of state. Even then, there was a big difference between technical knowledge and practical skills – the latter acquired by trial and error. Because of these limitations, resources accessed were done with a self-reliant model of organizational start-up.

Unlike entrepreneurial ventures where individuals might possess unique product knowledge prior to the organization's start-up, the new winery owners had merely financial and time resources that enabled them to experiment. Demographically, they were typically middle aged (45 plus), a male or husband/wife team and from a professional background. Their investment was part of a desired 'lifestyle change'. Because of imperfect information, knowledge acquisition was initially haphazard but eventually the growth of a marketplace did facilitate the exchange of operational details and a degree of cooperation.

It was also unclear whether the appropriate 'demand' conditions for such entrepreneurial ventures existed at this time. In the second two cited examples the counties where they were located remained dry, effectively limiting wine sales to the wineries themselves. Even if the wineries could make wine, there remained the nagging question of whether there would be an actual market for it. This was after all the area of the country dubbed the 'Bible Belt' where prohibitionist sentiments prevailed. Entrepreneurship studies suggest that the key to successful small firm growth is both the supply of risk-taking individuals *and* the requisite demand or space in the economy for the product or service that they are producing.[10] It was unclear that was the case for wine in North Carolina in the 1990s, despite the recent initiatives. Biltmore could survive on the basis of tourism; there was a less predictable customer base elsewhere.

Despite such cultural and legal obstacles, these early entrants were nonetheless able to gain access to sufficient knowledge through formal channels to maintain their enterprises. Better able to adjust to economic disequilibrium because they were less risk averse and well educated, they were more likely to innovate and to do so successfully. This is consistent with findings on self-employed farmers of similar backgrounds,[11] yet it is important nonetheless to note that the expenditure indifference associated with winery development places a longer-term orientation than normal farming.

It was these individuals who were responsible for creating an informal embryonic network since they were forced to discuss operational details with each other. Viticultural knowledge was available from outside sources but not tacit details specific to local idiosyncrasies. Each of these early owners whom I interviewed reiterated how crucial their own learning was from talking with others in the industry locally. They would discuss planting issues, vineyard maintenance, pruning and spraying. They discovered who was a good source of information on vineyard management, who key personnel were locally for the numerous tasks that need to be done but not on a regular basis. They shared ideas on crushing and fermenting and newcomers would look to the established wineries for winery layout and design. In many respects this was the classic example of 'following someone around and imitating their behaviour' that occurs with trainees in the manufacturing sector where there is no formal training programme. But here there was also a sense of reciprocity as individuals acknowledged that to survive they had to figure out how best things were done.

> Even if you didn't make the best decisions by following someone else's example, at least you avoided making dumb mistakes that were all too frequent at this early stage. Remember that most of us had little in the way of winemaking knowledge and what

we had learned was often from courses taken elsewhere or from books. Vineyard planting and management was a huge challenge and we knew that some had made mistakes and they were honest in admitting that and telling us what not to do. In fact at this stage it was learning more of what not to do than what you should do. (winery owner, interview with author, 2006)

These early entrants structured knowledge exchange as a way of informally brokering access to requisite operational details. That they could do this on a face-to-face basis was also due to the growing geographic concentration of wineries in the central Piedmont region around the Yadkin Valley. The physical proximity did facilitate informal exchange of valuable localized information but this was further aided when several larger wineries opened in this area. The entry of larger wineries shaped market formation in ways unattainable by the smaller wineries. They were able simultaneously to bring attention to the embryonic industry and create an identity that would sustain interactions and a sense of belonging by most of the industry participants. The role of larger wineries is crucial in this phase, as are their collective leadership actions in the next phase discussed in Chapter 6.

Capital-Intensive Wineries

We have already seen how Biltmore winery, established in 1977, was able to become established and expand production quickly because of the considerable resources it dedicated to the project. Now, two other wineries (followed by a third shortly thereafter) brought similar extensive financial resources and long-term horizons that stimulated industry growth in ways that small boutique wineries could not. The first, Shelton Vineyards, was founded in 1999; the other, RayLen Vineyards, opened the following year. They were followed by Childress Vineyards in 2004. Each of these enterprises differs from the small start-up wineries referred to above inasmuch as they were resource rich, both in capital and in their ability to gain immediate access to operational knowledge via experienced, professional winemakers and vineyard managers. Using these resources to establish an almost immediate presence in the area they nonetheless were instrumental in network building since each was forced to buy grapes from current growers until their own vineyards matured. This 'outsourcing' had important implications for cluster growth and ultimately shaped cluster governance.

At auction brothers Charlie and Ed Shelton purchased a 383-acre dairy farm near Dobson in 1994 with the aim of acquiring land close to where they had grown up. They were interested in doing something agricultural, having had a grandfather who was a tobacco farmer. After having an interest in winemaking stimulated by seeing a television promotion for the University of California at Davis viticulture programme, they searched locally until they found a consultant who could do soil tests and advise them about turning their farm into a winery. With money from one of the area's major construction business that they owned (Charlotte-based Shelco), they decided to turn their hobby interest in wines into a real commercial venture, building a 33,000-square-foot winery that opened on 23 June 1999, named Shelton Vineyards.[12] The initial plantings of European varietals covered 60 acres. Ambitious and optimistic about winemaking in the region, they claim the Yadkin Valley area where the winery is located is a perfect site, with its rolling hills, rich soil and moderate climate. It is, they say, a place well suited to growing grapes and becoming a region they consider 'Napa Valley of the East'.[13]

The winery construction was supervised by Sean McRitchie who took on the role as general manager/vice president when the winery was started. His previous experience had been as winemaker in the development of Benton-Lane winery in Oregon and he brought his vineyard team from that winery with him to Shelton. Matt Dyer, the winemaker, came from Firestone Vineyards in California, having worked earlier at Viansa Winery in Sonoma. In 2000 George Denka was hired by the Sheltons as vice president of sales and marketing, and in the next few years he spearheaded the sales expansion with a 50 per cent growth in the first few years alone. His experience working in the distribution industry was clearly an asset, as was his abiding interest in wine (earlier in the 1970s he had become the only wine steward in South Carolina).

The Sheltons signalled their intent by assembling a professional team and then spent millions building the gravity flow winery. With far greater resources than the other small wineries that were growing around them, the willingness to hire full-time specialists with a track record in oenology and viticulture, and the ability to forgo immediate profitability has meant that Shelton was able to establish an expansion goal that would put them in the forefront of wineries in the state. The combined technical and practical knowledge of their staff would enable them to establish requisite levels of quality in their wines that would short cut much of the learning curve experienced by other wineries in the area. The Shelton brothers have been unwavering in their commitment and determination to bring all their resources to bear on this project. They were once quoted as saying to McRitchie when he arrived that 'we want to do it right. If it improves the wine even a bit, let's do it.'[14]

One of their goals was to prove unambiguously that the region can become a major wine-growing area, and in doing so provide jobs for individuals in declining traditional occupations such as textiles, furniture and tobacco. But they recognized that a major impediment to the growth of this sector was the lack of systematic available knowledge. To overcome such a problem they started (through significant funding support) the Enology and Viticulture Program at nearby Surry County Community College and funded it for the first two years. This had been deemed essential given their own initial frustration in finding local technical advice when they began their endeavour. They argued that if the area was to develop a wine industry a local educational facility that provided even basic training and resources would be necessary. Such a facility would be attractive to would-be growers and winemakers but perhaps as important only then could winemaking become a legitimate agricultural activity in the region and thus sustain the industry's further growth by creating a skilled labour force. Subsequently, the Sheltons went on to spearhead the application for Yadkin Valley's appellation status (AVA), of which more will be discussed in the next chapter.

Inspired by the example of the Sheltons, as well as personally encouraged by them, Joe Nealy and his wife Joyce decided to start their own winery in the late 1990s. Joe had recently retired from a vice president position at Hanes, a local apparel and knitwear company, but also had experience of building successful start-ups. They bought a 115-acre dairy farm approximately 15 miles west of Winston-Salem and planted vines for their planned winery named RayLen which was officially opened in 2000. Like Shelton the 11,000-square-foot facility is designed for growth. They also hired an experienced full-time winemaker and general manager, Steve Shepard, whose earlier stint at Westbend had demonstrated his aptitude at making wines in this region of North Carolina. He was involved in the design of the winery and the choice of wines to make. Currently there are 35 acres under vines which still do not provide all of the fruit that is needed for the wines that they make – the remaining 20–30 per cent is bought from local growers.

Both Shelton and RayLen are examples of wineries that are resource-rich enterprises for which a long-term approach towards profitability has been possible. They both have been able to invest extensively in physical capital and human resources, hiring professional full-time winemakers to develop and manage operations. Their business plans are different from the small or boutique wineries, whose capacity can be between 500 and 2,500 cases. Their larger production volume (up to 30,000 cases) is predicated on achieving economies of scale which in the long run can be crucial in realizing profitability as well as offering lower price points on the wines they produce.

Even though they are atypical of the type of winery that has emerged in the state in recent years, their role has been important for establishing the industry's visibility as well as providing quality benchmarks. The emphasis upon professionalism and a formal approach to operational issues imposed a structure on relationships within the local winemaking community. This was done in two ways.

First, because they needed to buy grapes from local growers until their own vines matured or, as is still the case, to provide a degree of production flexibility, they very early visited local growers and became familiar with growing variations and the 'personalities' of the growers. The limited volume of available grapes in the early years often left them with little choice but spot market buying. Gradually they were able to establish more formal relationships with growers, selecting those who appeared more knowledgeable, proficient and/or willing to work with them to their specifications. A typical problem was that growers wanted to maximize their yield because they were paid by the ton but in doing so often minimized the quality of the final grapes. Buyers want better quality and demonstrated that they would be prepared to pay for it and likewise became more selective about what they did and did not purchase. For the growers, it became clear that adhering to basic guidelines would furnish a desired product and even a guaranteed price. Many growers said they learned a lot from these buyers about vineyard management, cropping, canopy management and various techniques designed to reduce the quantity of grapes but improve their eventual quality. In turn, the winemakers at these two big wineries said they had to impose quality standards to ensure appropriate harvests. While initially it was difficult, within several years they had established good relationships with certain growers who learned quickly what needed to be done. There is anecdotal evidence of some growers who evidently were not prepared to accommodate the quality imperatives and they lost their contracts, at least two locally known to the author having subsequently abandoned grape growing altogether.

Second, winemakers at smaller wineries would frequently contact the professionals at the large wineries and solicit advice. This could be informally at winery visits or formally through associational meetings that were beginning to take place. According to several small winery owners interviewed, such discussions were intentional and limited to procuring operational knowledge and seeking advice on specific aspects of viticulture and winemaking. It was not that the professional winemakers explicitly told them what to do; it was more of an exchange of ideas about what might work in a particular setting. Several indicated that through such interactions they learned more about canopy management, spraying regimes, appropriate fungicide usage and even vine layout when they were planning their vineyards. They felt they could trust the professionals because, as one said, 'it's not as if they're competing with us'. As for the professional winemakers, both said that they saw their role as building expertise in the community. They recognized that if the industry is to develop locally then everyone has to get better and be more consistent in what they produce. This means helping others to understand some best practices as well as directing them to official sources of information that would be helpful to their specific problems. As one said,

> I'm not holding their hands; I'm trying to get them to understand what you have to do. Some listen and others don't. One winery for instance just didn't get it that you have to keep the place clean. His is messy and I'm not surprised that his wine is all over the place in terms of quality. It's often just little things like this that can make the difference.

What transpired was not a form of contractualism that might inhibit knowledge sharing or undermine trust. Instead, it was informal, directed initially at the professionals and then subsequently shared with others in ways that helped the industry as a whole identify common problems and shortcomings. The professional winemakers and the owners of the larger wineries thus increasingly played an active advocacy role for the industry. One small winery owner interviewed in May 2003 told me

> They brought attention to the industry and that's been great but their winemakers have been really helpful in disseminating crucial practical information. I'd call him [the winemaker at one of the large wineries] up on numerous occasions and get tips or even borrow some equipment. He told me about some new spraying techniques, suggested different practices. It was really helpful.

Another said that 'the real difference between them [large wineries] and us [small wineries] is that they knew the problems before they hit whereas we were always reacting to them. In time though I'd get tips that would help me avoid certain things and do others correctly' (interview with author, February 2004).

The large wineries had resources that enabled them to build an identity, not only for themselves but also for the regional industry as a whole; their strategy part of a broader agenda of demonstrating the viability of a wine industry in North Carolina. If that was to happen they prudently recognized the need to establish as much transparency in their relationships with the other wineries as they could to facilitate the dissemination of knowledge or at least best practices from their professional operation to those smaller ventures. But the problem was the industry's infancy as even the two professional winemakers acknowledged that it was a learning curve even for them, trying to figure out which grapes grow best in what locations. In that respect, they also relied upon trial and error, thus somewhat hindering the development of the cluster. But at least they had the resources and support to experiment, which is what they often did.

After the vicissitudes of diseases, conflict and then Prohibition that plagued earlier attempts to establish winemaking in the state, the establishment of small wineries by enterprising individuals was given a boost by the presence of professional and resource-rich actors. While the small winery owners were driven by a passion for their enterprise, the large ones pursued a systematic and rigorous plan to establish a nascent wine marketplace in the state. Only that way could they realistically attain profitability. A 2003 interview with one of the winemaker/general managers captures the essence of these operations and the philosophy of the owners that underlie them

> I've been fortunate in that I was given a free hand and generous resources to develop the winery. That is one of the reasons I came in the first place as I like to see something develop from the ground up. But in the early years it was difficult experimenting with

what grows well here and what doesn't and what sorts of styles are best. Although cheaper than buying land out west, it's still not cheap here. At around $6000–12,000 an acre for vines and the knowledge that it will take 3–6 years before you see viable fruit, that's a lot more than the $2–3,000 an acre for other forms of agriculture. I'm not surprised that more tobacco farmers didn't choose this option, or others for that matter. This sort of thing takes a lot more capital and a lot more patience. And there's a lot more constant maintenance than with other crops.

When you harvest and make the wine I found it challenging convincing folks that the styles could be unique to North Carolina and wouldn't necessarily taste like a California wine. But the industry is new, locals who like wine have certain ideas about what varietals should taste like; those that don't know wine tend to prefer sweeter wines than I make. But I feel pretty secure in what I'm doing and continue to get a lot of support which is important. People have said we're pioneers and therefore we get to set some of the agendas but I think it's going to be a while before we can see how successful we've been. And I'm not talking about just winning medals at state fairs; I'm referring to when the industry as whole takes note. That will take time, perhaps a decade or more. So we've got to be patient.

They could afford to be patient; others had more prosaic attitudes towards profitability, especially farmers who were trying their hands at grape cultivation.

From Farmers to Winery Owners

The third category of new vineyard owners comprise existing farmers who decided either to supplement their current crops with commercial grape production or even start a winery of their own. Fewer in number than was at first anticipated, they nonetheless provide another set of stories that merit consideration because of their unique perspective as actual farmers rather than non-agricultural entrepreneurs. However, I also discuss those who had land but did not actively farm it until they planted grapes. Some of this area had been tobacco land that perhaps had been leased; now the owners discovered in grapes a crop that might be a substitute for tobacco.

One of the foremost examples of farmer turned winery owner is that of third-generation tobacco farmer Frank Hobson Jr. He had seen his tobacco allotment decline by 53 per cent during the late 1990s whilst other crops such as soya and wheat were not reliable income earners. It was the growing uncertainty surrounding tobacco, however, that caused him to search for an alternative crop.

When Hobson met the owners of Shelton Vineyards and discussed with them what they were doing he decided to try grapes as a supplemental crop on his farm, where he continues to grow tobacco, wheat, corn and soya. He planted his own vines and, despite not knowing much about viticulture, as a farmer he understood some basic operational practices that saw him through the initial years. Because of his oenological inexperience, however, he decided to hire a professional winemaker, Linda King, who had most recently worked at the largest estate winery in Ohio, Chalet Debonnet. He opened his winery, Rag Apple Lassie, in 2002 in Boonville, about 25 miles north-west of Winston-Salem. He admitted that it was expensive to start the winery, especially because, unlike most crops that have annual harvests, it takes several years before there is a proper grape harvest. On top of that was the cost of building the actual winery. But he believes wineries can be the future for the area, proving employment opportunities for locals who would otherwise leave rural areas, as well as a practical solution for tobacco farmers or those with tobacco land for sale.[15] It should be noted, however, that he was atypical of farmers in that he hired a professional winemaker from the outset.

Other farmers were to follow this trend but few adopted the professionalized approach and the extensive capital expenditures of Rag Apple Lassie. One such family in the eastern part of the state decided to build a winery on their 75-acre farm, having for several decades grown grapes in addition to other crops. For them the stimulus came from the realization that more people were drinking wine (particularly sweet wines in their region) following the widely advertised health benefits. However, what clinched the decision for them were the financial incentives that were available after the tobacco settlements in the late 1990s. That and the declining price for tobacco plus their experience of growing muscadine grapes made it easier to offset some of the costs of developing the winery. But they preferred to teach themselves winemaking, relying upon their past amateur endeavours and the occasional advice from people at Duplin. The rationale for their decision to develop a winery was told to me in a July 2003 interview with the owner

> Our tobacco allotment had declined significantly and now is about 5 acres. We had been thinking more and more of starting a winery, especially since Duplin had become so successful. We had earlier bought a press to press the grapes and then sell the juice since that proved more profitable than just selling grapes. But since we had the land [for additional vines] and believed we could sell wine locally we decided to give the winery a try. So when golden LEAF money was available it was like manna from heaven. We used it to buy all of our new vines so there was no cost other than planting. That was a huge saving and meant we could invest more in the actual winery building. Even if we couldn't make wine we could always sell grapes as the price per ton had gone up and our harvests were big so we'd make a profit. But the winery has been good and we've done well.

His sentiments are similar to other farmers/turned grape growers who were responding to events of the late 1990s that were transforming the landscape for tobacco farming.

The Decline of Tobacco

The policies that precipitated this agricultural transformation had their origins in public policy decisions in the 1930s as the country faced the ravages of the Great Depression. In attempting to alleviate the problems of price fluctuations that adversely affected rural areas, the federal government had established quotas on the amount of tobacco that could be grown whereby individual farmers acquired the rights to grow and harvest tobacco prior to it being sold at auction. In place since 1938 this system has governed tobacco farming, effectively restricting the supply of the crop and ensuring *de facto* price supports. As a major tobacco-growing state, North Carolina continued to be one of the major beneficiaries of these programmes. With high dollar value yields (approximately $4,300 per acre from an annual investment of $1,400–1,600 in seed and fertilizer) it remained a lucrative crop, suited for small plots and for part-time as well as full-time farming.[16] Quotas were passed down amongst families, further restricting an open market for the supply of the product. In addition its fairly predictable demand meant it was in fact the principal crop by value in state at this time.[17]

With growing health concerns over the use of tobacco products, more and more non-tobacco-producing states were seeking ways to limit the product's availability. The tobacco industry faced a series of litigation challenges starting in 1996 when Washington state Attorney General Christine Gregoire sued the country's biggest tobacco companies over alleged misrepresentation of the risks of smoking and the targeting of children in advertising.[18] Together with other state suits in the years following, the result put the whole tobacco industry on the defensive. Following spiralling litigation costs as well as potentially bankrupting settlements with class action lawsuits, the big four tobacco companies (Philip Morris, R. J. Reynolds, Lorillard and Brown and Williamson) eventually settled with 46 states in November 1998.[19] Because the suits were a coordinated effort on behalf of the states' Medicaid systems, there was pressure to have the tobacco companies place money in a fund that could be used to cover health-care costs. The terms of the actual settlement resulted in the companies paying $206 billion to the states over a 25-year period. Under Phase II of the agreement $5.15 billion was to be paid by the companies into over 12 years to states that produce tobacco. The Golden LEAF foundation was formed from half of the MSA funds received by North Carolina to assist tobacco farmers financially to find alternative crops. The attendant stimulus package was also intended to encourage alterative industries such as bio-technology as a way to address broader economic problems of other declining industries (textiles and furniture).

Are Grapes an Alternative?

With the inevitable erosion of markets for tobacco, it was assumed that some farmers would plant grapes as an alternative to tobacco or even in addition to other crops. Given the fiscal incentives and a smaller grape cultivation learning curve for farmers over that of non-farmers, it seemed a logical next step. But despite the hype associated with the settlement and the corresponding growth of wineries starting around this time, the number of farmers who actually switched from tobacco to grapes appears to be quite small. According to the viticulture extension agency at North Carolina State University, only 1–2 per cent of vineyards in the state in 2002 were owned or operated by tobacco farmers. If farmers were going to accept funds from the tobacco settlements and plant vines, one would have expected them to have done so by this time. That they did not suggests that they are perhaps more risk averse than entrepreneurs who started small wineries and/or they simply had fewer funds to cross-subsidize such a venture. For many though it was also a question of age.

Although market uncertainty about established crops persists, most tobacco farmers are in their fifties and unwilling to accept the risk and time frame for an investment in vines to be realized. Even with LEAF funds there was still market uncertainty about grapes in contrast to realistic and immediate profits from more established crops or activities. For example one farmer who is 53 was quoted as saying

> I've been doing this [tobacco farming] since I was big enough to pull tobacco leaves. Most tobacco farmers are my age or older. Why would we want to take on a whole new concept? This is a way of life. With a vineyard you're talking about seven years [before there's a return on investment]. I'll be 60. What kind of income would you have coming in to live on for five or six years? It's just not realistic for us.[20]

That farmer invested in the expansion of a chicken-breeding operation in 2001; an investment comparable to establishing a vineyard but with more immediate payback. Another said 'I thought hard about it and talked with folks around here but I'm just not sure this isn't another fad crop. I don't want to invest that much money and have to wait that long if there's not going to be a market for it' (interview with author, April 2003). He went on to say that it sounded like a lot of work and people were not really on the ball about knowing what they should plant. This sentiment of uncertainty was pervasive, meaning that those farmers who did plant vines hedged their bets and planted them as a supplement to their other crops. In general then, traditional farmers have not been enthusiastic converts to grape growing and winemaking, primarily because of the investment costs entailed and the longer-term growth perspective.

One of the few tobacco farmers who did decide to grow grapes acknowledges how difficult it is and what a change of pace it has been. He lost 75 per cent of his tobacco allotment and hopes that grapes will help make up for that loss. But he recognizes that it is not for everyone given that the pay-off for the investment does not come for 6 or 7 years. As he said, 'most farmers don't want to wait that long; they'd rather plant the seed, watch it grow during the season then pick it and get the money all in one year' (interview with author, August 2003). Another farmer with whom I spoke had decided to grow strawberries, seeing this as a more lucrative crop than grapes and with more immediate investment returns. He took LEAF money for this and said he considered grapes but decided that strawberries would be a more reliable crop year in and out.

Land Owners but not Farmers

Of those who owned land but did not consider themselves farmers, the Coes are a good example. Kathy and Van Coe decided in the late 1990s to plant 5 acres of vines on their 48-acre farm that had been in Kathy's family for over a hundred years. Tobacco had been raised there and Kathy remembered working part time in the fields when she was young; something she swore then that she would never return to.[21] Van runs a mortgage company and Kathy is a registered nurse. When the government quotas on tobacco were reduced their tobacco fields lay fallow for several years so the couple decided to try grapes as a possible alternative. Using savings, and with help from their brother-in-law Lynn Crouse, they invested over $600,000 to plant vines. They took classes at Surry Community College but were ignorant about many viticulture details when they planted their vines. After their first few harvests they discovered that the vines had been planted too close so every other vine had to be ripped out. Another time they forgot to apply appropriate levels of fungicide. By their own admission it has been a huge learning experience, with each harvest presenting new obstacles. As Van said 'So, it's a moving target. You don't know what you're going to encounter next.'[22] Their winery, Stony Knoll Vineyards, however, opened in 2004 and they now produce approximately 1,000 cases per year.

There are others like them who owned family farms, some of which had been under tobacco allotments but now were lying fallow. But since the current owners were non-farmers, returning to run an agricultural enterprise was daunting to say the least. Yet many of these people came from professional backgrounds and had the financial resources (or credit lines) that would allow them to make the necessary investments in vines. They also were motivated by the allure of a return to farming but without the connotations that are sometimes associated generally with farmers. While they did not necessarily come to think of themselves as gentlemen farmers, they did envision a winery lifestyle that evoked an almost Arcadian vision of rural enterprise. As noted earlier, grape growing and winemaking have a status that somehow transcends its reality as agricultural labour. It is perhaps this attraction that convinced them to make the necessary investments, although most retained their full-time job for economic security. Those that chose to revisit their family land and actively crop it were certainly possessed of a certain status desire even if it was masked behind rhetoric about local economic development. This is not to say that such people were naive, nor do I wish to infer that they were solely motivated by egotistical desires for self-aggrandizement. But they were driven by a desire to become players in an emerging industry in which a measure of one's success was predetermined by the resources one could bring to bear in the initial operation. In that sense they were cognizant of, and presumably motivated in part by, the challenges of structural transformation in rural North Carolina society.

The apparent viability of grape growing in the area, access to vital knowledge sources and general enthusiasm for reclaiming part of their agricultural legacy all came together to provide the motivation for what many discovered was extremely hard work. They persisted, although few of these wineries are currently profitable given the immense investment they made and despite the fact that they did not have to purchase the land. Unlike those who purchased land, the above were more likely to plant larger acreage; unlike their active farmer counterparts, they remained at least initially quite ignorant of agricultural practices. The latter all too frequently compounded the former.

This group constitutes an important sub-set of the farm owners since they have often been the driving force in the transition from tobacco to grapes. But their aspirations are somewhat different from active farmers who were less likely to be driven by overly romantic notions of what is inherent in rural commercial activity. For the latter, their evaluation of grape growing was seen through the lens of other viable options, and was frequently tempered by the realization that winemaking was not, at least initially, a likely profitable option.

Of the farmers that did decide on grapes, perhaps because they were located in the eastern part of the state where scuppernong was ubiquitous, most seemed to prefer muscadines. The allure of that grape had never dissipated. Furthermore, it needed little maintenance and was relatively inexpensive to cultivate. As we have seen in the previous chapter, state agricultural extension agencies had long worked with farmers to encourage this particular grape, with only market forces inhibiting an earlier production boom. Now with grape prices increasing and a ready market for the product, it was seen by some farmers as a viable alternative to tobacco. In interviews with two farmers who grow grapes and have farms close to the coast this sentiment was corroborated. As one said,

> I felt that this was a natural crop, easy to grow and with little maintenance. I mean people have been growing this or they've been growing wild for centuries. In the past it didn't really occur to me to plant any vines but with more of a market for muscadines I thought it would be worth trying. Now there are small wineries around here

that buy my grapes so that's great. I mean I don't want to make wine myself – too much trouble and all that government stuff – but I'm pleased that some do and they will keep buying my harvest. (interview with author, 2007)

Changing Grape Markets

From a farmer's viewpoint, understanding the relationship between crop prices, acreage and yields is difficult due to information lags because of the gestation time of vine development. The farmers with whom I spoke said that there was so much fluctuation in crop prices that it was difficult to make earnings projections based on predicted market value. Tobacco had provided much greater stability and predictability, plus high market value; other crops such as wheat and soya had seen price declines. Vines sounded intriguing in the mid-1990s but there was still uncertainty about the longer-term future for grapes given the lack of information about market growth potential. Remembering how often grapes were seen as a failed solution to rural woes in the past further stifled the enthusiasm of many.

Notwithstanding such caution, farmers were becoming aware of the steady increase in the price per ton of grapes during the latter part of the 1990s and this did sway some in favour of vineyard planting. The data for this period reflect changes in the demand for grapes as well as the transformation in practices pertaining to tobacco production. However, while the value utilized from the harvest has increased, the decade of the 1990s actually witnessed a decline in acreage although the yield remained fairly constant. As one can see from Table 4.1 there was a gradual increase in the number of acres since 1999 and a significant increase in the price paid for grapes at harvest.

As with any agricultural product there are seasonal variations for harvests and this is one explanation for price fluctuations even when demand is constant. However, there are several additional issues here that need explanation. First, *vinifera* commands a higher value per ton than muscadine – $1,100–$1,400 compared to approximately $500 per ton. Since the recent winery growth has been in *vinifera* plantings, and taking into consideration a lag for vines to mature and bear fruit, one should expect crop values to have increased by the late 1990s. This is reflected in the values indicated in the table. On the other hand, the increase in demand for *vinifera* during the late 1990s did not always result in a significant increase in the price that one might expect from the play of market forces since grapes and juice needed by fledgling wineries were brought in from out of state. Inevitably this distorts market pricing. In that respect *vinifera* prices are not as high as one might infer given the increased demand associated with winery growth in the state.

Table 4.1: North Carolina Grape Harvest Statistics, 1986–2001. Source: North Carolina Department of Agriculture and Consumer Services.

Year	Acres	Yield/acre (tons)	Price ($/ton)	Value utilized (per $1,000)
1986	800	1,875	385	539
1987	700	2,571	360	648
1988	700	4,714	330	1,057
1989	700	2,620	406	690
1990	600	2,500	533	800
1991	550	4,000	611	1,344
1992	520	2,500	780	1,014
1993	540	2,780	709	1,064
1994	530	2,830	729	1,020
1995	520	2,500	782	1,017
1996	480	2,500	757	681
1997	470	2,020	968	920
1998	470	3,190	1,030	1,538
1999	500	3,800	1,150	2,183
2000	600	3,830	1,160	2,661
2001	700	2,860	1,270	2,532

Second, muscadines are cheaper to grow given their resistance to most fungal attacks as opposed to *vinifera* which requires constant attention to pest and mildew control. Given this cost differential, plus the increase in demand, *vinifera* commands a higher premium than muscadine. Also muscadine yields are 7–8 tons per acre compared to 2–3 tons per acre for *vinifera*. Even with a lower market price, the costs per acre for muscadines are considerably lower than *vinifera* therefore making them an attractive option for more cost-sensitive farmers lacking in the resources that small winery owners had. This explains why many of the farmers who started (or increased) grape production did so with muscadines, and they were more likely to be located in the eastern part of the state where Duplin was driving demand and interest in sweet wines.

Conversely, former tobacco land that was planted with *vinifera* was more likely to have been bought by non-farmers for the explicit purpose of building a winery. Their goals were linked with aspirational lifestyle ambitions as opposed to the more fiscally prudent farmers. The few farmers who planted *vinifera* typically had sufficient acreage to maintain other crops that would subsidize such plantings and their aim was to sell their grapes rather than start a winery themselves. They would more likely be located in the Piedmont area of the state where the majority of new wineries were emerging.

In addition to the above caveats one should also note the different collection methodologies of state agricultural agencies and the United States Department of Agriculture (USDA) which indicate similar trends yet with different numbers. For example, the USDA counts all acreage, including hobbyist farmers who have small plots in their backyard. As a consequence the number of vineyards is inflated compared with the state agricultural agency figures. The role played by such individuals is not insignificant, as I noted earlier. Figure 4.2 provides a longer time perspective on the farm decline from the late 1970s through the 1990s and then shows rather dramatically the resurgent growth in farms and more so acreage after the late 1990s.

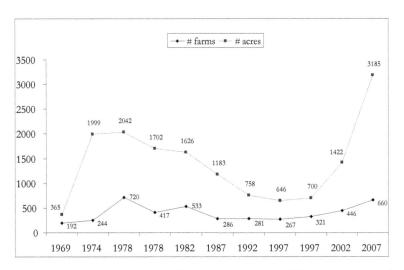

Figure 4.2: Grape Production in North Carolina, 1969–2007. Source: Census of Agriculture. NB. The years 1978 and 1997 are listed twice because of changing calculation methods in those years, with data from old and new methods recorded.

Despite the different figures, the trends are nonetheless similar. More grapes were being grown and prices were rising, plus a significant increase in the number of wineries was occurring. Land had come on the market for use in viticulture, either by farmers switching crops or by others selling their tobacco farms/plots. At the same time institutional forces were providing resources that were favourable for market growth.

Institutional Developments

Having largely ignored winemaking except for occasional targeted programmes for muscadine growers since the 1960s, State Agricultural agencies began to consider the viability of *vinifera* and hybrids and directed resources to studying appropriate viticultural methods. This new interest was sparked by the success of vineyards in Virginia that demonstrated that *vinifera* could be successfully grown and be commercially viable in the mid-Atlantic without the affliction of devastating diseases.[23] It was also increasingly apparent that there might be a local market for such a product in North Carolina. This new institutional interest prompted the founding of the North Carolina Grape Council in 1986 with funding from the state tax on wine. Originally under the North Carolina Department of Agriculture and Consumer Affairs, the Council was transferred to the state's Department of Commerce in 2000. The reason for this switch was that wine was increasingly seen as part of tourism promotions in the state and Commerce was deemed a more appropriate department to further the industry's development.

Despite the ambitious aims of the Grape Council, it proved more adept initially at marketing wine than facilitating the growth of technical education. As noted earlier, many of the early small wineries without professional wine-makers were forced to go out of state to get appropriate information for their ventures. Furthermore, the Council was not effective in the early years in con-tracting research services to improve viticultural practices, or even facilitating the coordination of activities of various state agencies. As such it was unable to identify ways of improving the quality of wine produced in the state as its man-date required. This would only come when specific educational facilities devoted to oenology were created.

In the decade that followed the Council's creation, an experimental vineyard was established at North Carolina State University but it was not until 1999 when an Enology and Viticulture Program was established at Surry County Community College that actual technical skills were available in-state. This pro-gramme is situated in the heart of the north-west Piedmont region where much of the growth of new wineries was occurring, and close to Shelton Vineyard. As noted earlier, the initiative and funding for the programme was from the Shel-ton brothers of Shelton Vineyards. They provided the seed money plus paid for the first two years of the programme's operating expenses. Robert McRitchie, who had been active as a winemaker and winery designer in Oregon for several decades, was hired in 2000 to direct and teach in the programme. The college provides training through degree and diploma/certificate courses for those interested in careers in grape growing and winemaking. The viticulture compo-nent includes plant science, vineyard stock selection, soil and pest management as well as vine nutrition courses. It also teaches basic economics of vineyard management as well as planning and layout of vineyards. The oenology part is devoted to the tools and techniques of winemaking and has a heavy laboratory component as well as field studies. Aimed at the local community, it has proved valuable for both farmers who are interested in grape growing and especially new winery and would-be winery owners. It is at this venue that most of the small winery owners without agricultural experience hone their skills.

This programme would provide a vital missing component in the develop-ment of the industry since it would be a vehicle for the dissemination of requisite technical knowledge. Both incumbents and new entrants could avail themselves, at relatively low tuition costs, of precisely the operational details that are necessary for successful start-ups. Furthermore, it helped initiate knowledge and information flows that could lower transaction costs for firms. The cooperative spirit that had emerged from the pioneering endeavours was becoming normatively embedded in the emerging network of winery owners and winemakers. To embrace this informal network as a newcomer was not seen as opportunistic; instead to ignore it suggested woeful ignorance of the relationship-based interactions crucial for survival.

Finally, Market Growth

One can see from the above how a series of intersecting events has produced circumstances that enabled an incipient market to develop. It did so through the growth of informal structured interactions based upon cooperation and knowledge exchange that provided allocative efficiency to firms. While learning was piecemeal with little attempt to coordinate and consolidate knowledge into formal repositories, it nonetheless provided a locus for future interactions that would substantiate the emerging architecture of this new market. It is remarkable that trust emerged quite quickly between individuals; but not to cooperate in a transparent way at this early stage would have been even more disadvantageous.

In all of the interviews that I conducted, with owners of small as well as large wineries, with winemakers, farmers and hobbyist grape growers, they all indicated a high degree of information sharing as well as tacit knowledge exchange during this growth period. New entrants went in search of operating details from the few established wineries. Nobody reported that such cooperation was inimical to competitive behaviour – in fact it soon became normatively established as appropriate. What is more, there were few if any formal mechanisms to structure such relationships. The North Carolina Wine Growers Association held workshops and an annual meeting and thus provided a quasi-formal setting for interactions. It facilitated contacts that could be pursued in informal settings. But its role was supplemental to the developing network of informal contacts that provided information about viticultural practices, equipment and supply procurement and even the loan of equipment or facilities in times of emergency.

The two large wineries, by virtue of their professional full-time staff, were able to play a more active role in solidifying market formation. They were able to demonstrate, via technical expertise, appropriate procedures that improved the quality of wine produced. And in their capacity as buyers of grapes in the initial years before their own vines matured, they could easily enforce quality guidelines when they made such purchases. Yet they too were victims of imperfect information since the industry was still in its infancy. The winemakers at these two vineyards struggled themselves in the first few years to find the right kinds of grapes to grow and how best to manage their vineyard during the growing season. Their resources and background enabled them to experiment and then share the results of these experiments with others. They were most likely to be the recipients of information requests, but their status inevitably made them a valuable resource. Because they were dependent upon other growers in these early years it was in their own best interest to encourage the dissemination of best practices. This is precisely what they did, sometimes in a more direct manner than others.

They did not, however, impose a structure on the emerging informal network of winery owners. It remained at this stage a free-flowing set of cooperative relationships; the result of numerous individual initiatives that resulted in collective organizational learning. In other words, as tacit knowledge emerged – a product of trial and error for some, of rational techniques for others – it became *de facto* community property. Such cooperation enhanced individual firm efficiency because it enabled informational coordination and minimized the impact of negative externalities. Because organizational learning became externalized it eliminated some of the imperfect information risks that entrepreneurs typically face. Not only that, we can see large and small wineries as partially integrated in an evolving network, the features of which are more cooperative than competitive. Rather than asymmetrical power relations hindering the growth of small firms and assigning them to subordinate status, large firms were actually instrumental in nurturing their growth. This is what makes this period so interesting and the behaviour of firms different from most competitive marketplaces.

The growing density of wineries in certain geographic areas also increased the variety of traded and non-traded inputs at lower costs. Furthermore, each of the respondents in interviews reported an increase in the frequency of their interactions with established competitors as well as with new entrants. Not only was basic information shared at the outset of one's operation, it became the basis for systematic exchanges that consolidated reciprocity. Density and frequency increases of interactions sustained the organizational clustering that was occurring. But even though they were trust-based, they did not present barriers to new entrants and remained fungible. This openness was crucial to market formation during the period.

In chronicling the intertwined histories of three organizational populations (tobacco farms, vineyards and wineries) I note the importance of a unique conjuncture of contextual processes. Without the legislation that forced the restructuring of tobacco farming there would not have been small plots of land available for wineries and vineyards. And without the financial subsidies offered to farmers, fewer would have started grape cultivation. Finally, without the existence of aspirational lifestyle individuals with the necessary resources and ambition for winery development, a winery cluster would not have begun to develop. The notion that externalities are a significant locus of entrepreneurial endeavours does not diminish the passion and fortitude of the early pioneers. But it does allow us to conceptualize market growth as the product of complementary events and processes.

Throughout this period institutional forces shaped the evolution of this emerging market but their impact was often to consolidate existing processes rather than be an incubator for them. When formal oenology and viticulture training became available at the local community college, it did provide much needed technical skills. But it was in the years after 2000 that more detailed educational programmes, at more locations, would help solve the practical problems that many wineries continued to face. By that time industry legitimacy was improving and an additional large winery would significantly reshape the network and impose more hierarchical relationships. Cooperation would remain, but with increased density, interactions would assume a more formal dimension. One would also see a difference emerge based upon grape type and this would further distinguish the network structure, rendering it less important in one segment than the other. As growth took off amongst *vinifera* growers, the muscadine market began to acquire its own identity, not necessarily separate but nonetheless distinct in terms of its relational properties. We will examine this parallel evolution in the next chapter.

5 MARKET GROWTH, DIFFERENTIATION AND LEGITIMACY

North Carolina's wine industry is in the midst of tremendous growth, and this will create opportunities for farmers interested in grape production. It is a win-win situation for agriculture in this state, boosting agritourism, creating job opportunities from the vineyard to the retail level, and offering farmers the opportunity to further diversify production.

Margo Knight Metzger, North Carolina Wine and Grape Council (2008)[1]

At a time when wine was barely sinking into the American consumer subconscious ... suddenly here's an alcoholic beverage rich in antioxidants and linked to cardiovascular benefit. At Duplin, it's neatly packaged in a sweet red wine sold amongst people already swimming in sweet coffee, sweeter tea and sweetest deserts. Even in the Bible Belt, this is lightening in a bottle.

Duplin's fate is changing overnight. Wine is selling out. Production is growing. More farmers are throwing in on a handshake. And as Duplin wine sales begin creeping across North Carolina, there is developing a parallel track. There are the first real rumblings among the popular press about vinifera grapes.

Ed Williams (2007)[2]

The 2000 transfer of the North Carolina Grape Council from the Department of Agriculture to the Department of Commerce signalled a new emphasis upon winery-related tourism. Building upon the popularity of 'wine trails' elsewhere,[3] the Grape Council has invested in improved signage and the promotion of regional clusters of wineries as well as hosting tastings in key consumer markets throughout the state. The growing density of wineries in key regions has facilitated this somewhat but so also has the general appeal of visiting a winery as part of a leisure activity. Rather than merely a basic tasting room, many of the wineries that have opened in recent years have constructed multi-purpose facilities that can be used for functions (weddings, banquets, management workshops, etc.). Such activities have provided revenue streams that are often more lucrative than the winemaking operations, and a source of financial survival as the winery builds its reputation. By embracing a 'wine tourism' model, in this instance selling the attractiveness of their location and facilities, they are then able to use this captive market to sell their wine.

Realizing that they can leverage their site-specific resources, some wineries have focused more attention upon building this part of their business and less detail on the actual winemaking. Because newcomers pursuing this strategy are more focused upon 'event planning' than oenology, it has somewhat constrained the development of consistent quality in the wines produced in the region. The more revenue streams flow through 'events', the more it could feasibly subsidize inefficiencies in vineyard management and winemaking since collective organizational learning in these areas could be stymied.

The second quote comes from a 2007 article in *On the Vine*, the publication of the Yadkin Valley Wine Country News. It mentions that Duplin celebrated the production of its one millionth case of wine in 2005 and that 200,000 cases were produced from the 2006 harvest. These are significant amounts of wine for a company and a region that thirty years ago struggled to establish a market for its product. As the major muscadine producer in the state, Duplin is recapturing the prominence and even the national market that Paul Garrett dreamed of a century earlier. That it has done this in a state, and a location within the state, where prohibitionist sentiments still linger, is a remarkable achievement. A significant part of the success, as noted in the quote and in subsequent comments by owner David Fussell Sr, comes from producing a beverage that is consistent with the taste preferences of many and by appealing to the recently publicized health benefits of the drink. He says 'The whole climate has changed. The reason we have such a strong wine industry in North Carolina today is that the wine has been accepted as a beverage of moderation and health.'[4]

The continued growth of muscadine producers such as Duplin is one of the stories that bespeak the increasing acceptance of wine as a consumer beverage for many citizens of North Carolina. Duplin is now firmly established as the largest winery in the state in terms of volume and continues to draw attention to its signature grape, the descendant of the famous scuppernong. However, in line with the first quote, it was further west that a new market identity was being forged with the growth of wineries who had mastered (or were in the process of mastering) the elusive *vinifera*. It is in this region, and with this grape, that cluster activities have been most pronounced, knowledge networks most vital and sector legitimacy most fragile.

In the Piedmont region of the state, where most of the recent growth has occurred, a new winery opened almost every other month after 2002 with most trying their luck with at least some dry wines. Although the learning curve for new entrants was less steep than before, there remained challenges that needed to be addressed if the industry was to establish a footing and gain credibility. Uppermost in the minds of critics was the issue of quality. 'I'm sure lots of people drink muscadines and it can be a good wine, but because it's so sweet it lacks the credibility amongst most wine drinkers to ever become a great wine', said an owner of a major wine store in Charlotte, the state's major city. But he went on to say,

> It's sad in a way because it's much easier to make wines from native grapes and folks have figured out ways to get rid of the foxy taste that was a problem with many of the early attempts. There's not a lot to differentiate the muscadine producers now in terms of quality and the price points are good. I sell a lot of it and that's a testament to how much things have changed around here. But if the state is going to be taken seriously as a wine producing area, say like next door Virginia, we're going to have to make some good dry wines and be consistent. It's started but the quality is all over the place. Folks are still learning, even after all of these years but I think that the bar has been set pretty high by some of the bigger wineries and this can only help. Now they've got to figure out what [varietals] grow best here and concentrate on that. Everyone wants to start making Chardonnay and Cabernet Sauvignon but it's not always the best grape for the area. My money is on the Yadkin Valley because that's where they've been playing around with *vinifera* and hybrids long enough to figure out what works and what doesn't. (interview with author, May 2005)

The lingering problem, as he so presciently states, is that muscadine-based wines just do not taste like fine wines and will always therefore have limited market appeal. *Vinifera*-based wines on the other hand have a difficult time competing on the basis of price with similar wines from elsewhere. How firms in North Carolina deal with these issues is the subject of this chapter and the one that follows. I will argue that differentiation occurs within the industry – between muscadine and *vinifera* producers, and between professional and semi-professional winemakers – and that the subsequent architecture of markets reflects how firms in these different categories develop operating strategies. I will also show how boutique wineries, those most characterized by semi-professional winemakers, have embraced wine tourism as a way of maximizing revenue flows and leveraging the emerging regional identity of the cluster.

Creating Regional Identity

On 7 February 2003, the Yadkin Valley became an official American Viticultural Area (AVA) – the first one to be established in North Carolina. The application for this status was spearheaded following a two-year effort by Patricia McRitchie of Shelton Vineyards with geographical research by Matthew Maybery.[5] At that time there were six bonded wineries within the Yadkin Valley AVA (Hanover Park, Rag Apple Lassie, RayLen, Westbend, Windy Gap and Black Wolf). Covering close to 2,000 square miles and 1.4 million acres, it incorporates an area with a unique climate and an approximate 1,200 feet elevation that seems suited to *vinifera* and hybrid production. AVA designations are defined by the Tax and Trade Bureau (formerly the Bureau of Alcohol, Tobacco and Firearms) and generally indicate distinct climatic and geographical features of an area. While not a guarantee of quality, the designation signifies that this is a good region to grow grapes and that there might be distinctive features associated with grapes that derive from the region. The latter is reinforced by the specification that 85 per cent of appellation grapes must go into a wine that has such a designation.

The benefits of such a designation for Yadkin Valley, and the two more that would follow in 2008 and 2009, are numerous and go beyond mere classification of local growing characteristics (*terroir*). It creates a regional identity for the industry, legitimates its presence amongst oenophiles, and generates a certain 'buzz' around the firms located therein. From a production perspective, it creates a local community of knowledge and one expects an increase in the informal knowledge exchange that occurs amongst a sub-group of wineries. It also built upon a growth that saw increasingly successful viticultural experimentation and witnessed the emergence of two large wineries whose resources and capabilities helped solidify the reputation of the embryonic region. The latter provide 'core' skills that can be diffused as a 'club' good within the network.[6] Finally, it is a step towards establishing a vibrant industry because it attracts new entrants to the area as well as fostering growth of subsidiary and ancillary industries (suppliers to the trade, agritourism such as restaurants and bed and breakfasts). But above all it signifies that the state could be thought of as a serious contender in the regional wine industry, and with a grape, *vinifera*, that had proved so elusive in the past.

Market Differentiation

At the beginning of the new millennium, the state was actually witnessing a parallel growth of wineries; the eastern part focusing almost exclusively upon muscadine and sweet wines whilst in the central and western regions *vinifera* and hybrids (plus some sweet wines) were the driving force. In this respect two markets were emerging simultaneously since the different types of wines appealed to different consumers and the markets' structural dynamics were somewhat dissimilar. Sweet wines were more likely to find their appeal amongst people unfamiliar with wine but with a predilection for sweet beverages. The drier wines were the preference of more traditional wine drinkers. While both together constitute an overall market formation, the mechanisms and dynamics of how the two sectors have grown are sufficiently different to merit distinction.

The ease with which muscadine grapes can be grown, and the larger quantity per acre, means that once a market can be established for the product, production volume on a scale much greater than *vinifera* was possible. With lower costs because of the larger acreage output, retail prices could also be less than *vinifera*, hence appealing to price-sensitive consumers. Finally, the ease with which such native grapes could be grown and more of an established tradition of making wine from them meant that the learning curve for industry entrants was less steep than for hybrids and *vinifera* growers.

The corollary of such apparent beneficial aspects is that muscadines are still stigmatized as 'sweet wine', therefore lacking the wider status of dry, French varietals. As a result, they will most likely remain a niche market product. The prices charged by producers are thus limited by the absence of sufficient status to merit a higher price point. Finally, the challenges (and costs) of growing the grape are minimal compared to other varieties, hence there was less pressing need for the creation of networks to facilitate knowledge transfer. The absence of the latter has meant that a collective identity for muscadine growers, of the type associated with clusters where density attracts new entrants, has been slow to emerge. The wineries that specialize in muscadine and other fruit wines[7] are scattered throughout the eastern part of the state and have only just begun to formulate strategic plans to advance the collective status of the industry.[8]

If one claims, as I do, that the emergence of networks for the transfer of knowledge crucial to industry growth leads eventually to density and ultimately legitimacy, then the absence of such networks might hinder the collective identity and reputation of sectors where this is less important. And without such an identity, it is difficult for the marketplace to evolve and capture a wider audience of consumers. This is not to say that interactions have not occurred that facilitate knowledge transfer between muscadine growers; merely that they are less embedded in localized networks that enable collective learning. For the more complex process involved in *vinifera* growing, the tacit knowledge that became increasingly codified was transmitted through knowledge networks that became part of the geographic clusters. As a consequence one finds that non-muscadine-specific wineries tend to be clustered because proximity is necessary for the diffusion of innovation-related knowledge. The subsequent regional identity of dry wine producers has been a product of cumulative individual successes that have forged a collective reputation, not dissimilar to what organizational scholars have claimed in studies of friendship ties as identity-building mechanisms.[9]

In this chapter I examine ways in which the two, often inter-related but sometimes separate, segments of the industry have evolved in the past decade. Specifically, I argue that predominantly muscadine wineries are part of business networks that facilitate generalized information and knowledge exchange but do so in less hierarchical structured settings. On the other hand, *vinifera* and hybrid producers are part of knowledge networks that are deeper, more interdependent and hierarchical because organizational learning is more complex, trust-based and reciprocal. As a consequence, the knowledge domain in the latter is thicker which results eventually in marked differences in the capabilities of producers as some find it harder to absorb requisite knowledge than others. This is further compounded by the presence of distinct types of winemakers – professional versus semi-professional; the former associated with the resource-rich larger wineries, the latter with boutique operations. Such resource heterogeneity results in the uneven diffusion of knowledge within the network and eventually an emerging hierarchical set of relationships. Among muscadine producers, the interactions remain far more informal and unstructured, with less need for relational proximity to facilitate routine information transfer.

This approach builds upon the recent work of Giuliani whose analysis of innovation capabilities in wine clusters in Italy and Chile emphasizes the salience of network structural properties.[10] Unlike that study, however, I find that leader firms emerge to impose production benchmarks. In working with grape growers such firms have been able to demand better quality and develop more appropriate governance mechanisms within the network. Such a strong presence has shaped the way knowledge spillovers have filtered down as well as creating a framework for the growth of socio-institutional ties that have formalized interdependencies.[11] During the 1980s and '90s as the industry was emerging, significant variations in quality were to be expected and even tolerated somewhat given the infancy of most wineries. Now, the reputational effects that accompany identity result in *de facto* demands for consistent quality that have been delivered by some wineries but left others still deficient. What this has meant for relationships within the network, innovation capabilities and overall cluster evolution is examined in this chapter.

Muscadine Resurgence

The growth of the muscadine segment is mostly associated with individuals who have agricultural backgrounds, either directly as farmers or as landowners. The following narratives typify the actors in this segment and provide an illustration of their operational rationale.

The Dennis family has owned land near Albermarle, in the south-central part of the state, for generations. Those earlier generations also had a knack for making wine out of the native muscadine grapes that grew in abundance in the area, and sold it for medicinal purposes to a grateful local population. In the 1980s, Pritchard Dennis was making wine from grapes picked in the woods, using his grandfather's recipe. The more he made the better he felt he became at it and started tweaking the recipe so that by the mid-1990s he judged the wine good enough to consider production on a more commercial scale. His son Sandon shared his enthusiasm for winemaking and together they decided to plant vines systematically in 1996. Such was the beginning of Dennis Vineyards, bonded in 1997 and now producing approximately 10,500 cases annually.

Their story is a classic family business start-up venture, the growth of which has been predicated on hard work, tradition and the identification of a niche that could be exploited locally. In a May 2003 interview, Sandon told me

> It made perfect sense for us to start the winery because we had been fairly successful at making wine and giving it to friends. We had the land and buildings to use as a winery and tasting room and I was really fed up with my other job. We quickly grew and were really able to capitalize on the health benefits study that came out of Cornell in 1998 in which Dennis Vineyard's Noble wine was found to have one of the highest amount of revesterol tested. But this really just reinforced what a lot of local people had been saying about our wines for a long time. So now we really emphasize the cholesterol lowering properties of our wines and this has helped sales a lot. We have expanded quite rapidly and currently sell about 90 per cent of our wines from the tasting room; the other 10 per cent is sold in local stores and by mail order.

Their initial planting of four and a half acres of muscadines is supplemented by grapes from several local growers. The latter's numbers have increased in recent years and Dennis has been able to work with them as well as be more selective in what they buy. This gives flexibility to try new types as well as compensate for occasional low yields from their own vines. However, as Sandon noted in another interview, muscadines grow with little trouble and are far less prone to disease.[12] Unlike European varietals which have to be sprayed, thinned out and almost constantly tended, muscadines are smart vines and they do not overload themselves. He wonders why anyone would bother with *vinifera* because it is so much more work. And he is convinced that with age, muscadines make really flavourful wines. He also makes some fruit wines (blackberry, blueberry, strawberry, peach and cherry) but sees muscadines as his real bread and butter.

A measure of Dennis Vineyard's success is that in 2001 they had to tear down a family property built in the 1940s to accommodate their first tasting room. In 2006 they expanded again, this time adding a facility where they could host weddings and various meetings. The latter has been a growing feature of wineries as they capture the rural idyll and market it as a site for special occasions. I will return to this theme later.

Dennis Vineyards, alongside Duplin and Hinnant Family Vineyards, had by 2000 already established itself as a major producer of muscadine with a growing regional reputation. With the other two mentioned wineries, it had reinvigorated the market for sweet wines and provided an operational template that would attract others to the industry. As in many emerging sectors, informal ties provide an impetus for new entrants and this was clearly the case with the three accounts that follow.

Muscadine Farmers

Farms that provide 'self-pick' options for fruit dot the landscape in many states and are hives of activity during summer and early autumn. In North Carolina strawberries are one fruit that has attracted interest in the last decade as a cash crop that might be a viable substitute for tobacco. For decades, however, some farmers have grown muscadines and then allowed the grapes to be picked by the general public. That fruit can then be eaten or in some ambitious cases even made into wine by amateur winemakers. Never a major source of revenue, it was nonetheless a fairly easy crop for most of these farmers and a nice supplement to their other crops or activities.

Close to Wilmington on the south-east coast was one such set of farmers, the Bannerman family, who had been growing muscadines since 1973. People would come and pick the grapes and even bring large drums to crush the fruit at the farm. A loyal clientele had developed and recipes for winemaking were shared by customers at the farm during harvest season. Such interest inspired owners Scot and Colleen Bannerman to try making wines themselves, and they offered samples to their customers and invited comments. They had recognized that their grape-growing operation yielded revenue only for several months yet the costs incurred were monthly. This, and the positive comments made about their early winemaking experiments, stimulated their interest in opening an actual winery and making their own wine. They had also noted the tremendous success of Duplin which was down the road from them. Even after start-up costs were incurred, they hoped that a regular sales pattern would at least provide them with a more consistent and less seasonal source of income.

The winery was bonded in 2005 and their initial 3 acres has now grown to 18. Production currently is at 1,100 cases a year, large enough for them to have a reliable revenue flow but small enough for them to maintain daily oversight of operations. By their own admission, the first few years were difficult as they struggled to learn not just winemaking but the operational details that accompany volume production. Acquiring and then using the winemaking equipment was a constant challenge; understanding and completing the paperwork for licensing was equally daunting and time consuming. It was not that the actual process was necessarily difficult, merely the scale of what they were attempting with little or no experience. For many muscadine growers this constituted the biggest challenge. They currently have their son Chris working for them as vineyard manager and hope his siblings will follow suit. This way they can keep the winery a family operation but have the labour resources to manage an expanding business.

Bannerman Vineyard remains a small, family-run operation. They attribute their success to the numerous hours of familial self-exploitation that characterize many such ventures. However, they also note that part of their growth lies in the lack of competition for muscadine wines which has given them a niche to exploit. In an interview quoted in Mills and Tarmey, Chris Bannerman talked about the advantage of muscadines over European varietals from a marketing perspective: 'Muscadine has the luxury of not having complete and total market saturation'.[13] He noted that retail shelves are full of wines but very few of them are muscadines. By making a sweet wine that satisfies the local population, they concentrated on providing a product to the burgeoning local market.

Less than one hour's drive from Bannerman's Vineyard, in Tabor City, Sheila Suggs Little and her sister Amy Suggs have their winery, Grapefull Sisters Vineyard. This is the area where the industry thrived somewhat in the last century and where it was thought that a revival might have come after Prohibition's repeal. Although this did not happen until recent years, the Suggs sisters' 45-acre farm that they inherited from their parents in 2003 was in fact originally a vineyard 90 years ago. Their uncle had grown grapes in the area and the sisters noted that muscadines grew wild on their property even though it had most recently been used to grow cotton. Recognizing that muscadine was effectively the state grape, they embarked upon the process of systematically planting vines to add to those that grew wild, and then learnt about viticulture. They started off with 1 acre and hope eventually to expand to 10 acres. By their own acknowledgement it was an expensive process, much more so than they had anticipated although their business plan includes the construction of a small inn and an RV campground. The idea of the latter two features is to make the winery into a destination, drawing customers from the nearby resort town of Myrtle Beach, South Carolina. Eventually, they plan to have such operations cross-subsidize the winery; an increasingly popular agri-business model for new wineries.

Currently their wine is made at Duplin Winery. Many small wineries where knowledge of actual winemaking is limited choose essentially to outsource key value-added phases of the operation such as grape crushing and winemaking. Given their inadequate knowledge base, the sisters realized it was better to pay someone else to make the wine until they developed the necessary skill sets themselves. Such a process contracts out this phase but by capitalizing upon the skill sets of nearby professionals eliminates much of the risk of a faulty final product. This adds to the costs and is a difficult trade-off for small businesses. But since wineries essentially have only one chance each year to make their product, it is a decision the more cautious or perhaps discerning prefer to take. It does, however, minimize flaws in the final product and contributes to the overall efforts to produce a wine that meets consumer expectations.

This pattern of hiring what amounts to a consultant winemaker is quite widespread in the industry throughout the United States. Small wineries decide that their skills sets might be in growing grapes and general viticultural techniques together with marketing the final product but see no point in investing in a plant to crush the grapes and/or blend the juice into a finished product. Since such capital expenditures result in equipment that is used for only several weeks a year, it is felt that the more prudent approach is to pay someone for such a service. We will see later how this model has developed more in *vinifera* production where winemaking skills are more crucially linked with producing a crafted product. There industry newcomers often lack confidence and acknowledge the implications of failure; hence the decision to let someone who has already mastered the learning curve perform the final stages of the operation.

Finally, in the heart of the Piedmont in what has now become *vinifera* country, is Garden Gate Vineyards, near Mocksville. Founded in 2000 by Sonya and Bob Whitaker, it was the sixteenth winery in the state to receive a licence. On a 3.24-acre farm, they grow exclusively fruit and muscadine grapes. Bob took early retirement from a power company, Sonya is a potter. Together they thought a small winery was possible in this area and since his grandfather had grown Norton grapes they decided they would focus upon muscadines since they knew they grew well locally. Their initial aim was to make about $50 a week from sales at the winery and festivals. In 2002 their initial production of 600 gallons (approximately 250 cases) sold out and their current production is 2,000 gallons (840 cases). Their aim is to remain a small and according to them 'a friendly environment'. In a March 2007 interview, they told me

> We built this tasting room next to the house because we want to offer a nice place for the novice wine drinker to drop by. This sort of person might not know anything about wine but they might like the casual atmosphere they find in the winery and feel comfortable buying a bottle. It's important to de-mystify wine and not be too snobby about it otherwise the market will not grow.
>
> We make sweet wines and believe that is what a new market for wine in North Carolina wants. Since it is such a new market the customers need to get used to drinking wine and they're likely to do this with sweet wines. Our typical customer might be a farmer who pulls in on his tractor on the way home from work and buys a bottle for dinner that evening. Also we want to stay small because big wineries can be intimidating and also bigger is not necessarily better for them.

These comments capture the sentiments of many new entrants who have modest ambitions. They are self-financing their winery and using their own labour so it is imperative that the operation remains manageable for the two of them to do everything. The difficulties they encountered were largely of a bureaucratic nature – especially permits since this was a dry county when they first started. They also complained of the lack of state support for the industry, noting that if wineries are to be conceived as part of tourism, then the state should pay for signage. Small wineries cannot afford the capital expense of putting signs on the major highways directing traffic to their location.

Are Networks Important for Muscadine Producers?

In my interviews with muscadine wineries and growers, I asked questions about the nature of information exchange and knowledge acquisition plus whether they thought of themselves as part of an emerging wine network. Amongst firms producing exclusively muscadine-based wines and fruit wines, the results were notable inasmuch as there was a greater likelihood of general information being shared between wineries than detailed technical knowledge. Daily and weekly interactions (e.g. phone calls or visits), when they occurred, were more likely to focus upon broad issues affecting the industry, equipment loan or general farming questions. The owners saw their interactions as part of a knowledge-generating set of relationships, very loosely structured and contingent upon informal ties of friendship and mutual cooperation typical of farming communities. There was little or no sense of collective learning occurring although they did acknowledge that ideas were exchanged and they felt free to call upon other wineries in the area for advice. They identified with other wineries and saw their actions as being part of an attempt to resuscitate the industry in the area. But there was no sense of a cohesive sub-group of firms within what might be construed as a regional cluster that was advancing the identity of the industry. In fact it was precisely the lack of such a collective identity that led to recent efforts by the North Carolina Muscadine Grape Association (NCMGA) to develop a strategic plan for the industry in 2007. This involved an effort to market their brand better, develop a clearing house for the dissemination of data on the sector, develop best management practices, establish quality standards for grapes and more generally identify their key stakeholders.[14] In other words, precisely the absence of such coherence has stimulated institutional actors to proffer efficiency measures in the hope of further developing the sector as part of regional economic development initiatives.

When asked specifically how they learned their viticulture and winemaking skills, several said that for the latter they relied upon modified recipes that were handed down through their families. For others it was through trial and error and the remainder consulted what books they could find as well as help from the Agricultural Extension agency.[15] Some attributed their overall success to their farming background; others indicated that their reason for choosing muscadine was because it was easy to grow and make into wine. With one exception the general consensus was that the skill sets to grow the grapes and make the wine were not insurmountable even for a person who is self-taught. As to viticulture methods, the grape's long history in the area, plus its ubiquity, meant that production knowledge was modest and widespread. Finally, most growers were able to farm essentially organically since there was little or no need for fertilizers, spraying and fungicidal control for the grape given its natural suitability to the climate and region. This not only saved costs but also labour hours and resources that could be diverted to other activities surrounding the winery operation.

Some looked to Duplin but as an example of what could be done rather than necessarily how to do it. Several had started business selling grapes to Duplin and therefore learned from them some cultivation techniques to meet requisite quality standards. But Duplin did not necessarily exercise a leadership role in shaping sector governance, framing network activities or structuring interactions. As easy as it was to grow the grape, there was less need for such a coordinating role than for *vinifera* producers to the west. There were no barriers to knowledge exchange because the perception was that operating knowledge could be acquired fairly easily and systematically through state agencies. Farming techniques were understood although most who entered the industry underestimated the degree of work involved and the capital necessary to sustain their vision.

Vineyard development costs averaged about $5,200 an acre and the actual planting was generally done by the owners themselves rather than using vineyard consultants. By 2005 muscadine wine-grape prices were averaging $534 per ton and, with average yields of 7 tons per acre, provided an attractive income for those who chose to remain merely growers as well as those who had decided to make wine themselves. Some still chose to supplement their own winemaking with 'you pick' operations; others sell to nearby wineries that lack their own production needs.

Interestingly enough, many of the muscadine growers thought of themselves as farmers first and winemakers/winery owners second. There appeared to be a greater sense of attachment to the land and recognition that they were part of an established tradition in the area. They knew of the scuppernong history and seemed determined to write another chapter in its long story. But they were also pragmatic enough to realize that for their venture to be successful, they needed to be more than just a winery. Almost all of the wineries were adding additional activities to make their tasting rooms a 'destination'. Whether this was modest bed and breakfast operations, a bistro or facilities for weddings and meetings, the idea was to offer more than a place to come and taste/buy wine. This pattern is similar to that found in *vinifera* wineries that have opened in the central and western parts of the state.

When asked about their interactions with others they often indicated that tourism related questions were frequently uppermost. One small winery owner told me in 2007,

> I wanted to know how [nearby winery] was doing with their bed and breakfast business because it's something that I'm thinking of. I also keep asking whether a restaurant is more of a pain than a profit because I think it would be good here but I don't know much about that side of the business.

Another told me in a 2005 interview,

> I would like to see another winery open down the road as that would bring more people. As it is it can be difficult to get people to visit since we're a bit out of the way. I've got to find something else that will make a visit special and I think a restaurant like Duplin's might be the answer.

Where Networks Matter

Much of the state's rapid growth of wineries in the last few years has occurred in the Piedmont region (central part of the state), centred initially on the Yadkin Valley but spreading outwards in adjacent counties. It is here that over 50 per cent of North Carolina's wineries are currently located. These include the multi-million dollar Childress Vineyard that was opened in 2004 in the southern part of the Yadkin Valley AVA as well as smaller, but still capital intensive wineries such as Rock of Ages (2006) and Uwharrie Vineyards (2005). In each of these the owners have used extensive resources from previously successful business ventures to build wineries that are on a grander scale than the typical new start-up. Here short-term profitability goals are subservient to long-term product development strategies. The aim, according to the owners of these wineries, was to build a profile for winemaking in the state and supply that demand by quality wines at mid-level price points. Their extensive resources permit a long-term approach to return on investment and with that security, they are able to focus upon building market legitimacy for the product. In the case of Childress this has come largely through the influence of their winemaker, Mark Friszolowski, and the professional vineyard team he has assembled.

The majority of new wineries in this area, however, are small family-owned, self-financed operations. Theirs are the epitome of entrepreneurial operations, replete with familial self-exploitation and a constant preoccupation with financial uncertainty. Most have far more enthusiasm than resources, have encountered difficulties in mastering the varied tasks (grape growing, winemaking and then wine marketing), but have demonstrated remarkable perseverance. However, they have entered an industry when more knowledge is widespread, institutional support structured and ancillary industries (suppliers) more locally established. It is this recent group of new entrants who have added density to the network, and whose success can be attributed to their access to knowledge networks and their pressure for more formalized learning and skill acquisition. It is individuals in many of these wineries who have availed themselves of the modest viticultural and oenology resources at local community colleges and have become active members of industry associations. In the latter they see a way to formalize the network of winemakers and grape growers that will further disseminate knowledge sharing. They also realize that the industry will best be served if it can develop a coherent collective voice. Finally, it is through such formal organizations that issues of quality can be addressed. Achieving the latter, however, raises issues of cluster governance that have not always been favourably embraced by all wineries. But as the industry evolves, key firms (and individuals within those firms) have played a leadership role that has structured the network and imposed a more formalized dimension to interactions.

Adding to the Knowledge Network: Can Scale Make a Difference?

On 14 October 2004, the 36,000-square-foot Childress Vineyards in the southern part of the Yadkin Valley opened. A $10 million, neo-Tuscan facility, it dwarfs many of the wineries one sees even in established regions of the country such as Napa and Sonoma Valley and is the largest in North Carolina. On a 70-acre site, the winery is the brainchild of NASCAR owner Richard Childress (together with his business partner Greg Johns), who lives nearby on a 25-acre property planted with Syrah, Cabernet Franc and Vidal Blanc grapes.

Originally conceived many years earlier when Richard developed a passion for wines during his own racing career, it came to fruition in the 1990s with the purchase of the property in Lexington. Having bought the land, Childress planted vines and had his grapes custom crushed so he could give the resulting wine to his friends. But he also realized that to succeed in this business he needed a professional winemaker, preferably with east coast winemaking experience and someone who could oversee vineyard management. He approached Mark Friszolowski, who had worked for the previous eighteen years as winemaker at Pindar Vineyards in Long Island. Friszolowski had a reputation for making good wines, his Viogniers having consistently won gold medals at various competitions, and he had worked extensively as a consultant for other wineries. Initially reluctant to move, Friszolowski eventually agreed because he thought it would be an opportunity to build an industry that had potential and with someone who had the resources to match the challenge. He was familiar with several of the winemakers in the state and knew of the growth of wineries there. As he said in an interview about North Carolina wines, 'I had tasted all the wines, and I knew there was potential'.[16] Now he would have the opportunity to craft production on a grand scale.

There are currently 26 acres on the winery site under vines although in the initial years most grapes were purchased from local growers. His experience growing grapes and making wine allowed Friszolowski to be exacting in his selection of grapes to be purchased. Recognizing that good wine needs good grapes he worked with local growers to help them improve various facets of their operation so that the quality would ensue. Too often the emphasis had been upon quantity, he told me in a 2007 interview, which he attributed to typical agricultural mindsets. However, with grapes sometimes less is better and he pays people not just by the ton but also by the quality of the harvested grapes. He routinely inspects growers' vineyards and is not hesitant to bring faults and problems to their attention. He has even cancelled contracts when the final harvest does not meet the prearranged specifications. This had led some growers to be frustrated and angry but it has also allowed others to learn techniques rapidly that were previously unfamiliar to them. It forces them to pay more attention to vineyard management details, acquire appropriate methods to improve the quality of their grape harvest and ultimately embrace higher production standards than in the past.

As Childress Vineyards' own vines have matured, he is less reliant upon bought grapes although is still willing to buy because of the flexibility it offers. This pattern mirrors the other big wineries that no longer need the quantities of purchased grapes that they required in their earlier years. What grapes are bought are of high quality and smaller quantity, the result of which has been some growers have been unable to sell their fruit and abandoned it on the vine.

As with any newcomer to the area, Friszolowski has experimented with different varietals to discover what grows best but also acknowledges that it will take at least ten years to determine more precisely the region's signature grapes. Even then, each harvest is so different there will be considerable fluctuations. He recognizes the difficult learning curve for newcomers but also stresses that broad support mechanism are now in place to aid fledgling wineries. He currently makes wine for several local wineries, enabling them systematically to access the tacit knowledge that enhances their own reputation as well as that of the local cluster.

Childress currently produces approximately 30,000 cases, divided roughly amongst three different categories: house wines, mid-range varietals and a third tier of reserve wines. This enables them to market to different constituencies, from neophyte wine drinkers all the way to connoisseurs. Their facility also contains a bistro and extensive banquet rooms for private functions, plus there is a chain hotel located next to the winery. Clearly the reputation of Richard Childress and his NASCAR links has enabled the winery to garner public attention disproportionate to the initial modest production output. However, through extensive marketing efforts (such as promotional events at races or billboards on highways), the winery has been able to promote not only its wines but North Carolina wines in general. Together with Biltmore, Shelton and RayLen, Childress has played a crucial role in further legitimizing the industry's identity and organizational form in North Carolina, plus, as we shall see later, exercising leadership in overall governance. By dramatically increasing the stock of knowledge, they have codified many practices, imposed new operating logics and furthered the asymmetrical relationships within the network.

Directly or indirectly, the recipients of this changing organizational landscape have been the many new boutique wineries that have opened in recent years. It is amongst this size category that the sector's growth has been most vibrant, adding to the density and intensity of network interactions. Here one can find examples of firms who are able to benefit from industry and institutional growth in the previous decade, who are able to access a richer set of resources and whose presence has benefited from, as well as contributed to, organizational learning and firm heterogeneity.

Incremental Additions to the Knowledge Base and Knowledge Network

Robert Wurz comes from near Calistoga in the northern part of the Napa Valley in California. As a boy he made wine from an old ciderwood press and went on to obtain a PhD in wine chemistry from University of California at Davis. He had planned to work in the California wine industry but the downturn in the mid-1980s saw him relocate to North Carolina and take a job as a research chemist with Ciba Geigy (now Syngenta). Biding his time until a return to California he decided to make some wine himself and with grapes bought from Phil Hammond, a grower in nearby Pinnacle, he made his first vintage in 1999. His second the following year was better and this convinced him and his wife Natalie that they might be able to start their own winery. With funding secured from a partnership of investors, they acquired a 12-acre estate of former tobacco land 12 miles north of Greensboro and planted vines on 1.5 acres of their property. They built a 5,000-case capacity production facility, preferring to put their capital into that rather than extensive vineyards. In 2006 they opened Stonefield Cellars.[17]

Robert had earlier realized that one needed to experiment with winemaking techniques since conditions were not the same as in California where he had learned his trade and so much of the technical publications focused upon. As a consequence he decided to buy grapes from local growers as well as those in Virginia and Georgia, determined to find the right kinds as he perfected his own local winemaking techniques. He currently buys 90 per cent of his grapes, growing the remaining 10 per cent on his own property. Of that 10 per cent there are currently 11 different varieties; his localized way of deciding what might grow best in the region. By buying grapes he has the flexibility to switch production quickly. He also works with growers to determine quality standards that he expects and together with an assistant visits growers at least once a year to check out their vineyards.

By accessing local growers whose vineyards were already mature Robert did not face the 3–5-year gestation period that other new wineries encountered as their vines developed. He could also be selective about the grapes he buys. Growers who supply him know what his standards are and are prepared to meet his specifications whenever possible. Issues such as canopy management or spraying schedules are typical of the information exchange that occurs between him and growers as he works to ensure the best possible fruit at harvest. He signs one-year contracts with growers but the latter know that by delivering high-quality fruit they can be assured of repeat business. However, he also recognizes that each year can produce very different growing conditions so allowances have to be made for the final quality of grapes and overall harvest.

Current production at Stonefield Cellars is 2,700 cases and they hope to reach their own production capacity of 3,000 cases in the near future. However, they continue to operate as a custom crush facility for other local wineries and Robert acts as winemaker/consultant to several area wineries. He believed that this was a way to ensure the financial viability of his own operation and simultaneously to help sustain other local wineries that perhaps lacked the resources that he had. He also saw it as a way of using his technical knowledge to provide assistance to those learning winemaking, particular the sorts of tacit on-the-job skills that even the local oenology programme cannot offer.

Robert retains his full-time job with Syngenta but Natalie now works full time in the winery as vice president of sales and marketing. The latter's role has been crucial since once wineries have mastered the winemaking part of the operation, often their biggest challenge is actually selling the wine. Her ability to devote all of her time to this task has aided the winery's growth but, like many others, renting out their facility for events has been a vital revenue source. When asked about the biggest challenge facing the winery and the North Carolina industry in general, Robert said

> It's important that we make consistently good wines. We would like to make rich, full-bodied wines but that is always going to be difficult in the state because of the shorter growing season [than say California or Washington State]. But people have come to expect this type of big wine and what we have to do is convince them that there are good alternatives that are not so fruit forward. We need to adapt winemaking to the local conditions and not vice versa. (interview with author, 2009)

Approximately 35 miles east of Stonefield Cellars is Benjamin Vineyards and Winery, opened in 2004 and owned by Andy and Nancy Zeman. They bought a 10-acre plot in 2001 after searching for land with the right soil composition for a vineyard and put in 5 acres of vines. It is located in Graham and is close to

Chapel Hill and the Research Triangle – an important location choice for them given the potential market of wine drinkers in that area. They initially planted an acre of muscadines because as the native grape they thought it would be easy to tend and resistant to disease.[18] They subsequently added hybrids and then *vinifera* (Merlot and Cabernet Sauvignon). Their current production is 1,500 cases but they hope to reach a capacity of 2,000 cases, which they believe is the optimal size for a small winery that remains family-run.

Benjamin Vineyards continues to offer a range of sweet and dry wines, believing that this provides a choice for any customer. They sell their wines through an upscale market in Chapel Hill and some restaurants but otherwise rely almost exclusively upon sales from the tasting room. When asked about the problems they encounter with their operation, Andy said

> Sales and marketing are our biggest challenge. It took me a while to learn how to make wine but I was able to practise a lot before we even had the winery. We chose to grow muscadines, hybrids and *vinifera* and to do it as organically as possible to save on spraying costs. It's still easiest for us to sell muscadines but the problem is we can't charge a lot for such wine because it's not perceived as a value-added product. We are a micro-winery with a local market so we've tried to attract customers who will be repeat buyers. We have a special distributor's permit which allows us to sell to stores directly and thus bypass the costly distribution channels that have the mark-ups. This has been an important cost saver for us. Still our competitors are Total Wine and the superstores that can sell quality wine for $10 – we cannot match that because our cost structure is higher and volume lower.
>
> If the industry is to prosper we have to pay attention to quality since you cannot make good wine from bad grapes. Too many grape growers still work with the quantity mentality of let's see how many tons I can grow per acre. We need to better manage yields although that might start to happen now since there are more grapes available than there are buyers. Childress used to buy a lot of grapes but now their own vines are maturing and producing they don't need to as much. (interview with author, 2006)

He went on to say that the shift of the Grape Council from the Department of Agriculture to Commerce would help wineries since now there would be more available expertise in marketing and selling. These are the things where help is needed since most of the small wineries lack the staff to devote time to promotional activities. It has helped that his winery is located on the Haw River wine trail (and, since 2009, the Haw River AVA) and this brings in tourists who otherwise might not come to an individual winery. As several of the other wineries on the trail commented, the more wineries there are in an area the better it is for each one. In this case the density of the cluster is commercially beneficial because it makes them a 'destination'. It also adds to the visibility of the industry locally.

Nearby is the Winery at Iron Gate Farm, a 61-acre former tobacco farm that was opened as a winery in 2004. One of the co-owners, Debbie Stikeleather, had coveted the land following the death of the previous owners and after buying it looked for something to farm on it. She discovered the viticulture programme at Surry Community College and although not a wine drinker herself thought that a vineyard might be a suitable venture for the property. In pursuing this goal, she enrolled in the programme and planted 3.5 acres in 2001. Her original aim was to be a grape grower, selling her fruit to local wineries. After graduation from the programme in 2002 she began an internship with Linda King, the winemaker at Rag Apple Lassie and by that time she and her husband had decided to start their own winery.

There are currently 8 acres under vine and they produce approximately 3,100 cases. Eventually they would like to be a 5,000-case winery and they will supplement their own grapes with those bought from two growers in the Yadkin Valley. Her husband Gene runs a fencing business and this has helped subsidize the costs of the winery. Like many other in the area, they have built up a network of locals who volunteer their services in the winery, act as unofficial tasters in blending trials and provide general 'moral' support for the venture. They have also developed a multifunctional tasting room that caters to weddings and special events, as well as being a venue for local artists to display their wares. Currently Debbie serves as director at large for the North Carolina Winegrowers Association, sits on the Farm Bureau Board of Directors for Alamance County and is a member of the Cooperative Extension Advisory Board. She remains a staunch advocate for this rapidly growing viticultural region and is an active facilitator of this subnetwork of wineries and grape growers.

Further west in the Yadkin Valley is Laurel Grey Vineyards in Hamptonville, located on the family farm belonging to Kim and Benny Myers. Their 85-acre farm has been in the family for several hundred years and it was in the 1990s that they thought it would be a good site for grape growing. They had watched others in the area develop wineries, talked at length with people such as Michael and Amy Helton (Hanover Park Vineyards) and noticed the growing local interest in wine.

Kim started taking classes at Surry Community College and they planted vines (currently 10 acres are under cultivation). Recognizing that *vinifera* was not high yield and expensive to grow, they nonetheless felt that this was the sort of wine that the region could become known for. And, as they told me in a 2006 interview, 'if one makes a quality wine then you can charge more for it'. As with many small wineries the start-up costs far exceeded their expectations, and the sheer amount of physical labour was much greater than anticipated. They particularly cited the need for capital to sustain the operation in the early years when the vines were not producing fruit and this slowed down their plans somewhat. After several years of making their wine in custom crush facilities elsewhere, they built their own winery which opened in 2007. They currently produce approximately 1,600 cases but hope to reach a 2,500–3,000 capacity in the near future. However, they maintain a commitment to high quality, believing that the only way the industry can have lasting success is if it becomes associated with a high-quality product. One cannot compete with the lower-cost wines that are in the supermarkets, they said, so one has to have something special that makes a person spend over $20 for a bottle.

They approached this venture slowly, acquiring the skill sets and then the physical resources to develop a functioning winery. They were fortunate in having family land and this clearly helped in the initial start-up period although neither of them were farmers so there were many aspects of agricultural operations that they had to learn. However, their story is similar to several other wineries in the area where the inheritance of a farm and a search for sustainable agricultural practices eventually led to winemaking. Often disinclined to pursue traditional farming, for many newcomers winemaking appeared a more desirable agricultural activity although one with high start-up costs and much longer profitability goals.

Many of the area's small wineries that have started in recent years have stories similar to those told above. Two such wineries in Yadkin Valley are Flint Hill and Buck Shoals; further west closer to Asheville is South Creek Vineyards, and to the east on the Haw River wine trail is Creek Side Winery.

Tim and Brenda Doub opened Flint Hill Vineyards in 2005, on the farm where Tim's grandfather was born and lived and which they inherited. Not being farmers themselves (both had professional jobs), they took the introductory viticulture course at Surry Community College. They had planted vines in 2002 and supplied grapes to the now defunct Old North State Co-op in Mt Airy of which they were members.[19] However, using funds from their separate corporate jobs, they decided to open their own tasting room in the original family farm building, hiring Sean McRitchie to make their wines for them. In 2007 they opened a restaurant in their facility; a way of cross-subsidizing the winery operations.

In a similar vein, Terry Crater grew up in a farming family in the Piedmont; five earlier generations had grown tobacco, grain and corn as well as raising cattle and chickens. When he and his wife Joanne decided to start a winery (called Buck Shoals Vineyard) on the family farm that opened in 2004, it was to continue this agricultural legacy and keep the farm in the family. Since he had limited agricultural knowledge (like the others mentioned above he had a corporate background), he and his wife took classes at Surry Community College. Convinced that vineyards could strengthen the local economy and keep people in agriculture who might otherwise leave for nearby cities, he became an advocate of the industry. They subsequently formed a venture with nearby Raffaldini winery to share equipment and resources. Although their current production is 1,000 cases they hope eventually to reach 5,000.

Following his retirement as chief financial officer of the Siecor Corporation, Frank Boldon bought a 30-acre former cattle farm in McDowell County where he planted 2 acres of *vinifera* grapes. Resolute in his belief that good wines can be made in this area, close to Asheville, he has won various medals for his wines at the State Fair in Raleigh and currently produces 500 cases, almost all of which are sold directly from the winery.[20] Unlike the others mentioned here, he makes the wines himself at his premises, having learned the skills through courses, trial and error and long conversations with other local winemakers.

Finally, to the east of Greensboro, is Creek Side Winery, owned by Fred and Angie Wallace and situated on their 52-acre family farm. Self-professed 'weekend farmers', in 2002 they were looking for something else to grow on 22 of the acres and decided to plant vines after discussing the issue extensively with neighbouring grape growers and industry experts. They also were part of Old State Co-op but because of their location to the east, their grapes ripened sooner and this made coordination of their harvesting with the rest of the co-ops rather difficult. They subsequently opened their own winery in 2005 and currently produce 1,200 cases. Despite much on-the-job learning they did not feel comfortable making their own wine so use the services of consultant winemaker Robert Wurz (of Stonefield Cellars).

Learning and Remaining Small

The above narratives tell individual stories but ones that are typical of the new boutique winery owner, albeit differentiated slightly by the added resources some were able to bring to their operation. Many were looking for a viable way to utilize existing family farms, some of which had been partially devoted to tobacco; others realized a long ambition to start a winery following a professional career and bought farms (again some of which had been under tobacco production). Their production is typically modest with the majority under 1,500 cases a year although the aim for some in this category is eventually to reach 2,500 and even 5,000 cases.[21]

Financially most have cross-subsidized their winery with one of the owners' full-time employment income, sought investment from a small group of partners or used bank financing, or a combination of all three. Typically they have 5–9-year break-even goals, and they all underestimated the steep learning curve involved in the various facets of the business. As small operations they struggle with sales and marketing, find dealing with distributors an intimidating and costly experience, yet recognize that to grow they need a way to get their wines to wider markets. Most feel that the state does a poor job in providing an infrastructure that would be beneficial to them as small businesses and that there is still an inadequate support service from the Department of Agriculture, although it has improved in recent years as additional specialist viticulture staff have been added. Most have relied upon the formal organizations such as the North Carolina Grape and Winegrowers Association as a crucial way to meet others in the industry, share information, establish contacts and get in touch with suppliers. They lament the difficulty in securing financing from banks that seem either reluctant or lacking in expertise to deal with such an agricultural venture.

A 2005 study by MKF Research commissioned by North Carolina Department of Commerce and Division of Tourism highlighted the preponderance of very small wineries at that time, a reflection of both newness and a desire to keep the operation as a family affair.[22] Table 5.1 provides a breakdown of the 54 wineries in the state at that time.

Table 5.1: Size Distribution of North Carolina Wineries, 2005. Source: MKF Research LLC, and *Triad Business Journal* (2005).

Cases Produced	Number of Wineries
1,500 and less	31
1,501–2,000	5
2,001–4,000	4
4,001–10,000	9
10,001–20,000	1
20,001–100,000	2
More than 100,000	2

The principal concerns of most wineries after 'learning the trade' continue to be staffing resources and marketing/sales. Most report the scarcity of time as they juggle various activities that embrace the disparate tasks of a winery operation, from the agricultural details through to wine selling. Add to that the administration of their business and the coordination of activities associated with other revenue streams (e.g. weddings and banquets at the tasting room) – all at a time when perhaps the income from wine sales is in its infancy. As to sales, most prefer to sell direct from the winery or self-distribute to local retailers and restaurants, thus avoiding the administrative details and costs of using a distributor. However, the liability of newness is their lack of reputation and their small size which makes it difficult to attract consumers. Most cannot afford to advertise, including using the signage that has been coordinated through the Department of Commerce. Instead they hope that by affiliating with a regional association (such as a wine trail) or being located close to metropolitan areas they can build a loyal, local customer base.

As with most products, gaining access to distribution channels is important. But because most of the wineries are small it is often difficult to get a distributor to take their wine and, if they do, their wine will probably be a low priority in that firm's expansive operation. As several winery owners told me, by avoiding distributors they can keep more of the profit for themselves (or in some cases actually make a profit rather than a loss). Distributors typically take up to 50 per cent of the retail cost, so by restricting sales almost exclusively to the winery the owner can keep that margin for him/herself. 'Cellar door sales' or wine sold directly from the property is twice as profitable as sales made through distributors, hence the emphasis upon creating attractive tasting rooms and event facilities. Not surprisingly most of even the smallest boutique wineries have paid great attention to this facet of their operation.

On the other hand many still struggle to sell their wine so a good relationship with a distributor can get their product out to a broader market. At 1,500–2,000 cases one can sell most of the wine from the winery but once one exceeds that 2,000 threshold it becomes more important to get into established distribution channels. As one 2,800-case winery owner told me,

> what I lose in per bottle income is compensated for by the increasing volume of sales since I've used a distributor. They're fairly small and are willing to work with me and they've done a good job. But I still have to do a lot of marketing myself and rely upon 50–60 per cent of sales direct from the winery. (interview with author, 2006)

It is clear that the educational facilities of Surry Community College have proved a vital resource for formal training and many of the new owners took classes there. In each of my interviews with winery owners/winemakers who had opened their facility since 2003, at least one key member of their operation had taken either short courses at the college or completed the two-year programme. They all indicated that this was for them a way of systematically acquiring skill sets that enabled them to frame the requisite tasks of vineyard management and winemaking. They were then better equipped cognitively to digest informal tacit knowledge that was developed through network interactions, especially when they sought out local experts whose own experiential learning dealt with similar problems. However, they nonetheless lament the absence of programmes that would deal with broader small business administration and marketing. Most identify this as a crucial next step if the industry is to gain a sound financial footing and prevent mortality rates from rising.

Most small wineries have relied upon the informal network that has deepened and consolidated in recent years, with many citing the community college as a vehicle for establishing contacts. They also indicate that there are far more ancillary services available now than apparently there were a decade ago, facilitating the ease of procurement and lowering some materials costs. One such example of a new service catering to the wine industry is that of Patria Properties, a realty company owned by hobbyist winemaker Robin Weant. The company is the result of her 20-year real estate business experience and fascination with and study of wine and viticulture.[23] She started her company in 2007 and offers specialist advice on potential vineyard properties, providing detailed information on what rootstocks work and how to get soil tests all the way to helping a client establish a vineyard on the property. She spends time talking with other winery owners and learns from them of problems and issues that she can then relay to her clients. Another Winston-Salem-based company (Stave Worldwide) markets Hungarian oak barrels at 30 per cent less than French ones and has found customers amongst the three large wineries plus some of the smaller established ones; other specialists in vineyard maintenance are now commonplace, providing key skill sets that are location specific and the product of accumulated knowledge – precisely the sort of tacit skill sets that clusters can facilitate.

The increasing density of wineries appears to have encouraged the development of innovation-oriented cooperation since the benefits are apparent to those whose knowledge base is still maturing. Because their business models are predicated on long-term growth, winery owners are likely to embrace a shared, long-term vision for the industry. Any uncertainty surrounding the benefits of cooperation is dissipated when actors realize that their individual success is predicated upon the growth of a collective identity. The more new wineries are established, the greater the likelihood of them coming together to find ways of assessing the benefits of cooperation and overcoming the liability of newness. In doing so, they solidify the horizontal interactions that occur in knowledge networks (sharing amongst actors with similar skill sets). But because different firms have different resource capabilities and skill sets, knowledge accumulation is inherently imperfect and path dependent which results in persistent firm heterogeneity.[24] Consequently, certain firms or actors emerge as key knowledge brokers who are able both directly and indirectly to impose their problem-solving skills upon the remainder of firms. Mark Friszolowski of Childress and Steve Shepherd of RayLen are key figures in this instance. These vertical relationships emerge partly because new less skilled entrants are more deliberate in their selection of knowledge sources and seek out such informants. They also emerge as informed actors impose more detailed operational procedures (vineyard management techniques for example) to ensure requisite quality for their inputs (grapes purchased). This has the effect of simultaneously overcoming governance problems and creating a hierarchy within the network. The more some firms seek out technical advice from technological leaders, the more formalized the hierarchy. This is not to say that informal interactions are no longer sources of knowledge transfer; merely that knowledge-seeking behaviour has become more purposeful and structurally embedded.

Renewed Institutional Support

The dramatic increase in wineries that started after 2002 was a response to the growing realization that *vinifera* could be successfully grown in the state, there was a market for the finished product and that resources for new entrants minimized the likelihood of grape-growing failure that had plagued new ventures in previous decades. Gaining access to knowledge networks was somewhat easier because the networks were deeper, more diverse and established. Trust-based relationships within such networks were still largely conditioned by informal reciprocal ties albeit framed regionally through industry associations. The latter's role was largely facilitative and complemented institutional support for the industry.

The success of Surry County Community College's viticulture and oenology programme was evident by the large number of new winery owners who took the two-year programme or at least attended classes and workshops. Several new educational programmes have recently started elsewhere. At Appalachian State University, the Chemistry Department has begun offering analytical services to wineries through a mobile laboratory as well as establishing programmes to help local winemakers better understand the chemistry behind their wines. Under the tutelage of Grant Holder, the Department has assembled a small team of specialists whose aim is to identify problems specific to wines made in the North Carolina climate and soil and then help overcome them.[25] The programme is in its infancy and some wineries have been critical of the high costs charged for the mobile laboratory testing service. However, others have lauded the opportunity to have access to facilities that were otherwise not available. Of my sample of firms in the central Piedmont, 60 per cent had utilized this service in the past few years and saw it as a crucial source of technical assistance.

Also affiliated with Appalachian State University is the recently created Center for Mountain Wine Growing under the direction of long-time North Carolina wine expert and enthusiast Norm Oches. The centre provides an outreach programme for and conducts research on wineries that are at or above a 1,600 feet elevation and/or with slopes in excess of 30 per cent. It borrows heavily from successful steep-slope growing in Europe, where it has partners, and has been an important stimulus for the recent addition of higher-elevation grape growing in the state.

At North Carolina State University a reinvigorated specialized viticulture programme within the Departments of Food Science and Horticultural Science and the North Carolina Cooperative Extension Service has led to the appointment of additional staff.[26] With a teaching and research focus in viticulture and oenology, and the development of an experimental vineyard, the programme provides a resource base that was conspicuously absent except for those interested in muscadine growth. The Extension programme offers short courses and web-based programmes for North Carolina winemakers that are designed to help them improve the quality of their wine and thus its regional and even national competitiveness.

The presence of the programmes is testament to the growth of wineries and a realization that there are significant economic benefits that can be best realized with a more professional and educated approach to winemaking. It is only in recent years that the state has been willing to invest resources in grape-growing and winemaking research, hitherto seeing it as a niche occupation that was inconsequential compared to the dominant agricultural activities of hog and poultry farming or more specialized crops such as strawberries. Part of the problem is that an alternative to the high-profit relatively low-cost tobacco farming is not likely, yet nostalgia for such largesse still lingers amongst many in the state agricultural offices.

On the legislative front, the North Carolina General Assembly passed a number of laws in 2005 that are favourable to wineries. The five bills passed in September of that year included an increase in the volume of wine that can be shipped direct to consumers, shipping orders are no longer subject to a $100 application fee to receive the appropriate permit, and allowing winery representatives to offer wine tastings in retail outlets. The latter has proved important for an industry that relies upon face-to-face interactions to stimulate interest in the product and sales.[27] However, because there are still legislators who are opposed to anything involving alcohol sales, broad consensus for industry support is difficult to achieve.

The large wineries in the state, particularly Shelton through the lobbying of its owners and Childress through the leadership of its winemaker, have been influential in promoting the industry and shaping the parameters of formal organizations that have emerged. Whilst not always consistent with the interests of small wineries, such activities have nonetheless built upon earlier patterns of enabling conditions that facilitated cooperation and lowered transaction costs. This has provided a structure for innovation to occur and encouraged co-location by new firms, the stories of which are relayed above. In essence this recent period of market formation, primarily in the central part of the state where the bulk of *vinifera* growers are situated, is one in which governance has evolved through the activities (and resources) of the large wineries. How that leadership has shaped the industry, increased firm heterogeneity and possibly even diminished cooperation is the subject of the next chapter.

Conclusion

During this recent phase of industry growth, one can see product differentiation (muscadine versus *vinifera*) as well as a distinction between professional and semi-professional winemakers. Both have shaped the evolution of the marketplace for wine, and produced variation in the structure of interactions as the cluster has formed.

Muscadine wines continue to be a niche market, with those growers in the eastern part of the state focusing entirely upon the grape as well as other sweet 'fruit' wines. Their appeal is mainly to a population unaccustomed to regular wine consumption, and one with a predilection for sweet beverages. Some *vinifera* and hybrid growers elsewhere have planted muscadines to reach out to those neophyte wine drinkers who prefer sweet wines. Their hope is that the latter will gravitate to dry wines eventually; in the meantime muscadines fulfil a steady sales pattern and help their bottom line. Many *vinifera* wineries acknowledge that their preference for making dry wines is somewhat stymied by the public clamour for sweet wines, with several noting that up to 50 per cent of their sales come from muscadines despite only accounting for 10 per cent of production. For such individuals, the status or 'snob' value associated with dry wines becomes quickly tempered when these figures pass through the accountant's hands!

Those that exclusively grow muscadines typically focus upon a local consumer market and have been able to capitalize upon continued favourable publicity of the wine's health benefits. This is used extensively in the limited marketing of their wines that they undertake. While embracing agri-tourism, they have sought to diversify into some service activities (e.g. banquets) but cognitively they remain farmers. Interested in honing their production skills, they nonetheless rely upon systematically disseminated information from state agricultural services rather than routine informal knowledge-seeking contacts with others in the area. In this sense they remain poorly connected within the cluster, although membership of a 'network' as a crucial knowledge incubator (muscadines remain fairly easy to grow) is less salient for them.

Vinifera and hybrid growers meanwhile see themselves as part of a more exclusive occupational speciality from which they derive a status-laden identity and through that affiliation obtain the requisite technical operational knowledge. Their mutual interactions are more frequent but also contingent upon their ability to absorb 'club goods' that in turn is determined by their respective resource and capability base. In other words exchange of knowledge becomes systematized between actors when there is consensus that both parties have either the ability to absorb such knowledge or are recognized as valuable sources of innovation-related information. Those who are perceived to be resource-rich are actively sought out; those whose capabilities are perceived to be deficient and perhaps incapable of absorbing knowledge (hobbyists) can be marginalized. What had hitherto been a network characterized by random searching and imperfect dissemination of knowledge has now become systematized, formalized and much more structured around either reciprocal knowledge exchange or contractual relationships. The increasing presence of experts who offer crucial innovation-related advice to actors with resource bases and cognitive skills that facilitate its transmission in a selective way results in a hierarchy within a sub-group of network actors. Peripheral to this group are others whose access to such communities of knowledge is limited until they can demonstrate a capability to absorb detailed knowledge and/or contribute to beneficial knowledge exchange. While the diffusion of knowledge between actors in the first sub-group continues and contributes to overall improvements in wine quality, and thus market legitimacy, the latter are more likely to continue with an unsystematic, trial-and-error approach to learning that is likely to result in continued product inconsistency. Such an emerging pattern of fragmentation has continued in recent years, although it has not completely eradicated an overarching cooperative framework that encourages new entrants from gaining entry to the broad network. It has, however, raised the spectre of whether or not most wineries can continue to improve the quality of their product; not to be able to do so could be problematic in the long run for sustained market growth.

6 CLUSTER CONSOLIDATION: NETWORKS, QUALITY AND WINE TOURISM

With a superb combination of sun, soil and soul, Yadkin Valley wineries are ideally located in the North Carolina region that is rapidly gaining a reputation for growing high quality grapes and producing world class wines. Located in the Piedmont area of the Tar Heel state, wineries in the Yadkin Valley benefit from what many winemakers consider the best terroir in North Carolina.

> Yadkin Valley wine trail, North Carolina Wine and Grape Council pamphlet

Biltmore Estate winery has come of age. Part of our expansion opportunity is for us to build our portfolio capability. Our goal is to be a national marketer of fine wine, and potentially a global marketer of wine. It will not be improbable for us to go to Australia and create a line of wine. Or to Chile or France or Italy. We see ourselves building a company that has an array of offerings.

> Jerry Douglas, Biltmore Estate Winery[1]

The above two quotes are heady words indeed, especially for an industry that had struggled to survive three decades ago. Since then, however, North Carolina has emerged as the state with the fastest rate of winery growth in the nation. It is an industry that currently provides about 6,000 jobs and has an economic impact of $813 million. A new winery has opened almost every month since 2002 with no apparent end in sight. Most of these wineries are small, and many have positioned themselves as multi-purpose attractions, offering restaurant and/or reception facilities. Of the early pioneers, their vines have matured enough for them, potentially at least, to be able to produce the quality grapes that are necessary for the industry to take the next step to acquiring an established regional identity. For those whose wineries opened in the new millennium, they are still learning what grows best and how to market their product.

Despite the self-congratulatory statements of the above quotes, however, many experts acknowledge that the industry still has a long way to go before it can rest on its laurels. Ensuring an adequate supply of quality grapes continues to plague the industry. For all of its hype Biltmore only uses North Carolina grapes in approximately 25 per cent of its wines, the remainder coming from

California and Washington and bottled under the American appellation label. For them and their ambitions, there is insufficient quantity of, and quality in, locally grown grapes. Their business model relies upon purchased inputs and economies of scale to keep their prices and quality at desired levels. They are developing more contracts with local growers in ways that might address some of these problems. But all too often climate and geography work against the achievement of this goal. They remain a winery located in North Carolina but their goal is to leverage the tourist potential of the house. In this respect they are not dissimilar to other wineries in the state; their difference being the scale upon which they can realize that goal, the resources they possess and the established tourism nature of their setting.

Despite a burgeoning of new wineries, quality continues to be of concern to some local critics and this potentially hampers the industry's reputation and possible future growth. As a local food and wine expert noted in a 2008 newspaper article,

> The North Carolina consumer still must patiently sift through the various wines and wineries searching for a bottle worth drinking. That's right. Not every bottle of N.C. wine is good. Of course, not every bottle coming out of France, California or any other established region is good, either. But N.C. wineries have more challenges. Any time grape growing and winemaking spreads to a new region, the learning curve is steep. North Carolina does have a long history with native scuppernong grapes, and some wineries are working with those. Most wineries, though, have planted *vitis vinifera* European grapes that have not been tried here much, if at all, and doing so means almost starting from scratch when it comes to winemaking. Perhaps the biggest challenges are figuring out what grapes to plant and what kinds of wines to make in this area. Some grapes and wines do better in certain climates, and even smaller considerations such as soil composition and sun exposure have a big influence on the wine. In short, it's a complicated business, and N.C. wineries are still learning the ropes.[2]

In that same article he notes that experts have named quality and consistency across the state as two of the biggest challenges facing the industry as it grows. This does not apply to muscadine growers; their obstacle is that the sweet wines they produce are not held in the same esteem as the drier *vinifera* ones. That they can successfully market their wines locally is accepted, but it is questionable whether the state's winemaking reputation can rest upon muscadines. Sweet wines cater to a distinct clientele, a niche market that can sustain the local growth of wineries that make it. But in oenophile circles the overall legitimacy of the industry might become compromised if excessive attention to muscadines is proffered. At the present time, the two sectors coexist and benefit from the broad institutional supports and the proliferation of service providers to the industry. Nonetheless they increasingly constitute two markets with some overlap but distinctive consumer segments.

Within the fast-growing *vinifera* sector a further differentiation is developing. In addition to the large, resource-rich wineries discussed in the previous two chapters, smaller operations are increasingly falling into several, not always completely distinctive, types. First there are boutique wineries that contract out winemaking to a professional winemaker. They tend to be committed to making high-quality wines in small quantities and have the resources to build a reputation for their wine patiently. The second group is those who remain semi-professional winemakers, generally subsidizing their winery with income from an additional career. Their commitment to quality is tempered by the limits of their own skills and general resources. Sometimes this group is referred to as 'hobbyist winemakers' which probably describes some but certainly not all in this category. However, it is within this group that quality and consistency of wines are most problematic, usually because they lack the knowledge base to do otherwise. Finally there are the grape growers. At this juncture, many of them have prospered by securing regular contracts with wineries and under professional tutelage have been able to improve the quality of their grapes. The guaranteed income provided by such contracts enables them to remain part players in the supply chain and for most this satisfies their often part-time viticultural interests. Their interaction with professional winemakers has clearly been a crucial part of the quality upgrading that has occurred.

In examining the evolving structure of interactions between these individuals within the cluster, one gains a better sense of whether governance is emerging or if loose affiliations are merely assuming a more normative character in which some actors choose to participate and others do (or can) not. Because different actors possess different resources, such variation will undoubtedly affect how the knowledge network evolves. What is also apparent is that specialist firms (such as contract winemakers and custom crush facilities) are emerging in the region that make the operations of smaller and newer entrants into the industry more efficient and less capital-intensive. Such firms give the cluster its connectedness and provide the basis for further development.

In this chapter I rely upon the above typology to examine the recent rapid growth of wineries. I note specifically how regional density is emerging around three AVAs in the central part of the state and how within these geographical boundaries a hierarchy of firms appears to have been created. I also discuss the emerging forms of governance and the leadership role played by several key actors at the larger wineries. This has been effective in some instances, less so in others. It has simultaneously upgraded skill sets and technical proficiency for some, and possibly marginalized others. I also show how the structural properties of networks help us understand how some wineries are better able to innovate than others.

This brings us to the second set of issues that surround the topics of quality and consistency. I take off from the previous 'governance' debate to discuss the search for a signature wine for the region. That and the institutional support for research is measured against continuing difficulties for small firms in the area of sales and marketing plus the lack of skilled labour. Finally I examine the ways in which many wineries have embraced wine tourism as a solution to their fiscal problems but, in doing so, might conceivably become distracted from a commitment to actual winemaking. Whilst ancillary activities can be important revenue streams for new entrants, it is possible that they divert energy and resources away from the singular tasks of making wine, subordinating the latter to an almost cosmetic role in the overall operational logic.

Increase in Winery Growth Rates

Since 2000 there has been a 400 per cent increase in the number of wineries in the state. Mortality rates remain low with three wineries having closed since 2007.[3] However, given the time frame to develop a vineyard it is likely that most newcomers would wait at least five years to assess their efforts. Even though most newcomers grudgingly acknowledge that the venture involved far more work and more expenses than they planned, they are reluctant to abandon their endeavour. As one owner told me in a 2007 interview,

> I've saved up for this and thought about it for a long time. At my stage in life, I've done the things that made me money, now I want to do something that really interests me. I realize that I'm not to going to make a profit for a while but I've planned for that. It's really a lifestyle choice.

Another noted,

> I've been careful and realize that it'll take at least 5 years to build sales to a sufficient level to cover my costs and make a profit. But by then I figure a 1,500-case production and five varietals will be good enough. It enables me to achieve my goal and enjoy it.

These comments are indicative of most of the newcomers to the industry in recent years. They possess a pragmatic assessment of the lengthy time frame before profitability is attained, a reluctance to quit made possible by the resources they have brought to the operation, balanced nonetheless by an awareness of a certain fiscal necessity to be profitable eventually. Some have longer-term profitability goals than others (as much as ten years in several cases but more likely five). For others the business plan envisaged profitability within three years of opening.

The wine industry is renowned for attracting individuals with 'aspirational lifestyle' interests. In established and costly-to-enter markets they are characterized as utility maximizers in that they typically eschew immediate profits in return for the utility obtained from product characteristics.[4] Engaging in 'satisficing' behaviour, such individuals enjoy certain aspects of owning a winery, in some cases for the status that accrues or others where finding sustainable agricultural practices for family land are uppermost. They are not, at least initially, profit-maximizing individuals. Instead they have invested in a 'lifestyle' to which they aspire.

In the case of North Carolina wineries, it is apparent that aspirational lifestyle interests are a motivating factor but the numbers of utility maximizers of the type found in established wine regions such as Napa Valley, California, are few in this case.[5] As a local market has emerged, it has conferred reputational effects that are linked to the broader national industry identity and thus attracted individuals who might wish to be associated with such a product held in increasing regard. This partially explains the tremendous rate of winery growth in recent years, bringing actors who are motivated together with what are perceived to be *de facto* demand conditions. As the wine cluster has become consolidated, it has created an awareness of a niche that has subsequently stimulated new entrants. In other words the more established the sector has become, the more attractive it is to new entrants. This includes both the resource rich and those with more modest means. However, utility oriented actors are much more likely to invest in *vinifera* than muscadine production because the former is inherently more status laden than the latter. Since the resources needed for successful operation of *vinifera* are greater, that is probably pragmatic; it also signifies further demarcations amongst the ownership structures of the two types of wineries.

It has been argued that utility maximizers generate or at least tolerate inefficiencies but that the higher quality products that result from their status attainment goals are beneficial for the industry as a whole.[6] Typically the marginal costs are higher for such actors than established firms because of the latter's experience. However, the former's commitment to a high-quality product can quickly reduce costs because they are more likely to seek out expertise that eventually allows them to differentiate their product in a crowded marketplace. The systematic search for and selection of knowledge sources encourages a contractual and formalistic dimension to the network. Firms that are specific in identifying operational needs generally have the capacity to absorb the information that is forthcoming; those that are less resource rich can find themselves increasingly in a marginal situation. This is especially the case with the growth of codified local winemaking knowledge and more sophisticated technical information that has emerged in the last few years.

An almost continuous upgrading of winemaking techniques that are region-specific, especially for *vinifera* producers, has made it difficult for some firms whose trial-and-error processes prevent them from moving up the learning curve. Relatively resource-rich small wineries are most likely to engage in contractual relationships as a way of gaining operating knowledge. Others search for it through random informal channels. The former can more easily, but more expensively, acquire knowledge whilst the latter run the risk of becoming progressively marginalized in the network.

One boutique winery owner in the southern part of Yadkin Valley AVA captured the essence of this trend when referring to his decisions,

> I wanted to make a good quality wine on land that I'd bought with the express purpose of starting a winery. I knew that I didn't have the skill sets to do it, except perhaps for some vineyard maintenance, you know the stuff that's just basically hard work. So I talked to each of the big wineries' winemakers, consulted folks outside of the state and checked reputations. I didn't want to just start planting vines and hope for the best. I really wanted to know what was necessary to make a really good wine in this area. Once I identified a winemaker, I was able to work with him on vineyard planting, trellising and get expert help in maintenance. I wanted to keep it formal and contracted out all of these services. I wanted someone to manage the vineyard, to be responsible for the routine things. When I need a plumber I'm prepared to pay for his expertise. Isn't this the same? I mean you can't just ask around and pick up tit bits of information. Well you can but it's not a very systematic way of running a business. I see my role as running the tasting room, talking with people. But I'm hoping that the wine will be good enough to sell itself. My aim is 1500 cases, at around $18–20 a bottle. (interview with author, 2009)

Another (also in Yadkin Valley) was equally systematic in his search for the best professional in the area; someone who could direct him and with whom he could enter into a formal contractual relationship. In his comments on how he went about seeking such an individual, he noted,

> You talk with a lot of people in the industry locally. You learn who is good, who thinks they're good and then there's the rest. I'd thought about this [winery] project for some time, had the money for it and backing from four investors who shared my passion for wine and a commitment to excellence. That was good since it meant we were all on the same page. When we signed contracts they were agreements that were based on a mutual understanding of shared responsibilities – our commitment to continue the pursuit of quality wines and a willingness to make the necessary investments and forego immediate profits; his to deliver consistency in quality, even if in small batches for the first few years. We've stuck to this and it's worked well. (interview with author, 2008)

In both cases we see evidence of systematic searching for information rather than random scanning; a more formal approach not so much to knowledge acquisition but a realization that key facets of the operation would need to be contracted out to specialists. What worked well as collective organizational learning through the 1990s, whereby informal and unstructured network relationships generated requisite knowledge, is now being gradually replaced by a more structured and formal set of relationships.

In my sample, 80 per cent of the wineries that had opened in the past four years indicated that they systematically sought the requisite technical information on viticulture and oenology from formal courses at the Surry Community College (either in the two-year full-time programme or through specific courses), through formal relationships with professionals in the area (generally winemakers at established wineries) and through routine informal contacts with local winery owners. The frequency of the latter varied; in some cases it would be weekly meetings or visits, in others phone calls with questions. Key to these interactions was the idea that specific questions could be pursued with the expectation that information would be openly shared. Admittedly many facets of viticulture, such as varieties to plant, trellising and vine maintenance, as well as winemaking, such as fermentation techniques, are not entirely secret and firms can relatively easily engage in imitation. However, the purposeful behaviour and systematic searching for detailed knowledge that has become increasingly available in the cluster is clearly different from the more casual information searching done by early entrants, or *ad hoc* knowledge gathering that small wineries felt they needed to do as they began their operation.

Typically the interaction with professional winemakers at the big wineries, perceived to be the source of the most precise and detailed technical knowledge, was predicated upon contractual agreements. Courses at the local college were inevitably fee-based and formal. It was only the more general information seeking that involved interactions with other winery owners that remained informal, but this was typically done prior to start-up as a means to gain access to local issues. In other words, the route for new start-ups seems to be accessing general information, formalizing winery development plans and securing contractual agreements with professionals in the area, whilst throughout this period taking viticulture and oenology courses. 'I took three courses at Surry College in viticulture because I wanted to get some idea of the basics but we've hired a vineyard consultant and have the wine made at the local custom crush facility' (2008-opened Yadkin Valley winery co-owner, interview with author, 2009); 'Before we bought the land we consulted two local winemakers and got their opinions, we then hired a vineyard development company to help us arrange planting, and we use a local winemaker at West Bend to make our wines' (Yadkin Valley winery owner, interview with author, 2009); 'We designed the tasting room ourselves but laid out the vineyard after consulting with a specialist firm. We do basic pruning but also rely upon a crew who work under a vineyard management company, and we use Yadkin Valley Wine company to make our wine' (2009-opened Yadkin Valley winery, interview with author, 2009). These comments typify the operational approach of the new wineries that have opened in Yadkin Valley, the most developed AVA in the state and the area where the greatest density of wineries exist.

Those that did not seek out professional help most likely have more limited resources, even though many nonetheless took courses in viticulture and oenology prior to start-up. One said 'it remains partly a hobby and I have a full-time job that can pay the bills but not too much or for too long. I plan on being profitable within a year or so' (interview with author, 2009). Another commented,

> I've wanted to do this for a while and took courses on winemaking but I have to be careful about expenses. The Grape Council had some good information on business plans that came out of Cornell and that was helpful. It gave me a grasp of the budgets necessary and I've worked with that. But I cannot afford to hire too many people except for some part-time vineyard maintenance. I think I can get by like this. (interview with author, 2008)

And finally,

> People have been really helpful but there's a lot of learning. I'm trying to do as much as I can ... making the wines myself which I can handle. I can get some help since I've only got 2 acres so it's manageable and the crop is not too big. (interview with author, 2008)

Wineries such as these face a steeper learning curve than in the past because of so much more local knowledge available and codified. Because they are unable or unwilling to utilize formal channels that are available within the cluster they inevitably remain marginal to the innovation benefits that have accrued from local practices becoming established.

The above pattern of differentiation is a normal part of industry evolution, with increasing specialization begetting actors who use their resource and capabilities more intensely than others. It is also significant because it provides an opportunity for professional winemakers in the large firms to exercise formal governance as well as transfer skills to benefit those under contractual agreements.

The emergence of specialist firms that provide technical services to incumbents and newcomers further indicates the growing heterogeneity of functions and the increased density of the cluster. It suggests that industry evolution will be more fragmented than in the past but also that a more rigorous professionalism might provide requisite quality and consistency outputs amongst key firms that can sustain the growth.

Informal networks remain a crucial part of interactions but they are complemented by formal arm's-length relationships that provide opportunities for knowledge innovation and further skill specialization.

Consolidation of Regional Identity

Effective 27 May 2008, Swan Creek was approved as North Carolina's second AVA. Part of the existing Yadkin Valley AVA, it consists of five wineries (Raffaldini Vineyards, Laurel Gray Vineyards, Buck Shoals Vineyards, Shadow Springs Vineyard and Dobbins Creek Vineyards) and encompasses 160–180 square miles. Of note is the growth of French and Italian varietals not widely available in the United States that characterizes many of the wines from these operations. All of these wineries have been bonded since 2004 and are in the central part of the state.

Despite the fact that Swan Creek is within the boundaries of the wider Yadkin Valley AVA, the area differs from it because of its distinctive microclimate, a slightly higher elevation, a mineral rich soil composition and less rainfall. The four original wineries that spearheaded the application argued that the subregional designation would reinforce the idea that North Carolina has varied and distinctive growing conditions and build upon the brand recognition that surrounded the Yadkin Valley AVA over the previous five years.[7] For the two newcomers (Dobbins Creek and Shadow Springs), being affiliated with two AVAs was important. Shadow Springs' owner Chuck Johnson purchased his 47-acre property from Laurel Gray owners Benny and Kim Myers in 2005 and finished the tasting room in 2007. Currently he has 10.5 acres under vines, six varietals and two American hybrids using an open lyre terracing system.[8] He wanted to try varietals that he thought were appropriate to the land, hence differentiating his winery from some of the others in the area, and hopes that his wine profiles in the future will be subtly different from his neighbours.[9]

To the east of Greensboro, in what is becoming another concentration of wineries, the Haw River Valley AVA was approved effective 29 April 2009. North Carolina's third AVA, this area encompasses 868 square miles in north-central North Carolina and currently has six commercial wineries. This area benefits from a longer growing season than the better known Yadkin Valley and this enables wineries there to grow grapes such as Cabernet Sauvignon which typically take longer to ripen fully. The AVA builds upon the successful Haw River wine trail that was earlier designed to capture the tourism market from the Research Triangle area. All of these wineries were bonded after 2004 so again are fairly recent entrants into the industry.

The existence of three AVAs in close proximity to each other provides a growing legitimacy and identity for the industry which ultimately is helpful for consumer sales. It also provides a density of operations that facilitates information sharing and stimulates other new entrants. On numerous occasions in my interviews with wineries in the three AVAs, I was told that individuals with an interest in starting a winery would come by their wineries and sit and watch them, talk with them and pick up ideas about what to do and not to do. This is not dissimilar to the sort of informal exchanges that occurred in the earlier period of growth but now there are many more actors to learn from. Prospective owners were taking classes, generally at Surry Community College, but they still sought out the informal 'hands-on' experience that existing owners provided. As one owner recently told me,

> X would come by at least once a week after initially telling us about what he was planning. He patiently sat and watched us, didn't say much, just observed. Then after about a month or so he said he was happy because he saw the cash register opening and closing a lot and that meant we were making money. Now he's just opened his own tasting room and restaurant.

Four other owners of wineries in the two AVAs commented on how the appellation designation helped sustain what they referred to in various words as a 'collective purpose'. It meant that the area would be a focal point for visitors, that it reaffirmed the cluster's identity and that it encouraged more support services to locate in the area and provide requisite specialist skills. I asked each of them if they felt it helped them benchmark their wines and if it in some way reinforced a collective commitment to promote quality. Two were emphatic about this, the others more sanguine although all acknowledged that it facilitates a more cooperative attitude amongst the members.

Locational attributes are often difficult to determine and it would be presumptive to assume that the mere presence of a winery in a particular region necessarily means that there is extensive interaction between its owners and others. This point has been made elsewhere in the research on clusters.[10] However, being part of a recently founded AVA, and in an industry in its infancy where norms of cooperation have been established, it would be churlish to doubt the value of routine interactions between wineries in the cluster. The AVAs are the framework for local communities of knowledge because they provide opportunities for technical exchange and knowledge seeking that is site specific. I asked if this meant that members were less likely to interact with those outside of the AVA and each said no. However, they did note that the intensity of interactions within their area was often predicated on finding solutions to specific local issues.

Did this mean that knowledge spillover to those new firms entering the industry but outside of the AVA was restricted? New entrants reported having access to generalized information and indicated that knowledge seeking was generally rewarded by openness. But, some new entrants deliberately sought out professional assistance through contractual means and such purposive behaviour differentiates them from those whose learning is more informal. This then raises the question of whether such contractualism diminishes cooperative endeavours throughout the network. If actors with powerful knowledge bases are rewarded financially for disseminating information that might be a disincentive for them to provide such resources gratis. This could result in innovation-related knowledge being less likely to be diffused throughout the growing network, with a resulting hierarchy of firms emerging.

It was apparent from interviews with wineries where actual winemaking (vinting) was contracted to a winemaker that this was part of a deliberate strategy to gain access to technical knowledge through formal channels. Such a conscious approach to what is one of the key value-added parts of the operation differs from those who attempt to master all facets of the production process. The latter learn by doing, acquire technical skills through formal educational programmes but also rely heavily upon being able to absorb innovation-related knowledge informally through network interactions. The former eschew many of these broad linkages in favour of atomistic relationships with key knowledge brokers. Inevitably this results in fragmentation and differentiation but does it diminish the overall cooperative framework?

We can partially answer that question by examining the behaviour of the most recent industry entrants. Three such wineries within the Yadkin Valley AVA are Allison Oaks (2008) Divine Llama (2009) and Brandon Hills Vineyards (2009). Their stories encapsulate the operational axioms of many new entrants where specialist activities are outsourced to locally established professionals.

Specialization within Clusters

Allison Oaks currently has 6 acres of an old airstrip under vines, part of a larger 60-acre property. Owners Gene and Pam Renegar purchased the old grass runway Yadkinville airstrip in 1997 in part so they could store tractors and other agricultural equipment in the hangers that were there. With a background in tobacco farming, Gene Renegar decided to try grape growing and planted their first vines in 2000, taking some viticulture courses at Surry Community College. Since they owned some property in Yadkinville town centre they decided to put their tasting room there rather than at the vineyard (1 mile to the east) and let it double as a site for functions. They offer *vinifera* wines plus two muscadines and acknowledge that it can be easier to sell the latter in more rural areas of the state whilst the former is more popular in the big cities. In an interview with the author in 2009, Gene said that while it was easy for him to figure out grape growing because of his agricultural background, he did not feel comfortable making wine. He investigated local winemakers and decided upon Mark Terry, the winemaker at West Bend, because he had the most experience. Terry makes his wines each year. Gene believes that the courses at Surry have become more rigorous than when he took them and this will benefit new generations of students. But when it comes to actual winemaking he believes it is best to leave that to someone with more extensive professional experience.

Divine Llama Vineyards, located 15 miles north-east of Allison Oaks in East Bend, is a 77-acre property that is part vineyard and part llama farm. Conceived by two architect friends and their wives, the 5-acre vineyard was planted in 2006 and the tasting room opened in 2009. Their focus is *vinifera* and they continue to buy grapes from Virginia until their own vines are sufficiently mature. But since they have full-time jobs outside of the vineyard and farm, and had rudimentary knowledge of viticulture from courses they had taken at Surry Community College, they decided that they would have their wine made by a specialist. They chose the newly opened Yadkin Valley Wine Company's custom crush facility. This 10,000-case production facility is a joint venture by two wineries in the Swan Creek AVA, Laurel Gray and Shadow Springs. Designed as a custom crush facility for other small wineries in the area – an example of the sort of specialist activities that are being spawned by the cluster – it is also the shared integrated winemaking facility for the two wineries. The winemaker there, Kent Egon Smith, comes from Georgia but has a degree in oenology from California State University at Fresno.

Divine Llama's strategy is indicative of the behaviour of several recent entrants. They wanted to do something with land that they had acquired outside of the city, having been interested in finding a rural setting for their families. They both took five classes at Surry Community College to learn about viti-culture but recognized that they lacked the requisite skill sets (and time) to do all but the rudimentary tasks. Before even planting their vines they talked extensively with other growers, winery owners and local experts to determine what would grow best. They also thoroughly considered the marketing aspect, deciding eventually to choose a range of wines from dry to sweet, with several distinctive varietals that could offer a good profile for a small winery and differ-entiate them somewhat from others. Having planted vines they hired a vineyard consultant (Ashley Myers) to work with them and she inspects the vineyard every three weeks and provides instructions on pruning, spraying, etc. They designed and built their tasting room and, while waiting for their own vines to mature, bought grapes from nearby RayLen as well as from growers in Virginia. They also experimented with Hungarian, French and American oak barrels in order to determine which produce the best flavour in the resulting wines. Finally they were resolute in drawing up a business plan that would see them profitable within a few years. According to one of the owners they are on target for this.

Their aims are modest yet their approach has been more professional than many others whom I interviewed. Above all they have availed themselves of the various specialist services that now exist in the area, using them as a way to achieve a quality product which they believe is essential if the industry, and their own business, is to flourish. In a 2009 interview with co-owner Tom Hughes, he said

> We want to make very good wines. We don't want to make mediocre wines. We thought very hard about what to plant and how much to plant of each varietal. There's too much Chardonnay out there so we didn't really want to do that and compete with others. We wanted to offer a range that would appeal to all different taste segments. So we went with seven wines, from dry to sweet. These include Traminette [a *vinifera* blend], our best selling and what we hope will be our signature wine, a white hybrid, then Merlot and a sweet wine for those whose taste preferences are for sweet wines.
>
> We realized that we're still amateurs so we hired professionals to do the skilled work. We think we're good at the marketing side so we've concentrated on this. In the early years we talked with as many people as possible and also developed many contacts at Surry [Community College]. Through the latter we learned of local grape growers and who had the best grapes. We also learned who were the best winemakers. The network is now extensive and you can gain so much by talking with people in the industry and sharing knowledge. But you also have to be practical and recognize that some services must be bought.

The third new winery in this area, approximately 3 miles south of Yadkinville, is Brandon Hills. Owned by airline pilot David Blackwell and his nurse anaesthesiologist wife, this 3-acre vineyard is part of a 100-acre property that the couple bought in 2005. They also used an open lyre trellis system because of the soil's fertility and resulting growth control needs. They decided to drop the fruit from their first (2006) harvest to let the vines better develop and waited until 2007 before they utilized grapes to make wine. They also took classes at Surry Community College (he in winemaking, she in viticulture) but when asked why they decided not to make wine themselves, David was quite forthright.

> We are not full-time winery owners and it seemed that the expense of building a winery with all that is entailed for use 2–3 weeks a year was not justified. We learned a lot from locals about how to work with the vines, spraying etc. so that was not difficult. But you only get one chance each year to make wine so there's not much margin for error. We let Yadkin Valley Wine Company make our wines. They have all the facilities, it's nearby and they have the level of expertise that we need. (interview with author, 2009)

I asked him if he plans to develop the vineyard more and perhaps do winemaking himself and he said no. Their aim is to keep it as a 1,000-case winery and produce all of their own grapes. That way they can focus upon quality but also easily manage routine viticultural activities themselves (spraying, problem identification and solving). They plan on planting some Viognier vines next year but the vineyard will not grow much beyond 4 acres. It remains a hobby at the moment, albeit an expensive and time consuming one, but they still believe in approaching it as professionally as possible and that is why they decided to use custom crush facilities.

What is interesting about each of these vineyards is their decision to source their winemaking to an external winemaker rather than do it themselves. This involves contractual negotiations and a formal relationship that structures knowledge exchange in ways qualitatively different from that which had occurred in the past. It also signifies further specialization and professionalization within the network, and the provision of technical services that earlier were learned on the job. However, the vineyard owners still access the knowledge networks and report a high degree of cooperation, made even more detailed and informative given the larger number of growers and wineries in the area. As one owner said,

> Any time I need detailed information about things like yeasts, or spray schedules I can get on the phone. In other instances people drop by and make comments about what could be done to improve my crop and even point out problems that I had overlooked. (interview with author, 2009)

In choosing a winemaker and the appropriate facilities they not only have a choice now but can rely upon recommendations from others in making that decision.

This sort of detailed tacit knowledge has improved as the industry has matured, become more complex but also more codified now that there is a better understanding of what works and does not work in the area. The creation and use of specialist facilities allows a division of labour to emerge and the concentration of key, value-added activities among certain individuals. Furthermore, some wineries have recognized that there are scale benefits that might be realized through further cooperation; the Yadkin Valley Wine Company being a good example of this.

Even though AVA designation is not a measure of quality, there was a strong agreement that it should be the basis for reputation building that can only occur if wine quality improves. Again, the partners of the Yadkin Valley Wine Company are emphatic that they will continue their focus upon quality as the driving force behind winemaking. Because so many newcomers have entered the industry with, by virtue of their newness, vines that have not reached their potential, it is inevitable that quality and consistency will vary. This liability of newness has been a problem for those who were forced to buy grapes in the early years of their own wineries.

Why is Consistency a Problem?

By all accounts there has been tremendous variation in the quality of grapes over recent years, a reflection not just of normal harvest variations but also of different skill sets and experience of grape growers as well as incomplete understanding of what will grow best in the long run. However, the buying power of the larger wineries, and the professionalized approach to winemaking there, led to increasing attention paid to grape quality. In a 2006 interview with the winemaker of a leading winery, I was told

> There has been a big problem with quality and quantity. Some know what they're doing, others are focused upon producing volume. It's all over the place and I really struggled to get good quality grapes in the first years before our own vines were producing. People would turn up with crap. So I sat down with the growers, visited their vineyards, told them what to do and when to do it. I inspected frequently to make sure they were doing what I told them to do. I told them I'd work with them but they had to be precise in following my instructions. I said it's not just about yield; it's about quality so we had to do a lot of canopy management and pruning. I signed contracts but told them if I wasn't satisfied with what they brought me I wouldn't buy their grapes. I did adjust prices when harvests were bad and it wasn't their fault but I wasn't going to buy grapes that didn't meet my standards. My reputation rests upon the wine that I make and that means I need to get the best grapes possible.

Because of the volume of local grapes bought by this winery between 2004 and 2007, it encouraged growers to agree to what one told me were often harsh terms. But several also said that they learned a lot and it improved their viticultural techniques. As a grower told me in 2007,

> I thought I did a pretty good job of growing. After all I've been doing it since 1998. But just when my vines were yielding a good crop I had the opportunity to sell to X. He was real detailed and rejected some of the grapes from the first harvest. That hurt me financially. But I realized that there were some things that I could do that wouldn't be too expensive and that I would have a better chance of selling them all to the winery. The following year he bought everything. I now know a lot of little things that hadn't occurred to me previously. After all, I had a farming background so I thought vines would be like some of the other crops. But it was much harder work and there's so much uncertainty. But at least I've figured out what needs to be done.

Another grower told me in a 2009 interview,

> It took me a while to figure out what was best, even which varietals to grow. I don't want the hassle and expense of a bonded winery but like growing grapes, some of which I use to make my own wine. I would sell the grapes through contacts made at the NC Wine Growers Association and then Biltmore said they would buy some. I worked with Bernard [DeLille, Biltmore's winemaker] and he was pretty clear what needed to be done to produce the best quality grapes. I just follow the instructions and he periodically inspects my vines. It works well and he seems to be happy. I've certainly learned a lot. Now I sell most of my grapes to him.

Each of these quotes illustrates how a form of governance has emerged around leader firms in recent years, addressing issues of quality but also providing a structure to the hitherto informal learning that occurred within the network. Key actors within the leader firms, pressed by their own occupational self-interest, have mandated technical standards that systematize and transmit codified knowledge, in this case to grape growers. But inevitably there are spillover effects as other winemakers better understand requisite viticultural skills because there are demonstrable consequences to innovative behaviour. At associational meetings, through periodicals that transmit technical details, and with the dissemination of research by extension agencies, a body of knowledge on best practices has become more widely established. The North Carolina Wine Growers Association provides numerous short and one day courses/seminars that deal with all aspects of viticulture and winemaking. These offerings complement the more extensive ones at Surry Community College. Access to such knowledge through formal educational programmes is still fairly open, although the ability to absorb it differs with the result that some firms become marginalized.

Winemakers and owners of large wineries have also assumed leadership positions in growers' associations such as the North Carolina Winegrowers Association and with this attempted to improve quality standards and general industry efficiency.[11] As with their interactions with specific growers or those with whom they have a contractual winemaking relationship, systematized practices and procedures have been introduced. This can provide specialized and distinctive capabilities for firms within the cluster providing they have the organizational capacity to absorb such innovation. Yet some small winery owners have argued that such individuals are more adept at, and enthusiastic about, furthering the industry in ways that benefit themselves. In this respect they do not have the interest of the 'small guy' at heart (as one small winery owner told me in a 2009 interview) and are often insensitive to the concerns of smaller operators without the resources of the large wineries. What small firms deem as insensitivity, the leader firms argue is often lack of knowledge or even incompetence. As a consequence, some small firms are perceived to be random in their search for knowledge whilst others are more purposeful and selective. Inevitably this is affecting the structural properties of the network cluster because a hierarchy is emerging and with that a process of possible marginalization of some smaller firms.

Undoubtedly, leader firms have helped lower transaction costs by facilitating various infrastructural changes and reduced uncertainty and opportunism. The latter has been a direct product of both contracts and attempts to impose control, albeit indirectly through coordination, over the cluster. They have stimulated collective organizational learning by providing tangible evidence of the benefits of technical innovation, but they have also sought to improve the overall legitimacy of the industry. Their resources enabled them to invest in worker training and education, market information and establish links with intermediaries in ways that have positive effects for all firms in the cluster. As Visser and de Langen similarly argue in their analysis of cluster governance of the Chilean wine industry, leader firms combine a superior strategic insight and an ability to raise funds that permit collective investments that have a positive impact on the quality of that governance.[12] Their ability and incentives to invest can enhance the capabilities and insights of other firms, especially those that work directly with them in collaborative ventures. Notable examples of where this has happened in North Carolina can be found in the activities of Childress, Shelton and to some extent Biltmore wineries.

In other instances, however, their imposition of technical rules and operational procedures has alienated smaller firms. They have done this by the rigour of their contractual stipulations and by establishing minimally acceptable production standards that effectively 'discipline' subordinate firms. Whether this constitutes a form of governance is difficult to discern. What is evident, however, is that they have heightened the vulnerability of firms that lack the resources and capabilities to function along these lines, hence generating resentment and even distrust. On several occasions in my interviews, individuals at the larger firms derogatively referred to some smaller ones as 'hobbyist' winemakers whilst simultaneously recognizing that others were 'boutique' wineries. The latter are more likely to recognize their technical limitations and have the resources to procure specialized knowledge and skill sets; the former prefer a trial-and-error approach, in part because they lack such resources and are forced to learn by doing. The categorization is not a casual one inasmuch as it reflects a significant distinction in capabilities and professionalism that has emerged in the industry and a corresponding firm heterogeneity.

Searching for a Signature Grape

After decades of relative institutional indifference to grape growing aside from a passing nod to muscadines, viticulture and oenology research and extension activities have increased in the last few years. North Carolina State University has invested in faculty with specialities in viticulture and oenology but most importantly funding for actual research has increased. In 2008 a record $222,647 was made available for projects that included an evaluation programme for North Carolina wines, various investigations into spraying techniques and fungicide sensitivity, plus one examining the re-establishment of a muscadine grape breeding programme.[13] Compared to oenology investments in other states, the amount is small. But it signifies an important symbolic departure from the agricultural establishment's earlier vacillation between disdain and indifference towards winemaking. It is also a product of pressure from the larger firms whose influence has been used to articulate the industry's needs and growing stature amongst the legislature. Finally, it is an official acknowledgement of how big the industry has grown and how commercially it can no longer be ignored.

The various research areas reflect many of the specific concerns affecting grape growing in North Carolina and build upon several decades of *vinifera* and hybrid experiments. One of the salient issues discussed at the 2009 North Carolina Wine Summit, and at various Grape Council and Winegrowers Association meetings, is whether North Carolina can be identified with a signature grape, one that apparently grows well in the area and is sufficiently distinctive to reflect the local *terroir*. For example, Oregon's relatively youthful and small wine industry is associated with Pinot Noir, a grape that flourishes there and matches the requisite quality associated with its Burgundian counterpart in France. New York State is associated with semi-dry white wines such as Riesling which, like their counterparts that originate in Germany and Alsace, France, do better in colder climates. This has enabled winemakers in both states to market their product collectively around the state's reputation for that varietal.

The industry's infancy in North Carolina precludes a final determination of a specific varietal, although experts have indicated that Viognier and Cabernet Franc appear to grow well and reasonable quality can be produced on young vines by relatively inexperienced winemakers.[14] However, many wineries prefer to try their luck at the established favourites such as Chardonnay, Merlot and Cabernet Sauvignon even though the latter's longer ripening season makes it difficult to produce consistently with the requisite rich flavour in the North Carolina climate.

Viognier is a Rhone style varietal that only became popular in the United States in the late 1990s as a backlash to the oceans of buttery and oaky Chardonnays that were flooding the market. Proclaimed by California growers a decade earlier, North Carolina growers started planting it and found that it yielded surprisingly good quality grapes even from young vines. It offered a crisp but full-bodied drier wine that people could drink as an alternative to Chardonnay. From a production point of view it offered some significant advantages. The grapes are thick skinned, grow in loose clusters and are better able to withstand the humidity and drought that are commonplace in the south.[15] In order not to mask its distinctive flavour it is better to age it in stainless steel tanks rather than oak barrels that are used for Chardonnay. This reduces materials costs (oak barrels are more expensive and have to be replaced more frequently) and a shorter ageing time means the wine gets to market sooner. However, it can also be a difficult grape to grow because it can succumb to problems such as bud necrosis, and the volume at harvest is often lower than that of other varietals, resulting in a higher cost per ton. This inconsistency has led some such as early enthusiasts Shelton to abandon Viognier as a stand-alone wine. Nonetheless, others, such as newcomer Junius Lindsay,[16] are building their reputations around it. This winery's attention to detail puts it firmly in the category of boutique wineries. They won several blind tasting awards when their wine was compared with Californian and French wines and it is featured at local high-end restaurants and specialist wine stores in the area – a notable fact for such a new, small winery. Many of the area's other wineries continue to grow Viognier successfully and make wine that is of good quality, despite the youthful vines. Most admit that much consumer education is needed to promote a grape they nonetheless remain enthusiastic about but of which the general public is woefully ignorant.

In many respects the widespread growth of this varietal is a direct product of local area network linkages in the Piedmont region. Early industry entrants successfully experimented with the grape and produced good tasting wines from youthful vines. They passed this knowledge on to new entrants who were able to benefit from the experiences of the pioneers; the latter detailing the sorts of problems that would be encountered and how best to manage cultivation. In other words significant technical details were readily available and shared through the informal network in ways that encouraged new entrants to plant this grape. The more immediate revenue stream that came from young vines was also an added attraction for those seeking a way for speedier returns on their investments. The resulting improvements in quality because of the incremental additions to technical knowledge derived from local experience was invaluable and has led to a greater consistency in product quality than many other varietals grown in the region. This assessment is best summed up by a small winery owner who has made Viognier one of its key grapes:

> When we were deciding what to plant we talked with others in the area and they all mentioned Viognier. We asked about the problems and why this particular grape would be good. Everyone told us that it was difficult to grow in some respects, but was fairly easy in others and seemed to do well in the soils around here. Since we were going to work with a winemaker to make our wines we talked at length with him and got tips on what to do and not do. He looked at our soil tests and advised on us our vine purchases and then made suggestions about trellising, spraying and cropping. What really clinched it for us was that folks told us that you can get a reasonable crop after a couple of years. We looked at what sorts of investments we had made and decided it would be good to get a harvest and then sell some wine sooner rather than later. Since we borrowed money from the bank for some of the winery we felt pressure to start getting some returns. We also figured that this could be a key grape in the area. It certainly has been pretty successful and people like it, but most importantly they buy it. (interview with author, 2007)

Despite the virtues of Viognier, its major drawback is the lack of name recognition. Whilst easier to sell in California where an established market provides numerous opportunities for niche products, an area such as North Carolina where the industry is still in its infancy often renders sales difficult. People are not familiar with the grape and while they might enjoy tasting the wine at the winery, still are more likely to buy Chardonnay if they want a white wine because that is what they are comfortable with, tasting and perception-wise. A virtually unknown (and difficult to pronounce) wine from a region with a limited winemaking reputation creates obstacles for many wineries. Consequently, if they grow the grapes they frequently do so in conjunction with the more popular Chardonnay. And yet, according to winemakers at established wineries such as RayLen, Hanover Park and Childress, Viognier can still emerge as one of North Carolina's signature white wines.

Similar things are being said about Cabernet Franc, although this grape takes longer for the vines to mature and produce requisite quality (and quantity) so it is still too early to establish its impact locally. It too suffers somewhat from name recognition. In many Californian (and French) wineries it is used as a blending grape and the larger wineries in North Carolina are using it for this purpose in their proprietary blends. The problem with blends, however, is similar to that of niche products such as Viognier. The majority of casual wine drinkers is familiar with single varietals (Cabernet Sauvignon or Merlot for example) and gravitate towards them when making purchasing decisions. A blend with a proprietary name, however 'funky' looking or bizarrely labelled, needs explanation and clarification for consumers and can therefore be difficult to sell.[17]

This brings us inexorably back to Chardonnay. According to a 2005 *On the Vine* article by Greensboro wine writer Ed Williams, Chardonnay is the cash cow for most North Carolina wineries. While representing 10–25 per cent of production it accounts for one third to one half of sales. It is fairly easy to grow in the soil and climate conditions of the state, it buds and ripens at the right time, is reasonably resistant to rot and disease and is sufficiently malleable so that winemakers can replicate their specific style each year despite different growing conditions.[18] It has many different styles, from flinty, austere and minerally to full-bodied, buttery and vanilla flavoured – each representing climatic and regional differences as well as winemakers' preferences. Above all it is a wine that neophyte wine drinkers recognize and one that for many is the virtual default option when ordering a white wine in a restaurant or bar. It is also hugely popular with female wine drinkers and since women represent the majority of wine buyers in supermarkets, proves a big seller in such locations. One can make it using stainless steel fermentation styles (resulting in a crisper, flintier style) or the more expensive barrel versions which are creamier and full-bodied.

Most *vinifera* producers in the state have some acreage of Chardonnay precisely because it is reasonably easy to grow, has immediate name recognition and sells. The downside, as Ed Williams and others have noted, is it ubiquity.[19] This raises the inevitable concern over competition and price points. As one specialist wine shop owner in Winston-Salem told me in 2008,

> It's difficult for me to sell NC Chardonnay at this store because of the price points so I don't bother. Why would someone pay $15–18 for an NC Chardonnay when you can buy a probably better quality one from California for around $10 at the supermarket. And then there are oceans of inexpensive Australian Chardonnay out there followed by even cheaper ones from Chile. People might buy a local one from a winery but it's tough to move the product at broader retail points. Is it really that distinctive? I don't think so no matter what the owner says. On the other hand, the NC Viogniers, while more expensive at say $18, are a little easier for me to sell because it's a niche product. But then again, the people who come to my store know wines and are likely to ask for suggestions that might meet their taste interests. I can recommend this Rhone varietal as an alternative to Chardonnay, because many of the latter have come to taste bland and mass produced at the lower price points. My Chardonnays are mainly in the $20–25 price range and even though some NC wineries have ones in this price range there's no way I can sell them here.

Because there is so much of this wine on the general market, at price points and quality levels that satisfy all types of consumers, it remains difficult for North Carolina wineries to establish a presence for Chardonnay outside of their tasting rooms. Admittedly most wineries rely upon direct sales or self-distribution which somewhat obviates this problem. One Swan Creek AVA winery markets a Chardonnay in the mid $20 range claiming that 'experts' have said that even at that price it is cheap given its quality. However, it was unclear in my interview with that winery owner that sales of this particular vintage were flourishing. One had the distinct impression that since some people had made laudatory comments on the quality of the wine, *ipso facto* the price could be raised to reflect that quality. But without attendant status or reputation such price points remain difficult to sustain to all but a few loyal locals and friends who covet their relationship with a winery owner.[20]

Most wine writers recognize that a region is more likely to establish itself successfully and develop if it has a signature grape.[21] People associate Napa Valley with Cabernet Sauvignon, Oregon with Pinot Noir, Spain with Rioja, Argentina with Malbec and Germany with Riesling. If one produces one of these wines outside of these regions, it will inevitably be evaluated and compared with the perceived 'authentic' product until one can lay claim to some legitimacy through expert validation. For an infant industry such as that in North Carolina, that remains a difficult task.

Overcoming Problems of Quality and Consistency

The above discussion on grape type raises a related set of questions regarding quality that continue to plague the industry's growth and broader legitimacy. While some wineries make some good quality wine some of the time, few are able to be consistent in their quality across their various products and over time. This could be still the liability of newness. But local wine enthusiasts have commented that too many of the established wineries are still incapable of making a good quality wine when, given the maturity of their vines and their material resources, they should be able to do so. The exceptions to this are the muscadine producers whose market appeal remains local and therefore less susceptible to the comparative evaluation that inevitably occurs for *vinifera* producers. Their market, as repeatedly noted, still remains local.

Consistency in the quality of the state's wines continues to be one of the biggest challenges facing the industry as it grows, according to Gil Geise who is an instructor at the Enology Program at Surry Community College. Most of that quality comes from what occurs in the vineyard and it is in this area that some newcomers have been deficient. Too many new owners have bought land, planted vines and then concurrently attended classes at the community college where they learn viticulture and oenology techniques. This means that they are learning while they are doing rather than before they embark upon the business venture. This can result in poor vineyard management, leading to poor quality grapes and finally wine that is inferior. Yet the cost structure of their operation dictates a certain price for the wine which is not, unfortunately, a reflection of its quality. Since most wineries are small (less than 2,500-case annual production) their overheads and other materials costs means their wine must be sold in the $14–18 price range if they are to break even let alone make a small profit. According to Appalachian State University's chemist, Grant Holder,

> The state has spent a lot of money marketing the wines that are being produced. Now they should concentrate on maximizing the quality of the wine, maximizing consistency so that those prices that must be charged for North Carolina wines are true reflections of the quality.[22]

The price/quality ratio will always pose analysis difficulties for embryonic industries where true measures of quality are somewhat indeterminate because consumers use different preference sets in making their purchasing decisions. Demand for a product may reflect underlying attributes of that product and be evaluated using hedonic price analysis. Purchase decisions can also satisfy self-identity needs and social affiliation rather than intrinsic quality aspects of the product. As a consequence, people will probably continue to buy wine at wineries that is not of good quality, and at price points that are undoubtedly greater than the commensurate quality merits.

If you enter a winery you are likely to see bottles with ribbons and awards proudly and prominently displayed. These are awards from local fairs, regional and sometimes national tasting competitions (e.g. 'San Francisco Chronicle Wine Competition', 'North Carolina State Fair in Raleigh'). They provide a mark of recognition that is supposed to confer status and be an indicator of quality and they remain important avenues for wineries to benchmark their product and perhaps even learn if what they are doing is right. They can aid winery sales as customers see this as a seal of approval and legitimacy. One-off successes, however, can all too often mask flaws in other wines by that winery. Success in such competitions can also seduce a winery owner into believing the elevated status of their wine can easily translate into charging a higher price for it. It can also delude them into thinking they have mastered the various flaws that so often lurk in North Carolina wines, especially red wines which all too often have that distinct vegetal smell and taste. Regrettably, as so often happens in such a case, it merely convinces them that they have truly realized the potential of their *terroir*.

Two well-known winemakers from California, who visited several local wineries for tastings, plus one well-known North Carolina winemaker, remarked to me about the tendency of many North Carolina wines to be flawed. There are several issues here. According to them, one of the major problems that particularly afflict red wines in the state was that of methoxypyrazine, a compound that results in a vegetal taste in the wine.[23] The compound exists in all red wines but at excessive levels can produce an off taste. Apparently, with greater attention to vineyard management, it can be controlled and almost eliminated. Experienced winemakers have either learnt to suppress it or at least minimize its occurrence. Murphy Moore, winemaker at Shelton Vineyards, however, says 'it's hard to get the brix to a high enough level and therefore the fruit doesn't fully ripen' (interview with author, 2009). It is a problem for Bordeaux varietals, and she went on to say how hard it is in the state to eliminate it totally from the red wines of that varietal because of the growing conditions. Steve Shepard (RayLen) said one has to work assiduously at every stage throughout the growing season, and be meticulous in one's efforts to control it. Unfortunately, too many winemakers in the state do not recognize it as a flaw, with some even going so far as to call it a product of *terroir*. It is possible that their own training was inadequate, or that they are still learning so they do not know how to identify the root cause of the problem or have the necessary skills sets to address it. It is also possible that they are simply refusing to acknowledge it, or, if noticed, they do not see it as being so problematic. But as one of the major winemakers in the state recently told me, 'You know it's a problem and I know it's a problem, but they don't. That's the bigger problem.' That same winemaker went on to comment that he keeps organizing workshops that could improve many facets of winemaking and viticulture but attendance is often sparse. When I suggested that time scarcity might be a problem for small wineries, preventing them from attending, he merely noted that if they want to stay in business they need to learn requisite techniques. In other words short-term sacrifices are necessary for longer-term benefits.

It was also clear to the above three North Carolina winemakers that many vines were too young to bear fruit with the result that wines were watery, weak-bodied and rather tasteless. Another winemaker from a major state winery told me that the growing conditions in the state do not really favour most red wines yet people persist in trying to make it. 'The season is too short, there's too much humidity, the nights are not cool enough, and then as if all of that was not bad enough, along comes a hurricane and the rainfall and hail virtually wipe out the crop' he said, all rather dismissively (interview with author, 2008). According to him all of this results in wines with weak structure and off tastes. What reds he uses, he does so as blends with juice from out of state. When I asked him about whites, he said that was less of a problem and one could make some good quality wines – but even this will take time.

Conceivably some of these problems will be addressed in time as vines mature, vineyard management techniques are improved and winemakers hone their skills. However, there is less confidence that the 'vegetal' problem will be quickly rectified since so many in the industry are unwilling to acknowledge it. According to some experts, it might continue to plague some wines because of inherent climatic problems in the area.

The presence of undesirable compounds that flavour wine reveals a broader issue of concern to some in the industry. If it was merely a problem that affected new winemakers, self-taught or recently graduated from the local community college, one might have confidence that with experience and better codification of tacit knowledge, they would be able to address it successfully. Unfortunately, this is not entirely the case. Several of the wineries that produce wine with this flaw have professional winemakers who should know better and yet apparently do not. Furthermore, several of these winemakers are used by new, small wineries to make their wines under contract; hence the problem is transferred to other wineries. This is alarming since the knowledge leaders whose role as conduits for the dissemination of requisite technical capabilities appear to be themselves deficient in a key aspect of production. And yet the absence of formal quality control prevents this issue from being addressed and the problem eliminated. Thus, what starts out as something undesirable that can be rectified, becomes instead almost institutionalized and undermines the governance benefits that have been an otherwise important facet of the industry's recent growth. For novice wine drinkers visiting tasting rooms this might not constitute an obstacle to purchases; for more seasoned enthusiasts whose role in helping the industry grow and attain regional stature is important, this can be a significant impediment.

In numerous discussions with wine experts who have tasted North Carolina wines, this problem has surfaced frequently and is seen by them as somewhat intractable. It applies only to *vinifera* wines; muscadines being native to the area have long since evolved in ways that create few such problems. It does raise serious questions about the effectiveness of network governance although it should be noted that the leadership of various associational groups have struggled to find ways of addressing it. One official, off the record, told me in 2009 that it is imperative that the industry be open about this problem and do something about it, whether through better training or even sometimes bluntly confronting the offending parties. After all, this official told me, there are enough good winemakers in the state who do know what they are doing to play a more effective leadership role in the industry. Whether this will be done remains to be seen.

That same official also told me that the state legislature needs to do more, providing research money for the industry and not just responding to the lobbying of several large wineries in the state. The latter can sometimes dictate agendas in ways that are not necessarily beneficial to the industry as a whole, I was told. If state agencies can establish greater credibility in systematically assisting wineries by providing the detailed knowledge they need to take the industry to the next level, this might be able to alter the received wisdom on some of these contentious issues.

Smaller winery owners similarly complained about the lack of state efforts to support the industry. Although the planting of experimental vineyards in Raleigh is a start, the bulk of the industry is located 100 miles to the west of the state capital. Kim Myers, of Laurel Gray and recent past president of the North Carolina Winegrowers Association, noted 'I would like to see research plots at several vineyards scattered about. We are considerably different here in the Swan Creek area. The soil's different.'[24]

The state recently embarked on a major upgrade to the facilities at Surry Community College, breaking ground in May 2009 on the $5 million Shelton-Badgett North Carolina Center for Viticulture and Enology, named after the family of Charlie and Ed Shelton of Shelton Winery in nearby Dobson. It will house a bonded winery, a resource library, a 4,000-square-foot events facility, laboratories and classrooms and an adjacent 5-acre vineyard. Located in the heart of the Yadkin Valley AVA, the centre is intended to serve the grape and wine industry not only in North Carolina, but also in the mid-Atlantic region and the south-east. It currently has 64 students enrolled in its viticulture and oenology programmes. In its co-op programme, students work for a semester at a commercial vineyard or winery and receive college credit. Students may choose an 18-credit-hour certificate programme, a 42-credit-hour programme involving two semesters and one summer, or an associate degree programme taking two years and one summer. In addition to oenology and viticulture courses, business management programmes will be offered to help would-be winery owners deal with the commercial aspects of their wineries.

In a recent report produced by the business school faculties at the University of North Carolina at Greensboro and North Carolina Agricultural and Technical State University, the need for better business management skills/time management were noted as being one of the principal concerns of winery owners, especially smaller ones who typically relied upon unpaid family labour.[25] Together with constraints imposed by limited finances and difficulties in gaining access to financing, time management and lack of basic business skills represented major obstacles to attaining and sustaining profitability, the report indicated. In order to sell their wine, wineries need to spend time and money marketing it and this, most acknowledged, was in short supply. Having mastered aspects of grape cultivation and even winemaking, many wineries faced the obstacle of actually selling their wine. In my interviews with winery owners over the past five years I asked the following question: 'If you break the whole winery business into three basic components – growing the grapes, making the wine, selling the wine – which one of these constitutes the biggest challenge?' Almost all said 'selling the wine'. In fact one small winery owner of a Yadkin Valley AVA winery told me in a 2007 interview,

> We were careful to make sure we purchased the right land, got the best person to design the vineyard, had a good vineyard manager, hired the best winemaker in the area to make our wine, built a nice tasting room adjacent to a main highway, paid for all of the appropriate signs ... and still we've had a really hard time selling the wine! In retrospect, instead of putting all of our money and time into the other things we should have paid more attention to marketing. But we just figured that if we got everything else right, the wine would sell itself. Well it didn't.

Another in the same general area the following year commented,

> The thing that has most surprised me about this industry is the way everyone shares information. I took (viticulture and oenology) courses at Surry, read a lot and perhaps most importantly talked a lot with other winery owners. I would go and spend time, volunteering in their vineyard, helping at harvest time. There was so much that I learned informally through these contacts and I'm a much better winemaker than I could have been. What was great was how I could learn many of the on-the-job skills by talking with others and this really complemented my book learning from the Surry courses. Sure I made mistakes, like the incorrect trellising that I put in and then had to rip out. However, what I was not prepared for was the paperwork and some broad business skills. That's not something you learn from others. In fact others typically don't share this information but perhaps they're in the same boat as me and also don't really know. What we really need as a group are some basic lessons in things like business strategy, marketing and even accounting. Dealing with the paperwork of getting bonded was not really difficult just amazingly time consuming ... and time is what I don't really have. Besides, I would much rather be working in the vineyard than sit-

ting at a desk sorting out the best source for bottles and glasses or what permits I need for the tasting room. That's been the hardest thing for me and I bet I'm not alone in thinking this.

He was correct in that he is not alone; such sentiments were expressed to me on many occasions, especially from small owners who still constitute the majority of the industry. It is not just a question of skill deficiency though, since given the professional background of many owners they are cognizant of the administrative imperatives they face. Their problem is usually one of time management. Balancing the agricultural responsibilities of vineyard management, oenological activities and marketing their wine is proving much more time consuming than many anticipated. There is a tendency to focus upon the agricultural dimension since that is the one area that is new to many of them and where they feel their learning is deemed most essential. In doing this, however, they often pay less attention to marketing and sales activities even though they recognize their importance.

Perhaps because such skill sets are deemed non-industry-specific knowledge, it means there is less emphasis upon creating frameworks for its dissemination. Or it is assumed that many owners possess such capabilities therefore rendering redundant any need for formal and even informal knowledge conduits in these areas. Yet, since many of the small wineries sold most of their wines direct from the tasting room or self-distributed, it required administrative skills and time, that many of them nonetheless acknowledge themselves to be deficient in. There are attempts to rectify this through the various state associations and the growth of wine tourism has given an added dimension to understanding and planning ancillary marketing activities. As a consequence more and more of the new wineries have unambiguously positioned their site as a tourist or event destination, devoting considerable resources to marketing it accordingly. Whether this adds to or detracts from the pursuit of improvements in wine quality is the subject of the final part of our discussion.

Marketing Wineries versus Making Wine

Since oversight of the North Carolina wine industry was transferred from the Department of Agriculture to the Department of Commerce in 2000, it is perhaps not surprising that winemaking would become subsumed under the general panoply of wine or agri-tourism. A 2008 Report on wine tourism, commissioned by the North Carolina Department of Commerce,[26] analysed the demographics of visitors to North Carolina wineries. Although 53 per cent came from North Carolina, the remainder came from states across the south-east and most of the latter availed themselves of overnight lodgings. Two thirds stated 'visiting a winery' as the express purpose of their travel and 61 per cent were first-time visitors, most of whom reported favourably on their experience. Such data indicate interest in wine tourism and positive experiences for those who did it. Wine tourism is crucial for small wineries since it allows them to make more money from 'cellar door' sales than distributing directly to wine stores and restaurants. Wine sold on the premises is twice as profitable as wine sold through distributors. The challenge is to get sufficient number of visitors to come to wineries.

The idea of wine trails has been used successfully in other states to encourage visitors to follow certain routes, visit wineries but also spend money at local restaurants and hotels. North Carolina wineries have certainly been made aware of this, having several sessions at the 2009 North Carolina Grape Growers annual conference devoted to the promotion of wine trails. An inaugural wine conference at Appalachian State University in 2006 similarly devoted numerous sessions to the development of advertising, marketing and promotion campaigns. Such activities are certainly beneficial to small wineries that otherwise might not appear on the consumer radar.

Two wineries that embraced the idea of being a destination that would complement their wine sales are Uwharrie Vineyards and Rock of Ages Winery. Both are good examples of recently opened wineries were extensive resources were put into building a tasting room that had multifunction use for receptions, weddings, conferences, etc., and located in areas close to major metropolitan centres.

Conceived just over seven years ago, Rock of Ages Winery is the brainchild of owner and winemaker Kevin Moore. Located in Hurdle Mills, north-west of Durham, it covers 225 acres of former tobacco land that has been in the Moore family for several generations.[27] Currently there are 26 acres under vine with 17 different varietals. Construction of the winery began in 2005 and it was opened in 2006. Its design is old English style with Italianate features and a Western Lodge feel that was purposely conceived to be a destination as well as a working winery. It has an extensive kitchen and staff, and landscaped exterior that lends itself to weddings and corporate events which have proved very lucrative since the winery opened. Kevin Moore, by his own admission, has used his capital resources from his tile and marble import business (Hard Rock Marble and Tile) to finance the grand scale of the winery and its buildings and firmly to establish its visual supremacy. He took a degree in Enology and Viticulture from Surry Community College when his interest in making wine was piqued and devoted the next few years in planning and building the winery. As he told me in 2007 interview,

> If I was going to do this I wanted to do it properly with a nice facility that we can grow into. Too many wineries start small because they're under-funded and then have to keep adding on. We built this with much greater capacity than we need now but we can grow into it. To be successful though you need a nice setting and that's what we've tried to do. If we can get people to come here we can hopefully convince them to buy

our wine. We wanted to create a space where events could be held. We have these great facilities, everything you could imagine and people do like it. Our bookings for weddings have grown and we host corporate events. In each case we require people to buy our wine so it's a nice way to simultaneously get rental income and wine sales.

He decided to make the wines himself and feels confident in what he is doing. In 2007 he was buying his grapes from elsewhere until his vines matured. He wanted to experiment with different varietals hence the large number (of both dry and sweet wines) that he has planted. After experimenting in this way he will eventually concentrate on those that he has found to grow the best. He did this because he says the area where he is located is drier than Yadkin Valley so he needs to figure out what grows best there. He is emphatic that attention must be paid to quality but that you also need a good marketing plan that includes a strong component of how to grow your market. 'Benchmarking your wine is important', he said, 'but so is pricing. One needs to compare oneself to the quality of what others are producing, then price your wines slightly lower.'

More than most of the smaller wineries, he embraced a coherent marketing plan and emphasis that reflects the capital investments made in the winery. He appeared more cognizant of what was involved in selling wine, perhaps more so than actual winemaking, but his indisputable professional approach to the business side of the venture separates him somewhat from many of the other small wineries in the state.

A similar story can be found in Uwharrie Vineyards, near the major city of Charlotte, where partners David Brasswell and general manager/winemaker Chad Andrews have an 85-acre property with 35 acres currently under vines that produce 6,200 cases. Their facility is geared towards banquets and weddings and in 2007 when I interviewed Chad he indicated that they were booked throughout the summer. They too invested heavily in marketing (bottle and label design; layout and design of the facilities) because they identified the revenue potential of their location. Thus far they indicate it continues to be a very good way of subsidizing their winery operation.

Many other small wineries have embraced this multipurpose function, albeit rarely on the scale and capital investments of the above two. But they have all recognized the financial benefits of providing rental space in their wineries and positioning themselves on the emerging wine trails. Most view this tourism-related activity as a way of solving their marketing and sales problems, actually encouraging people to visit the winery in the first place. 'If I can actually get people in the door, I can sell them wine', said one small winery that opened in 2008. He went on to say,

part of the problem is that we're doing this with another full-time job, so we can only open at weekends. It would be great to open weekdays but we'd have to hire someone to work then and we cannot afford that right now. Unlike some who have taken early retirement and put their savings into the winery and who have the time to be open more days a week, that's not possible for us. It's a real dilemma though.

I questioned owners about whether their efforts at tourism-related activities distracted them from time spent devoted to viticulture and oenology. Most acknowledged that the former did prove somewhat seductive because it provided an almost guaranteed revenue stream regardless of what wine they produced. Since most underestimated the cost of developing and sustaining a winery they welcomed this income source which came with low marginal overhead costs. They indicated also that such activities were easy because it was hospitality-related and therefore nowhere near as complex as the winery side of operations. Most of them recognized the need to interact with customers at the winery, the *sine qua non* of any sales-related endeavour, so this proved a simple extension of that function. Did it detract from the actual winemaking operations? Although they were reluctant to admit it one had the sense that this might be the case. The large wineries served as models of tourist-related, multifunctional spaces, but they had the resources to employ full-time vineyard managers and winemakers so it did not interfere with their core activities. Smaller ones lacked such professional assistance and therefore time scarcity once again reared its head. And yet the small ones saw the benefits associated with tourism, especially since the North Carolina Grape and Wine Council was making this more of a centrepiece to their promotion of the industry in the state. Not to embrace this 'business model' would be to ignore the residual effects of externally funded campaigns, as well as forgoing potential sales; but doing it rendered one vulnerable to further time pressures that could eventually hinder the commitment to product quality. This is the dilemma facing segments of the industry at this moment.

Conclusion

Inevitably as an industry grows and matures, attracting new entrants of very different capabilities, differentiation, specialization and a hierarchy of firms will emerge. One can expect that with such differentiation some firms will display more robust characteristics than others. In recent years we have witnessed the emergence of a critical mass of wineries with concentrations in certain parts of the state. This is a normal pattern of cluster evolution and provides requisite efficiency benefits and lower transaction costs for incumbents and some newcomers alike. In all probability firm mortality rates will rise as operational efficiency for the resource-richer firms will expose limitations for those without such resources and capabilities. We have also seen the growth of additional specialist firms in ancillary industries that cater specifically to wineries and growers. We now have several large wineries whose marketing plan is regional if not national operating alongside numerous small, boutique wineries who are content to sell the majority of their wine direct from the tasting room. Few wineries are currently profitable, mainly those that have been operational for at least 5 years, but that is consistent with such an industry that remains in its infancy and where aspirational lifestyle motivations are apparent. However, now that there are more actors, especially some with specialized skill sets that were conspicuously absent in early periods, one can expect an overall upgrading in operational skills if our earlier theorizing about networks and organizational learning remain viable. If nothing else, this could result in lower transaction costs that accompany production rationalization and this can have immediate benefits for financial stability.

Within the overall cluster of *vinifera* growers that is located in the central and western part of the state, it appears that interactions and reciprocal learning are now shifting to arm's-length contractual relationships, as opposed to the earlier pattern of informal access to knowledge. This is especially the case with innovation-related operational details. At one level this signifies the increase in technical complexity that is diffused as the industry has matured and the need for more formal and detailed ways of structuring such knowledge exchanges. Professional specialists, who constitute important knowledge bases, have replaced earlier 'amateur' practitioners and these key actors now facilitate and even direct such exchange. Their leadership role in attempting to establish some form of quality control has been important and provides opportunities for firms with whom they work to engage in operational upgrading. That they have often been resisted in these efforts is not surprising since they have often affected the financial outcomes of subordinate firms. But in structuring relationships within the network, they have nonetheless imposed operational practices that have improved the overall efficiency of the cluster.

At another level, it reflects different resources and capabilities that new actors have brought to the industry and the willingness of some to approach learning in a more contractual and dyadic fashion. This does not mean that a broad network for the informal exchange of operational details no longer exists; it clearly does since most newcomers comment on the high degree of cooperation and information sharing that continues. But increasingly the sort of codified and tacit knowledge that in the past was reciprocally exchanged is now subsumed under a structured and hierarchical set of relationships between 'experts' and those willing to purchase their expertise. Those who are unwilling or unable to participate in such contractual formalism are more likely to be marginalized. Does this mean that they cease to be significant actors within the network? Not necessarily, since they remain active in the various associations and rely upon cooperative and trust-based interactions with many fellow network actors. It means that they might be latecomers to key operational details that are no longer public goods; learning of such things after their counterparts. Given that there is only one opportunity each year for them to make wine, this deficiency can be a significant impediment to success.

Such operational problems relate clearly to issues of quality and consistency of final product that plague the industry. With the current systemic impasse in this area, a product of the above firm heterogeneity, it is difficult to see an early solution to these problems. In the absence of any formal quality control mechanisms, it is difficult to address other than to let the market determine winners and losers. Furthermore, the unbridled enthusiasm shown by many new wineries towards agri-tourism potentially constitutes a further distraction from attention to quality. Understandably, even the resource-rich operations have to answer to their accountants at the end of the day; hence their eager embrace of using their winery as a site for weddings and other service-related activities that are guaranteed revenue streams. But to continue doing this runs the risk of subverting the earlier successes of winemaking and potentially delegitimizing the industry as whole just when it was beginning to acquire an identity.

CONCLUSION

I know I'm not going to make any money out of this for a while but I'm doing it because I enjoy it. I'm passionate about wine. I think we can make some good wine here, have a nice environment for people to visit and eventually be profitable.

Owner of a recently opened small winery (interview with author, 2009)

It takes a long time to learn about winemaking and to understand what grows best in an area and what doesn't. We're still experimenting in North Carolina and have a long way to go.

Bernard DeLille, winemaker, Biltmore Estates (interview with author, 2009)

The rapid growth of the industry during the past few years continues unabated. Several new wineries are planned to open in the next few months and several non-farmers have bought land in the Yadkin Valley AVA with the specific intent of growing grapes for sale to local wineries. Wineries that have opened in the past few months have often done so with the explicit aim of offering multiple attractions. Sanders Ridge Vineyard and Winery, for example, is a Yadkin Valley winery and organic produce farm that in addition has a restaurant on the premises. It opened the first weekend of July 2009 to huge crowds. Others, such as Shadow Springs Vineyard (in the newly created Swan Creek AVA), have been creative in their marketing, in this instance offering the public temporary shares in a vine. For $45 one can adopt one of the grapevines for a year, receive a certificate and photograph of the vine, and after harvest receive two bottles of wine from that grape variety.

Most wineries continue to hedge their bets on the preferred grape to grow and plant multiple types, from as few as four varietals up to sixteen. Existing vineyards have ripped out some vines that fared poorly and replanted with others that either did well or were reputed to do well according to others in the area. Wineries now have access to routinely disseminated information about growing problems, spraying, vineyard management and a multitude of technical details that emanate from either the Wine Growers Association or the state's various agricultural research centres. This was conspicuously lacking in the previous decade. At the various conferences and workshops that are held for winery owners and growers, significant numbers of ancillary industry support services are present, meaning that they come to the area to service the industry rather than vice versa. At a February 2009 meeting of the North Carolina Wine Growers Association, several large conference rooms were devoted to such industry-specific vendors as chemical supply companies, equipment manufacturers, bottlers and label suppliers, logistic and supply chain specialists. I asked several how long they have been coming and most said only in the past couple of years because it is only recently that there has been sufficient local demand for their products to merit attendance. In April 2010 the same association sponsored a two-day seminar on the tourist potential for wineries, catering to a growing interest amongst winery owners in complementing their wine production with a site for functions. Wine trails continue to be promoted locally, and bed and breakfasts, small inns and rental cabins are all proliferating in the areas of the state where winery growth is fastest.

Many *vinifera* purists still either grow or buy some muscadine grapes to make into wine for sale in their wineries, realizing that the prevailing local preference for sweet wines is an opportunity to capture a reliable revenue stream that their drier wines might not provide. Despite the 'snob' value of being an exclusively *vinifera* producer, experience has a tendency to trump idealism for even the most sanguine of utility maximizers. Yet it is surprising that a few still adamantly resist selling sweet wines. Pragmatism has also enabled most to acknowledge that hybrids can do well in the region and so they continue experimenting with them, either as stand-alone wines or used for blending with *viniferas*. The realization that such grapes are more disease resistant and easier plus often less costly to grow has rendered earlier reluctance to plant them less resolute. Meanwhile, the exclusively muscadine producers continue to market their product successfully, albeit with a more local specialized market. Their attempt to foster a collective identity lags that of *vinefera* growers, but sales at all of the predominantly muscadine wineries in my sample have increased each year. The growth of this sector, however, is much less robust than that of *vinifera* growers and remains more of a niche market.

The two quotes at the beginning of the chapter reflect the current status of the industry. On the one hand there continues to be an influx of new entrants, many with resources that facilitate satisficing if not utility maximizing behaviour. They possess an unbridled enthusiasm and resolve for their oenological endeavour, a recognition of the arduous labour entailed and a commitment to the collective project that the regional industry now personifies. The learning curve remains steep, but the collective experience of a decade's worth of trial and error plus locally established educational and training facilities provide avenues of progress that were conspicuously absent in the early 1990s when the industry started its growth surge. They realize how difficult it is to make an immediate profit and for many their approach to business is conditioned by an 'aspirational lifestyle' goal. Those who are resource-rich typically fit the utility maximizer category and yet this group is more likely to contribute to the industry's improved reputation because they have the capabilities to absorb the requisite knowledge that will result in the production of quality wines. The others (a majority perhaps?) can be best described as pursuing profit-oriented behaviour, relying upon formal knowledge channels and informal linkages. Some have the resources and knowledge to meet modest production goals but others are lacking in the resource base to implement fully all that is required for quality production.

The second quote, from one of the most experienced winemakers in the region, is a telling comment on the industry's infancy and continued limited knowledge base. His words are indicative of the need for patience and to be cognizant of the complexity involved in learning, often by painful experience, of appropriate techniques and procedures. As I will show in this chapter, all too often this perspective is not always embraced by some newcomers. Their impatience and enthusiasm can easily mar an understanding of operational complexities, and their reticence in acknowledging imperfections in their own techniques can adversely affect the industry's growing reputation.

Market Stabilization

The historical narrative that I have provided can be seen at one level as an agglomeration of individual entrepreneurship stories; frequently characterized by the persistence of hope in the face of considerable adversity. When experiments with one type of grape that the early settlers knew best failed, undeterred, individuals decided to make do with the native grapes that appeared to grow so well with minimal human interference. Thus was born the commercialization of muscadine that came to its zenith with Paul Garrett's late nineteenth-century marketing bonanza around scuppernong. By then, North Carolina had emerged as one of the principal wine producing states in the United States. Prohibition stifled this growth and the industry became dormant for many decades. Its rebirth in the 1970s was initially centred on muscadines but persistent efforts to grow *vinifera* (and hybrids) finally paid off by the 1980s and it is with these grapes that the current boom is most associated.

It would be inaccurate and even excessively optimistic to claim that wine has become the alcoholic beverage of choice for North Carolina natives now or even during the scuppernong heyday of the nineteenth century. As noted in Chapter 2, the preference for hard liquor such as whiskey and brandy continued unabated, and would do so well into the twentieth century. Notwithstanding the moral fervour that accompanied Prohibition or the determination of revenue collectors to collect their tax on 'moonshine', if alcohol was to be consumed then probably it would be the product of the plentiful supply of corn and apples in the area. But such a 'market' remained informal, the product a profitable response to local demand but supplied in ways that circumvented official channels. When a marketplace for wine emerged in the nineteenth century and then again starting in the 1970s, whatever stability it had was a product of dominant firms such as that of Paul Garrett and later Duplin, Biltmore, Childress, RayLen and Shelton who were able in varying ways to develop a governance framework for the network relationships. They provided an identity to an otherwise disparate group of individual producers who often struggled to establish themselves in an embryonic industry.

I have argued throughout that markets are socially constructed and whilst not dramatically different from institutionalist perspectives, such an approach is at variance with neo-classical economic models which see markets as the constituent product of competitive behaviour. Similarly, markets are seen not as the product of historical accidents or even random starts such as neo-evolutionary theories assert.[1] Instead they have been a product of unique circumstances where actors met the growing demand for a new product at a time of resource availability (plus operational knowledge) and an emerging institutional support framework. As markets have evolved they have done so in such a way that a particular form of organization (in this case cooperative clustering) has proved advantageous to small firm growth as well as encouraging industry entrants. As the cluster has grown, institutions have emerged, as Neil Fligstein argues, to reinforce such an organizational advantage.[2] Cooperation has been crucial to market formation and continues to be the glue that holds an embryonic industry together. The growing concentration of firms in both grape growing and winemaking plus those in related industries in a particular geographical area has enabled clustering with its ancillary knowledge transfers. The more firms there are in the area, the more attractive it becomes for new entrants. Once a cluster becomes established and an infrastructure emerges, the density of knowledge exchange increases and the innovation process speeds up. Not only do clusters drive the direction and pace of innovation, they can also facilitate improved productivity by individual firms. Clusters also provide a framework for cooperation that sustains growth by reducing transaction costs.

Firms learn to cooperate even though the benefits are not always easy to discern. Doing so, however, provides ways of assessing associated benefits and understanding the ramifications of coordinated behaviour. In other words, knowledge sharing constitutes both individual benefits and a collective long-term good. Because this is an industry where innovation and learning are crucial, the constant exchange of ideas and even persons has been necessary for the market to grow. Earlier periods of industry growth were stymied by either lack of relevant operational knowledge (vine disease awareness and rectification) or by external events (Prohibition). In other words firms lacked crucial resources and capabilities necessary for survival or they encountered institutional hostility that curtailed their operation. With both of these no longer pervasive, opportunities for firm growth have contributed to increased stability for this organizational field and actors have recognized that their mutual interdependence can be a source of collective strength as well as a means of continued learning. This finding is certainly consistent with those who argue for the importance of organizational actors creating a stable world so that organizations can flourish.[3] What this study has shown is the dynamic process whereby such a field or market has been created, initially from a core of pioneers but then more recently through the coordinated efforts of key actors.

Crucial to the emerging stability of the cluster has been the growth of knowledge required for operational success in an industry that in the past had been plagued by failure. Whereas many studies of clusters attribute success and higher rates of innovation to localized knowledge spillovers[4] or that physical proximity means clustered firms are more innovative than isolated firms,[5] I have argued that greater agency should be attributed to the firms themselves as engines of change. It is their capability (and access to resources) that determines the extent to which they can leverage their position in the cluster to acquire requisite knowledge for sustained growth. There exists a greater degree of heterogeneity amongst firms in a cluster than is sometimes acknowledged; hence differential rates of learning occur. Asymmetrical relationships structure interactions because the knowledge base of some firms is greater than that of others. As a consequence, with growing density emerges a hierarchical interaction network structure that confers greater legitimacy upon those firms seen as technological leaders who are inevitably sought out most by those firms with a weaker knowledge base. Similar studies of wine clusters in Italy and Chile have also identified reciprocal knowledge exchange to be resource mediated.[6] As the marketplace becomes consolidated firms with a weaker knowledge base become more marginal to network activities although they are rarely excluded completely because there is no formal mechanism for expulsion.

As industry-specific local knowledge increases, interactions become more structured and, with that structure, a need for cluster governance becomes apparent. Resource-rich firms with extensive knowledge bases are perceived as technological leaders, with the greatest capacity for innovation. It is also assumed that they will be in the forefront of constructing a stable framework for the network since stability is crucial for actors to realize the mutual benefits of interdependence and cooperative behaviour. If firms are to survive they must be able to respond to environmental change; in which case their capacity to absorb information and be flexible in their responses is crucial. This means that actors must have both resources and a capability to extract information and implement it in efficient ways. Firms with larger knowledge bases are more likely to develop collective ways to control organizational fields and seek to impose it on smaller firms.[7] This can be facilitated by institutions that provide formal patterns of knowledge transmission which in turn can contribute to further legitimizing the leadership role of the larger firms. The emerging wine market in North Carolina constitutes an organizational field that has become institutionalized and, within that field, a set of shared meanings and operational definitions have become consolidated.

At this early stage it remains difficult to determine the extent to which firms with large knowledge bases can effectively impose governance in the cluster. Albeit in many respects informally sanctioned, such a role does appear to have acquired legitimacy following the increasingly prominent role played by individuals in such firms. As noted in other studies of status hierarchies,[8] one can see the gradual emergence of key individuals whose influence is conditional upon their prominent position as knowledge brokers in the large firms as well as through the reputational effects of their performance in the local industry. Winemakers at several of the large wineries brought industry experience to their current job but also demonstrated *in situ* that they could make a quality product. Status and quality thus become interlinked and hence deference is displayed to such individuals by others in the industry. Providing they continue to produce wines of consistent quality, such individuals' status remains intact and this enables them to exercise a governance role even if primarily of an informal nature. It also leads to more structured hierarchical interactions, with contractualism often replacing earlier patterns of informal reciprocity.

As industry associations have emerged (such as the North Carolina Wine Growers) the above professionals have often assumed a formal leadership position, shaping the agenda for discussions on how oversight can be implemented and improved quality assured. Their collective role in such associations can be beneficial because of their strategic insight, extra-network resources and linkages, plus their enthusiasm for acting as brokers in the cluster coalition. Because of their technical proficiency, they are able to formalize procedural guidelines and facilitate a more rigorous operational framework that new firms can follow. Since their own reputations rest in part on that of the region, it is incumbent upon them to push for improved quality and consistency whenever they can. However, they still lack industry-wide enforcement capabilities although their governance role has been exercised often in providing *de facto* benchmarks for many firms.

This brings us to the second feature of the story told here: that of incumbent firms providing a framework that encourages and facilitates new entrants which in turn reproduces the overall market structure and reinforces its vitality. We have seen how the interactions between actors in firms constitute the social relations that must exist if markets are to function. In this respect, networks are constituent of the social order, are based on norms of reciprocity and provide firms with resources that permit them to operate in unstable markets. As interactions became embedded in informal networks, institutional supports emerged to organize economic activities in ways that eventually led to structural stabilization. Thus market stability has been attained, albeit in two separate forms since the dynamic network features of *vinifera* producers differ from the less dense and weakly structured interactions of muscadine producers. In the former, networks continue to enhance allocative efficiency and adaptive processes that have enabled new entrants to avoid the steep learning curve that characterized earlier entrants. But as network density increased, a core group of established firms provided knowledge resources in more systematic and contractual ways with newcomers. The latter in turn are notable for their own resource bases that enabled them, first, to afford to enter into such relationships and, second, to absorb the knowledge that is transferred. The increased intensity of interactions in such contractual and formal relationships does not supplant the informal network linkages; it systematically structures them in ways that improve organizational learning. Firms without such knowledge-absorbing capabilities – and this includes some that have been established even a decade ago – remain peripheral and forced to acquire requisite knowledge through random diffusion of information. While the latter has increasingly become codified and accessible through formal educational channels, it is nonetheless not as detailed and site specific as that proffered by dyadic relationships.

As the market identity grows, new entrants continue to be attracted and this further adds to density. However, with organizational field stability dependent upon the reputation of firms within the market, product quality and consistency assume more importance than in the past. If too many firms are unable to produce goods that meet minimal quality standards, then the overall legitimacy of the industry can suffer. But because of the industry's infancy, there are insufficient institutional mechanisms that can provide comprehensive training for newcomers, nor are there acceptable frameworks for guaranteeing some form of agreed quality control. Notwithstanding the efforts of large firms whose winemakers make wines for smaller firms, and therefore impose their own quality standards that can spread through parts of the industry, it remains up to the market to determine whether or not products meet minimal quality standards.

It appears that there are still newcomers who enter the industry underestimating the amount of knowledge required to function efficiently and effectively. In the early days of the industry this was inevitable; today this can be problematic for the industry's reputation. Some newcomers simultaneously learn how to operate a winery and vineyard management whilst they are preparing their businesses. Others rely upon trial-and-error procedures following minimal formal education. While many acknowledge they are still learning, their ability to master the intricacies of vineyard management and winemaking remains mod-est. The result, all too frequently, is a finished product that is often flawed. As Stephen Rigby, winemaker for Raffaldini and a person who has worked in the Yadkin Valley for over a decade, told me in 2009 interview,

> Experience and paying attention to detail are crucial. You have to learn from your failures but in order to do that you have to be systematic in what you do so you know why certain things happened the way they did. You've got to learn to look at the vines, how they are growing. They don't always look pretty and that's not bad. But you've got to teach yourself to understand the fruit. Also to get the best quality grapes you've got to take more risks. Too many people pick too soon because they're worried about losing their crop. Sometimes it's best to wait. But this is what experience tells you.

As Bernard DeLille, winemaker at Biltmore, told me in a 2009 interview,

> The problem is that the NC industry exploded without the necessary base. SCC (Surrey County Community College) is good but this (education) needs to be done first rather than at the same time as developing the winery. People are often too impa-tient and sometimes blind to the reality of what's at stake. Overall we're learning a bit more each year about what will grow best in the area. But it's a slow process. One year can give a great harvest followed by two bad ones. It's a patient process. I think it's (the industry) grown too quickly without people knowing enough. Yes NC State, ASU and SCC are out there and the state is throwing money at it but the research is of limited value because it's still research and they're still trying different things. Unfortunately people want immediate confirmation and they're not going to get that straight away. So many struggle and do the wrong things.

Both of these comments, from established professionals with many years experience in the area, point not just to growing pains but possibly fundamen-tal problems that continue to plague segments of the industry. Because some incumbents still lack requisite knowledge yet continue to think that they have the necessary skill sets, while others are bereft of the knowledge and do not have the resources to acquire it, the industry continues to be beset with considera-ble variations in quality. This can damage the overall reputation of the sector if consumers come to think that most producers lack consistency in their finished product. As one winemaker told me in a 2009 interview, 'it's ok to make so-so wine and sell it at $6 a bottle; but when you do that with a $17 or $18 bottle then it's a problem'.

Under normal market conditions where competitive conditions punish poor performers, one typically sees high firm mortality rates. But in this instance, the newness of the market, pervasive satisficing behaviour by some incumbents and the continued novelty factor associated with local producers selling direct from their winery to consumers who remain intrigued at the concept of a North Car-olina wine have the affect of insulating firms from such perils. How long this state of affairs will persist is difficult to determine but as the industry matures one would expect firm failures to increase because long-term losses are difficult to sustain indefinitely. Inexorably, if this industry is to develop as others have, the quality standards set by some wineries will raise the benchmark sufficiently high that others will have wines that will compare poorly. As the latter's sales diminish, they will be forced either to improve their own quality or exit the business.

Industry newcomers, however, have access to far more detailed operational knowledge than their predecessors a decade ago. This has influenced recent start-ups who are able to balance informal information exchange with the formal acquisition of finely grained and increasingly codified knowledge. As a cluster grows, it encourages innovation and learning, with greater reliance upon formalized and established procedures replacing those of trial and error. But the emergence of asymmetrical relations between large and small firms might eventually erode the innovation potential of the cluster. Should this happen, one would need to reconceptualize the dynamics of cluster evolution as a hierarchy of firms act as growth engines.

Problems and Prospects

In reflecting on the current status of the industry, several issues can potentially sidetrack its growth or impair the consolidation of its reputation. We now have a situation where several large firms, with professional winemakers, are able to utilize maturing vines to make wines that meet minimal standards of quality and consistency. Their formal relationships with smaller wineries enable them to disseminate the requisite knowledge and operational techniques that permit those wineries to produce at similar quality levels. How effective they can be in persuading others to upgrade remains to be seen. Which brings us to the first issue, that of research.

It is clear that much knowledge about local conditions remains to be developed and both formalized and institutionalized. This will require a more active and extensive investment by the state in oenology and viticulture research and the provision of resources that enable continued upgrading of institutional support mechanisms. Informal networks will remain important for the exchange of ideas but, as tacit knowledge becomes more codified, a formal mechanism for its transmission must be institutionalized. This might require some established wineries to recognize their own current limitations and acknowledge the need for skills upgrading. Some will accept this, others resist.

Related to the above, as the industry has grown it has led to subtle transformations in agricultural structure but without the state necessarily recognizing the growing importance of this new sector. Like most small businesses, there are gripes about excessive regulations amongst winery owners. But the state has not been particularly proactive in supporting the industry and could do more by streamlining various regulatory and fiscal procedures. It could also recognize the growing importance of the industry by underwriting more marketing endeavours (currently this is done, but in a bare-bones fashion by the Department of Commerce). Unfortunately, the industry is still a marginal player in the eyes of the Department of Agriculture whose focus still remains centred on agri-business such as industrial-scale hog and poultry farming.

Third, many new entrants continue to view their winery as a tourist destination and a site for ancillary activities such as weddings or receptions. Whilst there is a utility to making one's business multipurpose, if it detracts from the core activity (winemaking) which is still in the learning stage, it could have longer-term deleterious effects on the provision of quality outputs. If owners find a guaranteed revenue stream from renting their facility, together with a captive market for their wines, it can easily cause them to be less thorough or committed to making the best wine possible. If this happens, they run the risk of becoming quaint locations but not necessarily the purveyors of decent wine. This can eventually affect industry reputation. Unfortunately, some of the explanation for this tendency lies in the current enthusiasm of promoting the industry as part of tourism initiatives. Agri-tourism and wine trails in particular are seen as ways of promoting the industry and building the 'brand'. But this can divert resources and attention by focusing upon service-related activities rather than technical skill development and upgrading in actual viticulture and winemaking.

Fourth, many wineries are still encountering difficulty selling their product. Small wineries generally self-distribute since they lack the resources and contacts to do otherwise, or are unwilling to cede a percentage of the sales to the distributors. When production volume is small (around 1,000 cases for example) this is not so problematic since most sales can be made direct from the winery. Winery visitors typically buy several bottles so it not inconceivable that a winery can sell 50–100 bottles per day. But moving beyond that capacity requires use of distribution networks. Wineries that use distributors, according to a recent survey,[9] report cash flow and financing to be less constraining for profitability than those that do not use them. In other words, not using distributors can create cash flow problems that inhibit profitability and this seems to be more likely to occur amongst smaller wineries that are moving beyond 1,000-case production. This can be something of a 'catch twenty two'; in order to expand one needs a formal distribution network but to do so requires resources and time that one might not have.

Pricing remains a potential hurdle for expanding production and sales. Price points are high relative to many other domestic and imported wines, but reflect the higher operating costs of North Carolina wineries due to limited production runs. In order to bring prices down to a competitive level, economies of scale are needed, with 30,000–35,000 cases seen as optimal. Few wineries anticipate such levels so high prices combined with the pursuit of a niche market will remain the best strategy for local producers. Key here will be the ability to offer a product that is somewhat unique, that differentiates the North Carolina wine from others therefore justifying the price premium. This brings us back to identifying and promoting a signature wine for the state which is still ongoing.

On the issue of scale and sales, some of the big wineries have had to scale back production this year because of excess inventory and a dip in sales associated with the current recession. Many people buy North Carolina wine when they visit a winery, but the industry has yet to establish itself in normal retail outlets as a beverage of choice. Part of the problem here is a general lack of widespread knowledge regarding the industry; part of it is the higher price points of NC wines relative to others on sale. In order for the industry to move to the next stage and become regionally known, attention must be paid to brand development. This in turn is predicated upon quality and consistency improvements and sustained marketing. The industry in Virginia has benefitted from close proximity to a major metropolitan area in Washington, DC. The North Carolina wine industry needs to expand its profile in the major urban areas of the state and the mid-Atlantic region. Under the umbrella of the Department of Commerce, some efforts have been made to further this expansion but more resources need to be invested.

Despite the above problems, new entrants still find the industry attractive. Most are self-financing which means they will probably remain small. But the lure of an aspirational lifestyle in an industry that is beginning to become established remains seductive. For those who are resource-rich and established, their concerns will probably soon focus on turning a profit. In the meantime they will continue to be key actors in forging the industry's identity. The name recognition and reputational effects they provide continue to help legitimize the industry and through that facilitate, one presumes, the operational parameters that will continue to consolidate this new market. If growth continues, conceivably quality guidance will increasingly be from exogenous forces such as out-of-state wineries where the industry is more established. This could result in further industry reshaping as the market becomes transformed and the early synergistic activities modified around a heightened professional winemaking culture.

APPENDIX: INTERVIEW QUESTIONS FOR NORTH CAROLINA WINERY OWNERS/ WINEMAKERS

Name of winery   _____

Date of founding _____

Owner(s)   _____

Location   _____

The following questions were asked under confidentiality:

1. Capital source for winery?
2. What did you do prior to owning/operating the winery?
3. Is this (the winery) a full-time or part-time occupation?
4. Capital expenditures (annual/initial)?
5. When were the vines first planted?
6. Size: total acreage and acreage under production?
7. Yields (tons per acre)? How much annual variation? How does this differ with different types of grapes?
8. What types of grape do you grow? Why did you make this particular choice?
9. Number of cases produced?
10. Profits; break-even plans?
11. Ratio of grapes bought to grapes produced? How has this changed?
12. From where/whom are the grapes bought? How has this changed? How did none establish the link? Is it a detailed contract?
13. Number of employees?
14. Skill level of employees?
15. How and where did you learn your viticulture and oenology skills?
16. What was the land prior to viticulture?
17. Sales volume: direct sales from winery; from retail outlets (how many and where are they); through distributors?
18. Sales: in state vs out of state?

General questions:

1. How have tobacco settlements affected your business? Did you receive Golden Leaf money?
2. How did you acquire your land (family property, direct purchase, switched crops)?
3. What motivated you to start the winery?
4. What made you choose the type of grape you grow?
5. How have you learned general information about grape growing and winemaking? Specific detailed knowledge?
6. How would you describe your relationship with other winery owners/winemakers in the area? Do you regularly exchange information with them and if so what sort of information? How much has such a pattern of interaction changed in recent years?
7. Do you utilize other local specialist agencies/suppliers?
8. Have you found the local educational facilities helpful in providing needed operational knowledge? State agencies? North Carolina Wine and Grape Council?
9. Describe how the industry has changed/is changing: has it become more professional or does it remain about the same?
10. Have you deliberately attempted to create your winery as a multifunction site (i.e. for weddings, receptions, etc.)? What is the difference in revenue from wine sales and event sales?
11. What are the major problems that you currently face in your winery?
12. What are the problems that the industry faces locally?

NOTES

Introduction

1. C. Gohdes, *Scuppernong: North Carolina's Grape and its Wines* (Durham, NC: Duke University Press, 1982), p. 29.

2. See Chapter 3 for a full discussion of policy measures that shaped early winemaking in the state.

3. According to legend, the idea of self-distilling whiskey was introduced into America in 1620 when an Englishman named George Thorpe acquired corn from Powhatan natives in Virginia and turned it into corn whiskey. Known by numerous other monikers such as hooch, mountain dew, white lightning, firewater, home brew and sheep dip, the beverage that most now refer to as moonshine has experienced something of a resurgence in recent years as people's interest in 'going local' extends to alcoholic beverages. For an interesting discussion of the drink and those who currently manufacture it, see D. Webster, 'Moonshine', *Garden and Gun* (June–July 2009), pp. 62–7.

4. References to wine and vineyards figure prominently in the Bible; wine is part of the sacraments and has been the economic basis of certain monastic orders; and in the case of France is a central part of the nation's culture and identity. As Tyler Coleman states, 'wine has come to epitomize what is good and what is French'. T. Coleman, *Wine Politics* (Berkeley, CA: University of California Press, 2008), p.8.

5. See, for example, H. Aldrich and R. Waldinger, 'Ethnicity and Entrepreneurship', *Annual Review of Sociology*, 16 (1990), pp. 111–35; and I. Light and E. Bonacich, *Immigrant Entrepreneurs: Koreans in Los Angeles, 1965–1982* (Berkeley, CA: University of California Press, 1986).

6. For a summary of this recent literature, see P. Thornton, 'The Sociology of Entrepreneurship', *Annual Review of Sociology*, 24 (1999), pp. 19–46; on the notion of 'opportunity structure', see the work of W. P. Glade, 'Approaches to a Theory of Entrepreneurial Formation', *Explorations in Entrepreneurial History*, 4:3 (1967), pp. 245–59.

7. E. Romanelli, 'Organization Birth and Population Variety: A Community Perspective on Origins', *Research in Organizational Behavior*, 11 (1994), pp. 211–46.

8. H. Aldrich, *Organizations Evolving* (London: Sage Publications, 1999), pp. 81–7.

9. A. Marshall, *Principles of Economics* (London: Macmillan, 1923); M. Piore and C. Sabel, *The Second Industrial Divide* (New York: Basic Books, 1984).

10. See studies by M. J. Enright, 'Regional Clusters and Firm Strategy', in A. Chandler, P. Hagstrom and O. Solvell (eds), *The Dynamic Firm* (Oxford: Oxford University Press, 1998), pp. 315–42; P. Maskell, 'Towards a Knowledge-Based Theory of the Geographi-

cal Cluster', *Industrial and Corporate Change*, 10:4 (2001), pp. 921–43; and E. Giuliani, 'The Selective Nature of Knowledge Networks in Clusters: Evidence from the Wine Industry', *Journal of Economic Geography*, 7 (2006), pp. 139–68.

11. N. Fligstein, *The Architecture of Markets* (Princeton, NJ: Princeton University Press, 2001), p. 31.

1 Districts, Networks and Knowledge Brokering

1.   Marshall, *Principles of Economics*; A. Weber, *Theory of Location of Industries* (Chicago, IL: University of Chicago Press, 1929).

2.   P. Krugman, *Geography and Trade* (Cambridge, MA: MIT Press, 1991).

3.   For a basic discussion of social capital, see P. Bourdieu, 'The Forms of Capital', in J. G. Richardson (ed.), *Handbook of Theory and Research for the Sociology of Education* (London: Greenwood Press, 1986), pp. 241–58; and P. S. Adler and S.-W. Kwon, 'Social Capital: Prospects for a New Concept', *Academy of Management Review*, 27:1 (2002), pp. 17–40. For a more extensive commentary of the utility of social capital for knowledge transfer in networks, see A. Inkpen and E. Tsang, 'Social Capital, Networks and Knowledge Transfer', *Academy of Management Review*, 30:1 (2005), pp. 146–65.

4.   Piore and Sabel, *The Second Industrial Divide*; A. Saxenian, *Regional Advantage: Culture and Competition in Silicon Valley and Route 128* (Cambridge, MA: Harvard University Press, 1994); M. Best, *The New Competition: Institutions of Industrial Restructuring* (Cambridge, MA: Harvard University Press, 1990); and B. Harrison, *Lean and Mean: The Changing Landscape of Corporate Power in the Age of Flexibility* (New York: Basic Books, 1994).

5.   Maskell, 'Towards a Knowledge-Based Theory of the Geographical Cluster'.

6.   Enright, 'Regional Clusters and Firm Strategy'.

7.   I. M. Taplin, 'Segmentation and the Organization of Work in the Italian Apparel Industry', *Social Science Quarterly*, 70:2 (1989), pp. 408–24.

8.   O. Sorenson, 'Social Networks and Industrial Geography', *Journal of Evolutionary Economics*, 13:5 (2002), pp. 513–27, on p. 513.

9.   R. Baptista and P. Swann, 'Do Firms in Clusters Innovate More?', *Research Policy*, 27:5 (1998), pp. 525–40; R. Baptista, 'Do Innovations Diffuse Faster within Geographic Clusters?', *International Journal of Industrial Organization*, 18 (2000), pp. 515–35; C. Beaudry and S. Breschi, 'Are Firms in Clusters Really More Innovative?', *Economics of Innovation and New Technology*, 12:4 (2003), pp. 325–42.

10. R. H. Coase, 'The Problem of Social Cost', *Journal of Law and Economics*, 3 (1960), pp. 1–44.

11. M. Bell and E. Giuliani, 'Catching Up in the Global Wine Industry; Innovations Systems, Cluster Knowledge Networks and Firm Level Capabilities in Italy and Chile', *International Journal of Technology and Globalisation*, 3:2–3 (2007), pp. 190–223.

12. Maskell, 'Towards a Knowledge-Based Theory of the Geographical Cluster'.

13. For an extensive discussion of the notion of trust and how it pertains to sociological theories of order and social stability, see B. A. Misztal, *Trust in Modern Societies* (Cambridge: Polity Press, 1996).

14. S. Breschi and F. Malerba, 'The Geography of Innovation and Economic Clustering: Some Introductory Notes', *Industrial and Corporate Change*, 10 (2001), pp. 817–33; R. A. Boschma, 'Proximity and Innovation: A Critical Assessment', *Regional Studies*, 39:1 (2005), pp. 61–74.

15. D. Keeble and F. Wilkinson, 'Collective Learning and Knowledge Development in the Evolution of Regional Clusters of High Technology SMEs in Europe', *Regional Studies*, 33:4 (1999), pp. 295–303.
16. P. Maskell and A. Malmberg, 'Localised Learning and Industrial Competitiveness', *Cambridge Journal of Economics*, 23:2 (1999), pp. 167–86.
17. M. E. Porter, *The Competitive Advantage of Nations* (London: Macmillan, 1990); and M. E. Porter, 'Clusters and the New Economics of Competition', *Harvard Business Review* (November–December 1998).
18. Krugman, *Geography and Trade*.
19. Maskell, 'Towards a Knowledge-Based Theory of the Geographical Cluster', p. 932.
20. Aldrich, *Organizations Evolving*; M. Ruef and M. Lounsbury, 'Introduction: The Sociology of Entrepreneurship', in M. Ruef and M. Lounsbury (eds), *The Sociology of Entrepreneurship*, Research in the Sociology of Organizations, no. 25 (Amsterdam and London: Elsevier JAI, 2007), pp. 1–29.
21. Glade, 'Approaches to a Theory of Entrepreneurial Formation', p. 251.
22. P. D. Reynolds, 'Sociology and Entrepreneurship: Concepts and Contributions', *Entrepreneurship, Theory and Practice*, 16:2 (1991), pp. 47–70.
23. R. S. Breckenridge and I. M Taplin, "Entrepreneurship, Industrial Policy and Clusters: The Growth of the NC Wine Industry', in L. A Keister (ed.), *Entrepreneurship* (London: Elsevier, 2005), pp. 209–30.
24. Ruef and Lounsbury, 'Introduction', p. 20.
25. M. Weber, *The History of Commercial Partnerships in the Middle*, trans. L. Kaelber (Lanham, MD: Rowman & Littlefield, 2003).
26. E. Giuliani and M. Bell, 'The Micro-Determinants of Meso-Level Learning and Innovation: Evidence from a Chilean Wine Cluster', *Research Policy*, 34:1 (2005), pp. 47–68.
27. B. G. Carruthers and S. L. Babb, *Economy/Society: Markets, Meanings, and Social Structure* (Thousand Oaks, CA: Pine Forge, 2000).
28. U. Staber, 'The Structure of Networks in Industrial Districts', *International Journal of Urban and Regional Research*, 25:3 (2001), pp. 537–52, on p. 537.
29. B. Uzzi, 'Social Structure and Competition in Interfirm Networks: The Paradox of Embeddedness', *Administrative Science Quarterly*, 42 (1997), pp. 35–67.
30. J. Podolny, 'Market Uncertainty and the Social Character of Economic Exchange', *Administrative Science Quarterly*, 39 (1994), pp. 458–83; R. Burt, 'The Contingent Value of Social Capital', *Administrative Science Quarterly*, 42 (1997), pp. 339–65.
31. Staber, 'The Structure of Networks in Industrial Districts'.
32. Uzzi, 'Social Structure and Competition in Interfirm Networks'.
33. R. Burt, *Structural Holes: The Social Structure of Competition* (Cambridge, MA: Harvard University Press, 1992).
34. Maskell and Malmberg, 'Localised Learning and Industrial Competitiveness'.
35. J. Podolny, 'Networks as the Pipes and Prisms of the Market', *American Journal of Sociology*, 30 (2001), pp. 311–34.
36. P. Marsden and K. Campbell, 'Measuring Tie Strength', *Social Forces*, 63 (1984), pp. 482–501; M. Granovetter, 'Economic Action and Social Structure: The Problem of Embeddedness', *American Journal of Sociology*, 91 (1985), pp. 481–510.
37. Staber, 'The Structure of Networks in Industrial Districts'.
38. Aldrich, *Organizations Evolving*.
39. U. Staber and H. Aldrich, 'Cross National Similarities in the Personal Networks of Small Business Owners', *Canadian Journal of Sociology*, 20 (1995), pp. 441–67.

40. Uzzi, 'Social Structure and Competition in Interfirm Networks'.
41. See F. Lissoni, 'Knowledge Codification and the Geography of Innovation: The Case of Brescia Mechanical Cluster', *Research Policy*, 30 (2001), pp. 1479–500.
42. E.-J. Visser and P. de Langen, 'The Importance and Quality of Governance in the Chilean Wine Industry', *GeoJournal*, 65 (2006), pp. 177–97.
43. P. DiMaggio, 'Constructing an Organizational Field as a Professional Project: US Art Museums, 1920–1940' in W. W. Powell and P. DiMaggio (eds), *The New Institutionalism in Organizational Analysis* (Chicago, IL: University of Chicago Press, 1991), pp. 267–92.
44. M. Guillén, *The Taylorized Beauty of the Mechanical* (Princeton, NJ: Princeton University Press, 2006).
45. Inkpen and Tsang, 'Social Capital, Networks and Knowledge Transfer'.
46. S. Schrader, 'Informal Technology Transfer between Firms: Cooperation through Informal Trading', *Research Policy*, 20 (1991), pp. 153–70.
47. Giuliani, 'The Selective Nature of Knowledge Networks in Clusters'.
48. A. Amin and N. Thrift, *Globalization, Institutions and Regional Development in Europe* (Oxford: Oxford University Press, 1994), pp. 14–19.
49. A good wine related example of this is the growth of organizations in Napa Valley California since the 1970s. As the industry developed in that area and acquired legitimacy and status, so too did the role of vintners' organizations as well as governmental regulatory bodies in establishing and enforcing operating practices. Both have had a significant impact upon how firms behave on a daily basis as well as creating parameters for best practices that have aided the sector's legitimacy and reinforced its high status. On the growth of such associations in Napa Valley, California, and for a full discussion of these themes, see J. Conaway, *The Far side of Eden* (Boston, MA: Mariner Books, 2003); and Coleman, *Wine Politics*.
50. S. Pinch, N. Henry, M. Jenkins and S. Tallman, 'From "Industrial Districts" to "Knowledge Clusters": A Model of Knowledge Dissemination and Competitive Advantage in Industrial Agglomerations', *Journal of Economic Geography*, 3 (2003), pp. 373–88.
51. J. Delacroix, A. Swaminathan and M. E. Solt, 'Density Dependence versus Population Dynamics: An Ecological Study of Failings in the California Wine Industry', *American Sociological Review*, 54 (1989), pp. 245–62; A. Swaminathan, 'Resource Partitioning and the Evolution of Specialist Organizations: The Role of Location and Identity in the U.S. Wine Industry', *Academy of Management Journal*, 44:2 (2001), pp. 1169–85.
52. F. Scott Morton and J. Podolny, 'Love or Money? The Effects of Owner Motivation in the California Wine Industry', *Journal of Industrial Economics*, 50:4 (2002), pp. 431–56.
53. W. Zhao, 'Social Categories, Classification Systems, and Determinant of Wine Price in the California and French Wine Industries' *Sociological Perspectives*, 51:1 (2008), pp. 163–99.
54. On Chile, see Visser and de Langen, 'The Importance and Quality of Governance in the Chilean Wine Industry'; Bell and Giuliani, 'Catching Up in the Global Wine Industry'. On Italy, see Giuliani, 'The Selective Nature of Knowledge Networks in Clusters'; A. Morrison and R. Rabellotti, 'Knowledge and Information Networks: Evidence from an Italian Wine Local System', *CESPRI* (Milan: Universita Commerciale 'Luigi Bocconi', 2005).
55. Giuliani and Bell, 'The Micro-Determinants of Meso-Level Learning and Innovation'.
56. R. Gulati, *Managing Network Resources* (Oxford: Oxford University Press, 2007).

2 From the Beginnings to Prohibition

1. W. L. Saunders (ed.), *The Colonial Records of North Carolina*, 10 vols (Raleigh, NC: P. M. Hale, 1886–90), vol. 4, p. 919 (1749).
2. Ibid., vol. 4, p. 6 (1734).
3. Ibid.
4. T. Pinney, *A History of Wine in America: From the Beginnings to Prohibition* (Berkeley, CA: University of California Press, 1989), p. 62.
5. Near the James River such vines were afforded a magnificent scale by one author who reported 'a great store of Vines in bigness of a man's thigh up to the tops of the Trees in Great abundance'. Cited in ibid., p. 13.
6. L. D. Adams, *The Wines of America* (Boston, MA: Houghton Mifflin, 1973), p. 43.
7. Pinney, *From the Beginnings to Prohibition*, p. 12.
8. Adams, *The Wines of America*, p. 19.
9. Ibid., p. 20.
10. Ibid., p. 19.
11. Pinney, *From the Beginnings to Prohibition*, p. 28.
12. Ibid., p. 28.
13. C. O. Cathey, *Agriculture in North Carolina before the Civil War* (Raleigh, NC: State Department of Archives and History, 1966).
14. Quoted in ibid., p. 13.
15. According to Leon Adams this grape variety is attributed to John Alexander, gardener to John Penn, Lieutenant Governor of Pennsylvania, who found the vine growing near Philadelphia and planted it in the Lieutenant Governor's garden. It proved resistant to the cold winters and pests that killed the European vines and was planted elsewhere, including Thomas Jefferson's garden in Virginia. Adams, *The Wines of America*, p. 43.
16. Quoted in ibid., p. 20.
17. As with any legend, much of the story about Raleigh seeking out such vines then planting them in his settlement on Roanoke Island, only for one such vine to remain to the present day, is undoubtedly a myth. It makes interesting reading and the fact that very large vines exist probably helps account for its enthusiastic retelling. Given the mysterious disappearance of the settlers of that early colony, perhaps subsequent generations were desperate to find some evidence of human continuity, albeit in the form of a vine. For further discussion of this story, see Gohdes, *Scuppernong*.
18. J. Lawson, *A New Voyage to Carolina*, ed. H. T. Lefler (Chapel Hill, NC: University of North Carolina Press, 1967), p. 108.
19. Pinney, *From the Beginnings to Prohibition*, p. 60.
20. Ibid., p. 62.
21. A. L. Fries (ed.), *Records of the Moravians in North Carolina*, 12 vols (Raleigh, NC: Edwards & Broughton Print. Co., 1922–69), vol. 3, p. 1083.
22. Ibid., vol. 3, p. 1084.
23. Diary of the Congregation in Salem, in ibid., vol. 4, p. 1604.
24. Ibid., vol. 4, p. 1782.
25. Ibid., vol. 4, p. 1722.
26. Salem Boards Ministries, in ibid., vol. 6, p. 2737.
27. Ibid., vol. 5, p. 2392.
28. Despite the abundance of vines throughout the Carolinas and the ease with which grapes grew and could be harvested, few rural natives made wine because the preferred alco-

holic beverages were applejack, whiskey or a persimmom beer. Other than for medicinal purposes or for flavouring, the demand for wine was quite small, and the hot weather prevailing in the region at harvest time made storage difficult if large quantities were for some reason made. For further discussion of alcoholic beverage preferences in colonial times, see Gohdes, *Scuppernong*.

29. *Guide Book of North-Western North Carolina* (1878).
30. *Records of the Moravians in North Carolina*, vol. 6, pp. 2974–5.
31. It is certainly interesting to note the ubiquity of this beverage by the simple fact that it was the only one that was not capitalized in the listing!
32. *Raleigh Star*, 31 January 1811.
33. Ibid., 21 February 1811.
34. A. D. Watson, 'Society and Economy in Colonial Edgecombe County', *North Carolina Historical Review*, 50 (1973), pp. 231–55, on p. 233. It should be noted that many of the early immigrants to the area were of Scottish and Irish descent and brought their whiskey-making experience with them. Furthermore, it was more financially lucrative to use corn to make spirits than it was to sell it as an agricultural product, hence encouraging the development of more and more stills for whiskey production. For further discussion of such agricultural diversification, see ibid.
35. Gohdes, *Scuppernong*, p. 13.
36. Ibid.
37. *American Farmer*, 29 April 1825; 21 December 1832.
38. Pinney, *From the Beginnings to Prohibition*, p. 140.
39. *Writings of Thomas Jefferson, Memorial Edition*, 20 vols (Washington, DC: Thomas Jefferson Memorial Association, 1903–4), vol. 18, p. 318.
40. Gohdes, *Scuppernong*, p. 12.
41. Pinney, *From the Beginnings to Prohibition*, p. 149.
42. C. O. Cathey, *Agricultural Developments in North Carolina* (Chapel Hill, NC: University of North Carolina Press, 1956, p. 155.
43. *American Farmer*, 6 April 1827.
44. Adams, *The Wines of America*, p. 44.
45. Pinney, *From the Beginnings to Prohibition*, p. 181.
46. U. P. Hedrick, *Grapes and Wines from Home Vineyards* (New York: Oxford University Press, 1945), p. 167.
47. Gohdes, *Scuppernong*, p. 17.
48. US Patent Office, *Report of the Commissioner of Patents* (Washington, DC, 1853), p. 39.
49. Pinney, *From the Beginnings to Prohibition*, p. 223.
50. Gohdes, *Scuppernong*, p. 18.
51. Quoted in J. Mills and D. Tarmey, *A Guide to North Carolina's Wineries* (Winston-Salem, NC: John F. Blair Publishers, 2007), p. 7.
52. Ibid.
53. *Wilmington Commercial*, 11 August 1849.
54. Pinney, *From the Beginnings to Prohibition*, p. 219.
55. Ibid.
56. US Patent Office, *Report of the Commissioner of Patents* (Washington, DC, 1860), p. 78.
57. Gohdes, *Scuppernong*, p. 19.
58. Mills and Tarmey, *A Guide to North Carolina's Wineries*, p. xxii.
59. The well-known Missouri wine grower George Husmann continued to deride the grape and many others commented derisively on its 'foxy' taste. Gohdes, *Scuppernong*, p. 26.

60. Gohdes, *Scuppernong*, p. 29.
61. J. A. Oates, *The Story of Fayetteville*, 2nd edn (Fayetteville, NC: Fayetteville Woman's Club, 1950), p. 538.
62. Gohdes, *Scuppernong*, p. 32.
63. Ibid.
64. Pinney, *From the Beginnings to Prohibition*, p. 416.
65. Gohdes, *Scuppernong*, pp. 39–40.
66. Pinney, *From the Beginnings to Prohibition*, pp. 431–4.
67. Ibid., ch. 16.
68. Ibid., p. 416.
69. Gohdes, *Scuppernong*, p. 66.
70. Ibid., p. 81.

3 Post-Prohibition to the 1990s

1. Quoted in Gohdes, *Scuppernong*, p. 77.
2. See T. Pinney, *A History of Wine in America: From Prohibition to the Present* (Berkeley, CA: University of California Press, 2005).
3. It should be noted that years of Prohibition did not necessarily quell the urge to drink for many Americans, with the result that people were willing to consort with 'criminals' in order to obtain the beverage of their choice. Whilst such activities did not institutionalize illegal behaviour they did create a climate of tolerance towards law-breaking by a sizeable segment of the otherwise law-abiding population.
4. Pinney, *From Prohibition to the Present*, p. 40.
5. Gohdes, *Scuppernong*, p. 78.
6. Ibid.
7. *Raleigh News and Observer*, 15 August 1937.
8. Census of Agriculture data-collection methods, at various time points, are sufficiently different to make longitudinal comparisons difficult. Initially they included all farms but of vine-bearing age only, then all vines, then those with farms of more than 20 vines and finally farms with sales of more than $2,500. For instance the decline in pounds harvested between 1934 (14,650,957) and 1944 (1,981,057) reflects differences in measurement rather than a dramatic reduction in crop sizes.
9. Pinney, *From Prohibition to the Present*, p. 187.
10. Gohdes, *Scuppernong*, p. 87.
11. Pinney, *From Prohibition to the Present*, p. 188.
12. Gohdes, *Scuppernong*, p. 88.
13. Adams, *The Wines of America*, p. 34.
14. Pinney, *From Prohibition to the Present*, p. 37.
15. His major adversary was Congressman Clarence Cannon of Missouri, chairman of the House Appropriations Committee and a lifelong Prohibitionist who was once quoted as saying 'no federal money shall go to any fermentation industry'. Since he was able to block appropriations to agriculture until he was assured there was no reference to winemaking, he was successful in stymieing Tugwell's initiatives. Ironically, it was only on Cannon's death in 1964 that two Federal wine-quality research projects were quickly approved and implemented. For further details, see Adams, *The Wines of America*, p. 30.
16. Quoted in ibid., p. 47.
17. Ibid.

18. After his death, his heirs continued his ambitious expansion by acquiring vineyards in California to complement those in New York State. Bottling was done in a Brooklyn plant until it was closed in 1958 and the famous Virginia Dare then became a largely California wine. They finally liquidated their business in 1961, selling off the numerous assets to a Fresno based firm, Alta Vineyards.

19. Pinney, *From Prohibition to the Present*, p. 41.

20. G. A. Mathia, *Economic Opportunities for Muscadine Grapes in North Carolina*, A. E. Information series no. 128 (Raleigh, NC: North Carolina State University, 1966).

21. Issues such as labour use and revenue stream comparisons with tobacco, cotton and strawberries were evaluated, as well as potential yields per acre. In each case models were developed for different farm sizes (5 acres, 15 acres, 29 acres, 56 acres and 153 acres). See ibid., pp. 23–36.

22. See http://www.ncmuscadine.org/html.

23. G. A. Mathia, A. Beals, N. C. Miller and D. E. Carroll Jr, *Economic Opportunities for Profitable Winery Operations in North Carolina*, Economics Information Report no. 49 (Raleigh, NC: North Carolina State University, 1977).

24. Information on Duplin Wine Cellars comes largely from the winery's own published history and the North Carolina History Project: Duplin Winery, at http://www.north-carolinahistory.org/encyclopedia/124/entry.

25. Of course there are many accounts of the preponderance of stills used by locals in the central and western parts of the state where dry counties were the norm. The early history of NASCAR in fact relies upon the not always mythical part played by bootleggers supplying large swathes of the region with illegal alcohol. For further details of this colourful history, see R. Hall, 'Before NASCAR: The Corporate and Civic Promotion of Automobile Racing in the American South 1903–1927, *Journal of Southern History*, 68 (2002), pp. 629–68.

26. R. Drew, *The North Carolina Muscadine – A Historical Timeline* (Wilmington, NC: Drew Image.com, 2006).

27. For a succinct discussion of the history and rationale behind hybrids as well as their current status in North Carolina, see N. Oches, 'Hybrids or Not?', *On the Vine* (May–June 2007), pp. 12–13.

28. Adams, *The Wines of America*, p. 29.

29. New York had taken the lead to understand many of the diseases that afflicted grape-growing in the east, publishing a bulletin on this is 1915. See R. D. Anthony, *Vinifera Grapes in New York*, Bulletin 432 (Geneva, NY: New York Agricultural Experiment Station, 1915). The programme advocated breeding and cultivation practices that would control the insect pests and native diseases such as black rot and mildew. Subsequent experimental work with *vinifera* was carried out by the United States Department of Agriculture at its Arlington, VA, station during the dry years.

30. In the case of the embryonic wine industry in Virginia during the 1960s, individuals were civil servants, gentleman farmers, lawyers, army officers and teachers – but no professional winemakers since there were none in that area. For further descriptions of winery growth in the Mid-Atlantic outside of North Carolina, see Pinney, *From Prohibition to the Present*; and Adams, *The Wines of America*.

31. L. Morton, *Winegrowing in Eastern America: An Illustrated Guide to Viticulture East of the Rockies* (Ithaca, NY: Cornell University Press, 1985).

32. Pinney, *From Prohibition to the Present*, p. 290.

33. Like North Carolina, the Virginia State Department of Agriculture had researched the viability and feasibility of grape growing and winemaking in that state. In 1977 the Grape Growers Advisory Committee had been formed and in 1980 the Farm Winery Act was passed to reduce taxes on local wineries, permit wholesale and retail sales without any minimum size restrictions. Further incentives for the emerging industry occurred in 1984 when the legislature created the Wine Marketing Program, followed by a state wine-tax supported Winegrowers Productivity Fund the following year that also provided a state oenologist and viticulturalist. Research and extension work has since developed at Virginia Polytechnic and State University. For further details, see Pinney, *From Prohibition to the Present*.

34. See Barbara Ensund's interview with Steve Shepard in Appellation America.com, 12 September 2006, at http://wine.appellationamerica.com/wine-review/217Steve-Shepard-Interview.html.

35. Interview with author, 24 July 2003.

36. William Cecil believed that a complete winery operation was consistent with his grandfather's intention of maintaining a working estate that was unambiguously in a European tradition. For more details on Biltmore's genesis, see B. Satterwhite, 'Biltomore Winery's Goal: Quality European Style Wines', *Vinifera Wine Growers Journal*, 12 (1985) pp. 85–9.

37. L. G. Somers, 'Grow Vinifera in North Carolina! But Where? Hope for the Tobacco State', *Vinifera Wine Growers Journal*, 13 (1986), pp. 90–7; R. de T. Lawrence, 'Helping North Carolina to Get Growing: One of the Most Viniculturally Undeveloped States', *Vinifera Wine Growers Journal*, 14 (1987), pp. 221–4.

4 Emergence of a Wine Cluster

1. Robert de Treville Lawrence was a retired State Department officer who had a small *vinifera* vineyard in Virginia and was one of the founders of the Vinefera Wine Growers Association in 1973. This quote is taken from the *Vinifera Wine Growers Journal*, the mouthpiece of the Association, volume 14 (1987), p. 221. He was a passionate advocate for *vinifera*-growing east of the Rockies and, like many of the vineyard owners featured in this chapter, brought resources from his previous job that allowed him to fund his vineyard operations.

2. F. V. Tursi, S. E. White and S. McQuilkin, *Lost Empire: The Fall of R. J. Reynolds Tobacco Company* (Winston-Salem, NC: Winston Salem Journal, 2000), p. 392.

3. Breckenridge and Taplin, 'Entrepreneurship, Industrial Policy and Clusters', pp. 201–30.

4. This is a somewhat curious omission since such registration would enable them to be taxed at a lower rate than regular land. Rather than an attempt to avoid taxation they are actually paying far more than they should given the rising tax values of potential residential land in these areas.

5. *On the Vine* (April–June 2006), p. 4.

6. Details come from interview with author, 26 May 2003.

7. Quoted in Mills and Tarmey, *A Guide to North Carolina's Wineries*, p. 15.

8. E. Williams, 'The Teachers are Learning', *On the Vine* (October–December 2005), pp. 4–5, on p. 4.

9. Ibid.

10. See Thornton, 'The Sociology of Entrepreneurship'.

11. T. W. Schultz, 'The Value of the Ability to Deal with Disequilibria', *Journal of Economic Literature*, 13:3 (1975), pp. 827–46.
12. Details come from interview between the author and Sean McRitchie, 26 May 2003.
13. Interview for *Triad Style Magazine* (20 November 2002), p. 10.
14. Quoted in Mills and Tarmey, *A Guide to North Carolina's Wineries*, p. 136.
15. Interview in *Triad Style Magazine* (20 November 2002), p. 10.
16. Breckenridge and Taplin, 'Entrepreneurship, Industrial Policy and Clusters', p. 214.
17. As the only tobacco farmer in Congress, United States Representative Bob Etheridge, D-2nd, said in 2003: 'I don't know anything else you can plant on an ace of land that's legal that will produce as much money in America', *Winston-Salem Journal*, 31 August 2003.
18. *Wall Street Journal*, 2 April 2003.
19. Known as the Master Settlement Agreement (MSA), it also contained stipulations to aid states where farmers were heavily dependent upon tobacco.
20. *Winston-Salem Journal*, 31 August 2003.
21. Quoted in Mills and Tarmey, *A Guide to North Carolina's Wineries*, p. 140.
22. Quoted in S. Youngquist, 'Field of Growth', *Winston-Salem Journal*, 2 October 2005, p. A10.
23. Pinney, *From Prohibition to the Present*, p. 289.

5 Market Growth, Differentiation and Legitimacy

1. M. K. Metzger, North Carolina Wine Summit, Raleigh, NC, 2008 (North Carolina Wine and Grape Council, 2009).
2. E. Williams, 'Duplin's Wild Ride', *On the Vine* (January–February 2007), pp. 4–5, on p. 4.
3. Wine trails have been particularly successful in the Finger Lakes Region of New York. Area wineries promote their proximity to each other as well as ancillary features such as restaurants and hotels in order to attract visitors who might not visit a single winery. Sometimes transportation is provided in the form of a bus that shuttles visitors between wineries and other sites of interest in the area. In North Carolina, the Winton-Salem Visitors' centre provides a map, self-guided compact disc and information on a series of Yadkin Valley wineries close to the city.
4. Quoted in Williams, 'Duplin's Wild Ride', p. 5.
5. For a discussion of what goes into appellation status, see P. McRitchie, 'Another First for North Carolina – but What's an Appellation?', *On the Vine* (July–October 2003), pp. 10–11.
6. The concept of club good refers to generally available information that is crucial to overall network efficiency and accessed by all actors within the network. For further elaboration of this concept, see Giuliani, 'The Selective Nature of Knowledge Networks in Clusters'.
7. There is a long tradition of fermenting fruits other than grapes and making them into wine. Examples included apples, berries and peaches. While many such enterprises were small and often for individual consumption or a restricted local market, there were notable exceptions. For example, the Tenner Brothers Winery that was established in Charlotte in 1935 made wine from blackberries, peaches and youngberries in addition to muscadine. By 1949 it was making large volume of wines, given its storage capacity of 600,000 gallons, but as noted earlier it moved to South Carolina in 1953 to take advantage of more favourable tax laws. Throughout the south there were many other examples

of mid-sized fruit wine producers. Today, many North Carolina vineyards make a fruit wine as a supplement to their other wines, sold at a lower price point and overtly appealing to consumers with a non-complicated sweet wine taste preference. For further examples and more extensive discussion, see Pinney, *From Prohibition to the Present*.

8. In 2006 The North Carolina Muscadine Grape Association (NCMGA) held a series of meetings and developed a strategic plan for the industry that would address image and economic feasibility issues.

9. E. Romanelli and O. M. Khessina, 'Regional Industrial Identity: Cluster Configurations and Economic Development', *Organization Science*, 16 (2005), pp. 344–58.

10. Giuliani, 'The Selective Nature of Knowledge Networks in Clusters'.

11. see G. Becattini, 'The Marshallian Industrial District as a Socio-Economic Notion', in F. Pyke, G. Becattini and W. Sengenberger (eds), *Industrial Districts and Inter-Firm Competition in Italy* (Geneva, NY: International Institute for Labour Studies, 1990), pp. 37–51; M. Storper, 'The Resurgence of Regional Economies, Ten Years Later: The Region as a Nexus of Untraded Interdependencies', *European Urban and Regional Studies*, 2 (1995), pp. 122–91; Porter, 'Clusters and the New Economics of Competition'.

12. Mills and Tarmey, *A Guide to North Carolina's Wineries*, p. 176.

13. Ibid., p. 239.

14. See 'Strategic Plan for the North Carolina Muscadine Grape Industry' (North Carolina Muscadine Growers Association, 2007). Also, SERA reports by the Muscadine Grape Research and Extension in North Carolina, put out by North Carolina State University's Department of Horticultural Science, provide routine information on growing conditions, research and extension activities of use to muscadine growers.

15. The NC Cooperative Extension Service at North Carolina State University published a detailed guide for growers in 2003 entitled 'Muscadine Grape Production Guide for North Carolina'. This guide offers precise instructions for vineyard development and management.

16. Quoted in Mills and Tarmey, *A Guide to North Carolina's Wineries*, p. 79.

17. For further background details on the winery, see E. Williams, 'Precious Stones', *On The Vine* (July–August 2007), pp. 4–5.

18. Mills and Tarmey, *A Guide to North Carolina's Wineries*, p. 162.

19. Old North State Co-op was started in 2001 by 21 growers in the area with grants from the United States Department of Agriculture's Rural Development Program and the Appalachian Regional Commission. The Co-op was located in a purchased building in downtown Mt Airy and its aim was to provide a winery for members to make and market their wine, as well as train people for the industry and be a business incubator. Eventual membership reached 50 until in 2006 it ran into serious financial difficulties. Just prior to foreclosure, it was purchased by several of the original members and operates now as Old North State Winery. It continues to serve as a *de facto* outreach service by providing a 'hands-on' extension facility for students at nearby Surry Community College.

20. For further details of this winery and its owner, see M. Conley, 'McDowell County Wines Win Awards', *Winston-Salem Journal*, 9 May 2009.

21. In numerous interviews I was intrigued at the persistent reference to a desired 2,500-case production goal for start-up wineries. I started asking about this particular number and was told that winery consultants who many had used had this (as well as a 5,000-case production) as their business model for a start-up winery. Those that did not use consultants nonetheless operated with such guidelines following discussions with existing properties that had adopted this model.

22. MKF Research, 'Economic Impact of North Carolina Wine and Grapes' (St Helena, CA: MKF Research LLC, 2007).

23. See C. Hodnett, 'Fruit of the Vine: Owner of Patria Properties is Using her Expertise to Help Clients Buy and Sell Wine Properties', *Winston-Salem Journal*, 13 July 2008.

24. For further conceptual clarification of how knowledge structures undergo change as network clusters evolve, see G. Dosi, 'Opportunities, Incentives and the Collective Pattern of Technological Change', *Economic Journal*, 107 (1997), pp. 1530–47; and Giuliani, 'The Selective Nature of Knowledge Networks in Clusters'.

25. For a further discussion of this programme and its staff, see N. Oches 'Appalchian State Chemist Looks for Ways to Help the Viticulture Industry', *On the Vine* (October– December 2005), pp. 8–9.

26. These include Trevor Phister, who teaches and researches in oenology (a 75 per cent research and 25 per cent extension appointment), and the recent appointment of Sara Spayd, who is the Extension Viticulturalist and teaches several courses in this area. She came from Washington State where she spent 26 years working as a Research/Extension oenologist and thus brings a level of expertise hitherto lacking in this division.

27. Further discussion on the various laws and their impact can be found in S. McDavid, 'State Legislature Fine Tuning Laws related to Viticulture', *On the Vine* (July–October 2005), pp. 10–11; and B. Corwin, 'State Legislators Back Industry with New Laws', *On the Vine* (January–February 2006), p. 19.

6 Cluster Consolidation

1. Jerry Douglas, Biltmore Estate Winery, lecture at Appalachian State University conference on North Carolina wine, 2008.

2. M. Hastings, 'Fine Wines of North Carolina: Growers, Vintners Learning, Patiently, What Works Best', *Winston-Salem Journal*, 24 January 2008.

3. It is difficult to determine the number of grape growers who have stopped production because many are farmers and they simply switch crops. Even examining harvest figures can be deceptive since growers have been exhorted to pay more attention to quality than quantity and this has resulted in yields per acre declining in many instances.

4. See Scott Morton and Podolny, 'Love or Money?'; Podolny, 'Market Uncertainty and the Social Character of Economic Exchange'; Podolny, 'Networks as the Pipes and Prisms of the Market'.

5. At least 50 per cent of winery websites in their 'about us/history' section profess a desire to realize a dream that embodies changing lifestyle references.

6. Scott Morton and Podolny, 'Love or Money?'.

7. B. Corwin, 'Something Special: Swan Creek's New Appellation Second in State', *On the Vine* (May–June 2007), pp. 4–7.

8. This resembles an inverted football goal and is designed to maximize growth potential by splitting the vine into two sides.

9. J. Bank, 'Seeing Double: North Carolina's Second Designated AVA', *On the Vine* (July– August 2008), p. 9.

10. I. M. Taplin, 'From Cooperation to Competition: Market Transformation among Elite Napa Valley Wine Producers', *International Journal of Wine Business Research*, 22:1 (2010), pp. 6–26.

11. I. M. Taplin and R. S. Breckenridge, 'Large Firms, Legitimation and Industry Identity: The Growth of the North Carolina Wine Industry', *Social Science Journal*, 45 (2008), pp. 352–60.

12. Visser and de Langen, 'The Importance of Quality of Governance in the Chilean Wine Industry'.

13. For further details, see 2009 North Carolina Wine Summit report from the North Carolina Wine and Grape Council. Other topics are crop-level management for certain varietals, clone and cultivar evaluations, analysis of phenolic compounds in North Carolina grapes, nutrient response in *vinifera* grapes and soil erosion in steep-sloped vineyards. Also, the Wine and Grape Council issues periodic emails informing members of technical issues that should be addressed at key times of the year. Such details are a product of ongoing research-reporting by various agencies and evidence of the public/private partnership that has been developed.

14. These are wines that typically win in State Fair contests. For example at the 2009 North Carolina State Fair Wine Competition, a Childress Cabernet Franc 2006 was 'best of show' and 'best red *vinifera* wine'.

15. For a discussion of various success stories in the growth of this varietal in North Carolina, see Williams, 'The Teachers are Learning', where he quotes interviews with some of the state's leading winemakers who have praised the virtues of this grape.

16. Junius Lindsay Vineyards was started with a 2-acre vineyard devoted to Rhone varietals planted in 2004 by Michael Zimmerman and his wife Lucia Gonzales. It is located in the southern corner of the Yadkin Valley AVA, approximately 15 miles south of Winston-Salem. They have gradually expanded their acreage and opened their tasting room in 2009. However, their wine is vinted by Mark Friszolowski at nearby Childress Vineyards who works closely with Michael in providing viticultural oversight. The close attention to detail inherent in this contractual partnership, and working with a winemaker with a very established reputation and understanding of the distinctive features of local terroir and growing conditions, has enabled the winery, according to local experts, to gain its reputation at such an early stage.

17. There are some exceptions to this, such as RayLen's Bordeaux blends Category Five (named after hurricanes that occasionally affect the state), Carolinius, Shelton's Reserve Claret, and Hanover Park's Michael's Blend and 1897, both Bordeaux blends that use the best grapes and are aged for a longer time period before release.

18. Williams, 'The Teachers are Learning', p. 4.

19. Ibid.

20. This raises an interesting side note on the notion of status as an attractive element for non-winery owners. People claim utility from close association with winery owners, even going so far as to volunteer their time at harvest or helping out at the winery. It is often these people who are the biggest customers for the wines of the winery.

21. If one peruses the major wine periodicals such as *Wine Spectator* or the writings of newspaper wine columnists such as the *Financial Times*'s Jancis Robinson and the *Wall Street Journal*'s John and Dorothy Gaiter, one is alerted to the name association of certain varietals with specific regions of the world. This does not necessarily mean that such varietals cannot be grown successfully elsewhere; it is merely that over time a certain brand recognition has emerged that has favoured the marketing of the signature grape in those regions.

22. Quoted by Youngquist, in *Winston-Salem Journal*, 2 October 2005.

23. It is a flavour and taste that has always concerned me and several friends who drink North Carolina wines. But we have also been amazed at how others seem either not to notice it or not to be concerned about it.
24. Quoted in *Winston-Salem Journal*, 5 October 2005.
25. See J. Bhadury and Troy, S. P. 'Business Development Needs of the Wine Industry in the Yadkin Valley, Swan Creek and Haw River Valley Viticultural Areas' (2008), at http://www.uncg/edu/bae/or.
26. M. Evans, C. Pollard and G. Holder, *Discover North Carolina Wines: A Wine Tourism Visitor Profile Study* (Boone, NC: Appalachian State University, 2008).
27. An interesting footnote is that Kevin Moore's grandfather, Ernest Moore, made communion wine for area churches on this property in the early 1900s. So in some respects Kevin is merely continuing a winemaking tradition.

Conclusion

1. B. Arthur, 'Competing Technologies, Increasing Returns, and Lock-In by Historical Events', *Economic Journal*, 99 (1989), pp. 116–31.
2. Fligstein, *The Architecture of Markets*, p. 31.
3. Ibid.
4. A. B. Jaffee, M. Trajtenberg and R. Henderson, 'Geographic Localization of Knowledge Spillovers as Evidence from Patent Citations', *Quarterly Journal of Economics*, 108:3 (1993), pp. 577–98.
5. Porter, *The Competitive Advantage of Nations*; Best, *The New Competition*; Baptista, 'Do Innovations Diffuse Faster within Geographic Clusters?'
6. Giuliani, 'The Selective Nature of Knowledge Networks in Clusters'.
7. Fligstein, *The Architecture of Markets*, p. 31.
8. See, for example, R. V. Gould, 'Approaches to a Theory of Entrepreneurial Formation', *Explorations in Entrepreneurial History*, 4:5 (2002), pp. 245–59.
9. Bhadury and Troy, 'Business Development Needs of the Wine Industry in the Yadkin Valley'.

WORKS CITED

Newspapers and Periodicals

American Farmer.

Guide Book of North-Western North Carolina.

Raleigh News and Observer.

Raleigh Star.

Triad Style Magazine.

US Patent Office, *Report of the Commissioner of Patents.*

Wall Street Journal.

Wilmington Commercial.

Winston-Salem Journal.

Published Sources

Adams, L. D., *The Wines of America* (Boston, MA: Houghton Mifflin, 1973).

Adler, P. S., and S.-W. Kwon, 'Social Capital: Prospect for a New Concept', *Academy of Management Review*, 27:1 (2002), pp. 17–40.

Aldrich, H., *Organizations Evolving* (London: Sage Publications, 2005).

Aldrich, H., and R. Waldinger, 'Ethnicity and Entrepreneurship', *Annual Review of Sociology*, 16 (1990), pp. 111–35.

Amin, A., and N. Thrift, *Globalization, Institutions and Regional Development in Europe* (Oxford: Oxford University Press, 1994).

Anthony, R. D., *Vinifera Grapes in New York*, Bulletin 432 (Geneva, NY: New York Agricultural Experiment Station, 1915).

Arthur, B., 'Competing Technologies, Increasing Returns, and Lock-In by Historical Events', *Economic Journal*, 99 (1989), pp. 116–31.

Bank, J., 'Seeing Double: North Carolina's Second Designated AVA', *On the Vine* (July–August 2008), p. 9.

Baptista, R., 'Do Innovations Diffuse Faster within Geographical Clusters?', *International Journal of Industrial Organization*, 18 (2000), pp. 515–35.

Baptista, R., and P. Swann, 'Do Firms in Clusters Innovate More?', *Research Policy*, 27:5 (1998), pp. 525–40

Beaudry C., and S. Breschi, 'Are Firms in Clusters Really More Innovative?', *Economics of Innovation and New Technology*, 12:4 (2003), pp. 325–42.

Becattini, G., 'The Marshallian Industrial District as a Socio-Economic Notion', in F. Pyke, G. Becattini and W. Sengenberger (eds), *Industrial Districts and Inter-Firm Competition in Italy* (Geneva, NY: International Institute for Labour Studies, 1990), pp. 37–51.

Bell M., and E. Giuliani, 'Catching Up in the Global Wine Industry; Innovations Systems, Cluster Knowledge Networks and Firm Level Capabilities in Italy and Chile', *International Journal of Technology and Globalisation*, 3:2–3 (2007), pp. 190–223.

Best, M., *The New Competition: Institutions of Industrial Restructuring* (Cambridge, MA: Harvard University Press, 1990).

Bhadury, J., and S. P. Troy, 'Business Development Needs of the Wine Industry in the Yadkin Valley, Swan Creek, and Haw River Viticultural Areas' (2008), at http://www.uncg.edu/bae/or.

Boschma, R. A., 'Proximity and Innovation: A Critical Assessment', *Regional Studies*, 39:1 (2005), pp. 61–74.

Bourdieu, P., 'The Forms of Capital', in J. G. Richardson (ed.), *Handbook of Theory and Research for the Sociology of Education* (London: Greenwood Press, 1986), pp. 241–58.

Breckenridge, R. S., and I. M. Taplin, 'Entrepreneurship, Industrial Policy and Clusters: The Growth of the NC Wine Industry', in L. A Keister (ed.), *Entrepreneurship* (London: Elsevier, 2005), pp. 209–30.

Breschi, S., and F. Malerba, 'The Geography of Innovation and Economic Clustering: Some Introductory Notes', *Industrial and Corporate Change*, 10 (2001), pp. 817–33.

Burt, R., *Structural Holes: The Social Structure of Competition* (Cambridge, MA: Harvard University Press, 1992).

—, 'The Contingent Value of Social Capital', *Administrative Science Quarterly*, 42 (1997), pp. 339–65.

Carruthers, B. G., and S. L. Babb, *Economy/Society: Markets, Meanings, and Social Structure* (Thousand Oaks, CA: Pine Forge, 2000).

Cathey, C. O., *Agricultural Developments in North Carolina* (Chapel Hill, NC: University of North Carolina Press, 1956).

—, *Agriculture in North Carolina before the Civil War* (Raleigh, NC: State Department of Archives and History, 1966).

Coase, R. H., 'The Problem of Social Cost', *Journal of Law and Economics*, 3 (1960), pp. 1–44.

Coleman, T., *Wine Politics* (Berkeley, CA: University of California Press, 2008).

Conaway, J., *The Far Side of Eden* (Boston, MA: Mariner Books, 2003).

Conley, M., 'McDowell County Wines Win Awards', *Winston-Salem Journal*, 9 May 2009.

Corwin, B., 'State Legislators Back Industry with New Laws', *On the Vine* (January–February 2006), p. 19.

—, 'Something Special: Swan Creek's New Appellation Second in State', *On the Vine* (May–June 2007), pp. 4–7.

Delacroix, J., A. Swaminathan and M. E. Solt, 'Density Dependence versus Population Dynamics: An Ecological Study of Failings in the California Wine Industry', *American Sociological Review*, 54 (1989), pp. 245–62.

DiMaggio, P., 'Constructing an Organizational Field as a Professional Project: US Art Museums, 1920–1940', in W. W. Powell, and P. DiMaggio (eds), *The New Institutionalism in Organizational Analysis* (Chicago, IL: University of Chicago Press, 1991), pp. 267–92.

Dosi, G., 'Opportunities, Incentives and the Collective Pattern of Technological Change', *Economic Journal*, 107 (1997), pp. 1530–47.

Drew, R., *The North Carolina Muscadine – A Historical Timeline* (Wilmington, NC: Drew Image.com, 2006).

Enright, M. J., 'Regional Clusters and Firm Strategy', in A. Chandler, P. Hagstrom and O. Solvell (eds), *The Dynamic Firm* (Oxford, Oxford University Press, 1998), pp. 315–42.

Ensund, B., Interview with Steve Shepard, in Appellation America.com, 12 September 2006, at http://wine.appellationamerica.com/wine-review/217Steve-Shepard-Interview.html.

Evans, M., C. Pollard and G. Holder, *Discover North Carolina Wines: A Wine Tourism Visitor Profile Study* (Boone, NC: Appalachian State University, 2008).

Fligstein, N., *The Architecture of Markets* (Princeton, NJ: Princeton University Press, 2001).

Fries, A. L. (ed.), *Records of the Moravians in North Carolina*, 12 vols (Raleigh, NC: Edwards & Broughton Print. Co., 1922–69).

Giuliani, E., 'The Selective Nature of Knowledge Networks in Clusters: Evidence from the Wine Industry', *Journal of Economic Geography*, 7 (2006), pp. 139–68.

Guiliani E., and M. Bell, 'The Micro-Determinants of Meso-Level Learning and Innovation: Evidence from a Chilean Wine Cluster', *Research Policy*, 34:1 (2005), pp. 47–68.

Glade, W. P., 'Approaches to a Theory of Entrepreneurial Formation', *Explorations in Entrepreneurial History*, 4:3 (1967), pp. 245–59.

Gohdes, C., *Scuppernong: North Carolina's Grape and its Wines* (Durham, NC: Duke University Press, 1982).

Gould, R. V., 'Approaches to a Theory of Entrepreneurial Formation', *Explorations in Entrepreneurial History*, 4:5 (2002), pp. 245–59.

Granovetter, M., 'Economic Action and Social Structure: The Problem of Embeddedness', *American Journal of Sociology*, 91 (1985), pp. 481–510.

Guillén, M., *The Taylorized Beauty of the Mechanical* (Princeton, NJ: Princeton University Press, 2006).

Gulati, R., *Managing Network Resources* (Oxford: Oxford University Press, 2007).

Hall, R., 'Before NASCAR: The Corporate and Civic Promotion of Automobile Racing in the American South 1903–1927', *Journal of Southern History*, 68 (2002), pp. 629–68.

Harrison, B., *Lean and Mean: The Changing Landscape of Corporate Power in the Age of Flexibility* (New York: Basic Books, 1994).

Hastings, M., 'Fine Wines of North Carolina: Growers, Vintners Learning, Patiently, What Works Best', *Winston-Salem Journal*, 24 January 2008.

Hedrick, U. P., *Grapes and Wines from Home Vineyards* (New York: Oxford University Press, 1945).

Hodnett, C., 'Fruit of the Vine: Owner of Patria Properties is Using her Expertise to Help Clients Buy and Sell Wine Properties', *Winston-Salem Journal*, 13 July 2008.

Inkpen, A., and E. Tsang, 'Social Capital, Networks and Knowledge Transfer', *Academy of Management Review*, 30:1 (2005), pp. 146–65.

Jaffee, A. B., M. Trajtenberg and R. Henderson, 'Geographic Localization of Knowledge Spillovers as Evidence from Patent Citations', *Quarterly Journal of Economics*, 108:3 (1993), pp. 577–98.

Jefferson, T., *Writings of Thomas Jefferson, Memorial Edition*, 20 vols (Washington, DC: Thomas Jefferson Memorial Association, 1903–4).

Keeble, D., and F. Wilkinson, 'Collective Learning and Knowledge Development in the Evolution of Regional Clusters of High Technology SMEs in Europe', *Regional Studies*, 33:4 (1999), pp. 295–303.

Krugman, P., *Geography and Trade* (Cambridge, MA: MIT Press, 1991).

Lawrence, R. de T., 'Helping North Carolina to Get Growing: One of the Most Viniculturally Undeveloped States', *Vinifera Wine Growers Journal*, 14 (1987), pp. 221–4.

Lawson, J., *A New Voyage to Carolina*, ed. H. T. Lefler (Chapel Hill, NC: University of North Carolina Press, 1967).

Light, I., and E. Bonacich, *Immigrant Entrepreneurs: Koreans in Los Angeles, 1965–1982* (Berkeley, CA: University of California Press, 1986).

Lissoni, F., 'Knowledge Codification and the Geography of Innovation: The Case of Brescia Mechanical Cluster', *Research Policy*, 30 (2001), pp. 1479–500.

McDavid, S., 'State Legislature Fine Tuning Laws related to Viticulture', *On the Vine* (July–October 2005), pp. 10–11.

McRitchie, P., 'Another First for North Carolina – but What's an Appellation?', *On the Vine* (Spring–Summer 2003), pp. 10–11.

Marsden P., and K. Campbell, 'Measuring Tie Strength', *Social Forces*, 63 (1984), pp. 482–501

Marshall, A., *Principles of Economics* (London: Macmillan, 1923).

Maskell, P., 'Towards a Knowledge-Based Theory of the Geographical Cluster', *Industrial and Corporate Change*, 10:4 (2001), pp. 921–43.

Maskell, P. and A. Malmberg, 'Localised Learning and Industrial Competitiveness', *Cambridge Journal of Economics*, 23:2 (1999), pp. 167–86.

Mathia, G. A., *Economic Opportunities for Muscadine Grapes in North Carolina*, A. E. Information Series no. 128 (Raleigh, NC: North Carolina State University, 1966).

Mathia, G. A., A. Beals, N. C. Miller and D. E. Carroll Jr, *Economic Opportunities for Profitable Winery Operations in North Carolina*, Economics Information Report no. 49 (Raleigh, NC: North Carolina State University, 1977).

MKF Research, 'Economic Impact of North Carolina Wine and Grapes' (St Helena, CA: MKF Research LLC, 2007).

Mills, J., and D. Tarmey, *A Guide to North Carolina's Wineries* (Winston-Salem, NC: John F. Blair Publishers, 2007).

Misztal, B. A., *Trust in Modern Societies* (Cambridge: Polity Press, 1996).

Morrison, A., and R. Rabellotti, 'Knowledge and Information Networks: Evidence from an Italian Wine Local System', *CESPRI* (Milan: Universita Commerciale 'Luigi Bocconi', 2005).

Morton, L., *Winegrowing in Eastern America: An Illustrated Guide to Viticulture East of the Rockies* (Ithaca, NY: Cornell University Press, 1985).

Oates, J. A., *The Story of Fayetteville*, 2nd edn (Fayetteville, NC: Fayetteville Woman's Club, 1950).

Oches, N., 'Appalachian State Chemist Looks for Ways to Help the Viticulture Industry', *On the Vine* (October–December 2005), pp. 8–9.

—, 'Hybrids or Not?', *On the Vine* (May–June 2007), pp. 12–13.

Pinch, S., N. Henry, M. Jenkins and S. Tallman, 'From "Industrial Districts" to "Knowledge Clusters": A Model of Knowledge Dissemination and Competitive Advantage in Industrial Agglomerations', *Journal of Economic Geography*, 3 (2003), pp. 373–88.

Pinney, T., *A History of Wine in America: From the Beginnings to Prohibition* (Berkeley, CA: University of California Press, 1989).

—, *A History of Wine in America: From Prohibition to the Present* (Berkeley, CA: University of California Press, 2005).

Piore, M., and C. Sabel, *The Second Industrial Divide* (New York: Basic Books, 1984).

Podolny, J., 'Market Uncertainty and the Social Character of Economic Exchange' *Administrative Science Quarterly*, 39 (1994), pp. 458–83.

—, 'Networks as the Pipes and Prisms of the Market', *American Journal of Sociology*, 30 (2001), pp. 311–34.

Porter, M. E., *The Competitive Advantage of Nations* (London: Macmillan, 1990).

—, 'Clusters and the New Economics of Competition', *Harvard Business Review* (November–December 1998).

Reynolds, P. D., 'Sociology and Entrepreneurship: Concepts and Contributions', *Entrepreneurship, Theory and Practice*, 16:2 (1991), pp. 47–70.

Romanelli, E., 'Organization Birth and Population Variety: A Community Perspective on Origins', *Research in Organizational Behavior*, 11 (1994), pp. 211–46.

Romanelli, E., and O. M. Khessina, 'Regional Industrial Identity: Cluster Configurations and Economic Development', *Organization Science*, 16 (2005), pp. 344–58.

Ruef, M., and M. Lounsbury, 'Introduction: The Sociology of Entrepreneurship', in M. Ruef and M. Lounsbury (eds), *The Sociology of Entrepreneurship*, Research in the Sociology of Organizations, no. 25 (Amsterdam and London: Elsevier JAI, 2007), pp. 1–29.

Satterwhite, B., 'Biltmore Winery's Goal: Quality European Style Wines', *Vinifera Wine Growers Journal*, 12 (1985) pp. 85–9.

Saxenian, A., *Regional Advantage: Culture and Competition in Silicon Valley and Route 128* (Cambridge, MA: Harvard University Press, 1994).

Saunders, W. L. (ed.), *The Colonial Records of North Carolina*, 10 vols (Raleigh, NC: P. M. Hale, 1886–90).

Schultz, T. W., 'The Value of the Ability to Deal with Disequilibria', *Journal of Economic Literature*, 13:3 (1975), pp. 827–46.

Scott Morton, F., and J. Podolny, 'Love or Money? The Effects of Owner Motivation in the California Wine Industry', *Journal of Industrial Economics*, 50:4 (2002), pp. 431–56.

Schrader, S., 'Informal Technology Transfer between Firms: Cooperation through Informal Trading', *Research Policy*, 20 (1991), pp. 153–70.

Somers, L. G., 'Grow Vinifera in North Carolina! But Where? Hope for the Tobacco State', *Vinifera Wine Growers Journal*, 13 (1986), pp. 90–7.

Sorenson, O., 'Social Networks and Industrial Geography', *Journal of Evolutionary Economics*, 13:5 (2003), pp. 513–27.

Staber, U., 'The Structure of Networks in Industrial Districts', *International Journal of Urban and Regional Research*, 25:3 (2001), pp. 537–52.

Staber, U., and H. Aldrich, 'Cross National Similarities in the Personal Networks of Small Business Owners', *Canadian Journal of Sociology*, 20 (1995), pp. 441–67.

Storper, M., 'The Resurgence of Regional Economies, Ten Years Later: The Region as a Nexus of Untraded Interdependencies', *European Urban and Regional Studies*, 2 (1995), pp. 122–91.

Swaminathan, A., 'Resource Partitioning and the Evolution of Specialist Organizations: The Role of Location and Identity in the U.S. Wine Industry', *Academy of Management Journal*, 44:2 (2001), pp. 1169–85.

Taplin, I. M., 'Segmentation and the Organization of Work in the Italian Apparel Industry', *Social Science Quarterly*, 70:2 (1989), pp. 408–24.

—, 'From Cooperation to Competition: Market Transformation among Elite Napa Valley Wine Producers', *International Journal of Wine Business Research*, 22:1 (2010), pp. 6–26.

Taplin, I. M., and R. S. Breckenridge, 'Large Firms, Legitimation and Industry Identity: The Growth of the North Carolina Wine Industry', *Social Science Journal*, 45 (2008), pp. 352–60.

Thornton, P., 'The Sociology of Entrepreneurship', *Annual Review of Sociology*, 24 (1999), pp. 19–46.

Tursi, F. V., S. E. White and S. McQuilkin, *Lost Empire: The Fall of R. J. Reynolds Tobacco Company* (Winston-Salem, NC: Winston Salem Journal, 2000).

Uzzi, B., 'Social Structure and Competition in Interfirm Networks: The Paradox of Embeddedness', *Administrative Science Quarterly*, 42 (1997), pp. 35–67.

Visser, E.-J., and P. de Langen, 'The Importance and Quality of Governance in the Chilean Wine Industry', *GeoJournal*, 65 (2006), pp. 177–97.

Watson, A. D., 'Society and Economy in Colonial Edgecombe County', *North Carolina Historical Review*, 50 (1973), pp. 231–55.

Weber, A., *Theory of the Location of Industries* (Chicago, IL: University of Chicago Press, 1929).

Weber, M., *The History of Commercial Partnerships in the Middle Ages*, trans. L. Kaelber (Lanham, MD: Rowman & Littlefield, 2003).

Webster, D., 'Moonshine', *Garden and Gun* (June–July 2009), pp. 62–7.

Williams, E., 'The Teachers are Learning', *On the Vine* (October–December 2005), pp. 4–5.

—, 'Duplin's Wild Ride', *On the Vine* (January–February 2007), pp. 4–5.

—, 'Precious Stones', *On the Vine* (July–August 2007), pp. 4–5.

Youngquist, S., 'Field of Growth', *Winston-Salem Journal*, 2 October 2005.

Zhao, W., 'Social Categories, Classification Systems, and Determinants of Wine Prices in the California and French Wine Industries', *Sociological Perspectives*, 51:1 (2008), pp. 163–99.

INDEX

For Product Safety Concerns and Information please contact our EU
representative GPSR@taylorandfrancis.com
Taylor & Francis Verlag GmbH, Kaufingerstraße 24, 80331 München, Germany

www.ingramcontent.com/pod-product-compliance
Ingram Content Group UK Ltd.
Pitfield, Milton Keynes, MK11 3LW, UK
UKHW021612240425
457818UK00018B/518